RACING

RACING

Full of Myself

Johnny Dawes

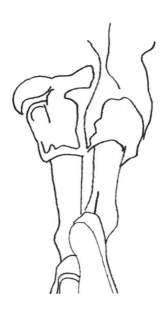

Published by
Johnny Dawes Books

Full of Myself

Author: Johnny Dawes.

Design: Johnny Dawes, Julie Hiam, Al Williams.

Mixing Desk: Al Williams, Cordelia Molloy.

Printing: TJ International Ltd, Padstow, Cornwall.

Distribution: Cordee and www.johnnydawes.co.uk

© Johnny Dawes December 2011

Johnny Dawes has asserted his rights under the Copyright, Designs and Patents Act 1988 to be identified as the author of this work.

A CIP catalogue record for this book is available from the British Library.

ISBN: 978-0-9570308-0-0

My EB's Photo: Ray Wood

Second Edition

Published by
Johnny Dawes Books

For Luke & Emma

Contents

The Absolute Epilogue

by
George Smith

Disco in the Dolbadarn. Lights flicker to pumping sounds. The crowd are losing themselves in their own cloud of cigarette smoke. Boozing and bopping.

The DJ suddenly spots a figure at the entrance; a wedge-shaped torso silhouetted by the light beyond. Stopping the music for a brief moment he makes an announcement on the microphone.

"Ladies and gentlemen…The Dawes."

Llanberis jeers.

He came into our midst, somehow burdened with brilliance. He dazzled us with his climbing and baffled us with his Dawes brain. His rants were a difficult journey for the humble listener. He would lead us down long, inconclusive tunnels of complex thought – the conclusions being disconnected from the start point.

"For crying out loud, Johnny", we have all exclaimed at one time or another: "Write it down".

He has. Those listening thoughts, those diatribes are freeze-framed now, so that we can at last keep up with him.

He was never happy. Ecstatic sometimes, but never content. I remember an early meeting in the quarries – on reaching the top of something there he was, loitering on the levels alone. Rolling around a barrel toward the cliff edge.

"What you up to, John?"

"Actually I was thinking of topping myself": he said in a matter-of-fact way. Down went the barrel. Crash. A week later, he had mustered whatever it took to climb *Indian Face.*

He and I would bristle through lack of comprehension. Both ways.

"You know George you're very competitive and you've absolutely no reason to be".

My, what a pompous little shit he could be, with his flamboyant clothes, his know-all ways and his car fetishes. Grit was the stuff – oh didn't I know?

"Oh yes – Snowdonia is really much more suited to scrambling".

He somehow made me feel like a docile heifer being confronted by a small, angry livestock judge on show day.

In this book, you do not see him climb. So let me tell you. If you ever saw Johnny Dawes in his prime, you never forgot what you saw. Could he move on rock! It wasn't just his raw talent – he knew how to try hard too. The passion! The anger. "For fuck's sake I am only trying to make a little rock climb", he would reprimand the rock. It's not the cruises that I remember most vividly, but the gallantry of his assaults upon the unknown. He'd attempt a manoeuvre that one had never thought to try. Then more: tiptoes on a slab, chimneying a blank wall, heels on a ledge where the rest of us might have used toes. Once – though dwarfed by the immensity of the endless corrugations of Strone Ulladale – I watched the little man leading, with a brush in one hand, pitons and hammer dangling, giant rack seeming not to weigh him down; miles above his gear.

Where we would not dream to go, he seemed strangely at home. Halfway up that same cliff I once spied him on a ledge, distractedly juggling stones he had found at the belay. He was never at rest.

His application of timing and agility were in no way confined to climbing itself. In the café he'd be bent double, sat in his chair. Fidgeting.

One day in the quarries I watched him step on to a slate slab the size of a car, poised, upon a slope of overly steep rubble. The slab began to slide dramatically. Instead of being marmalized by the offending thing, he simply ran up it as it slid away, and ceremoniously jumped off its top as it descended into a cloud of dust and destruction.

Once leaving Stanage for Sheffield in the thickest pea souper, he demonstrated his sense of distance by simply counting the seconds and then very decisively he steered into the nothingness – that turned out to be a road junction.

His regular descent of Zoë Brown's whole staircase in one flawless dive was an extraordinary feat (not properly documented in climbing history). Headfirst, he would glide like a flying squirrel, hands outstretched. Without slow motion, it is difficult to convey the intricacies of the landing procedure.

Amidst all the history, movement crops up everywhere as though it cannot be kept down. Those intricacies and the power of focus are put into words in a special way for us to soak up. In fact when I put this book down, I swear to God my balance…started to go.

Johnny's book is a love story of sorts. It seems to start out against a strange backdrop of disconnection within unsatisfactory affluence. Then there is the affair with the rock. In her, Johnny finds a perfect partner (though latterly their difference in age has become an issue, but we live in hope that a more moderate and mature relationship will endure for many years to come). Then there was the adoration of the climbing world – the distant, unreal love of an audience. His brilliance and compulsivity positioned him awkwardly in a predominantly reserved and modest culture.

"I am not supposed to rate myself – am I?"

We didn't help – most of us supporting the notion that yes, he was one of the very best climbers in the world – but that he shouldn't go on about it.

None of this assisted him in navigating through normal, everyday life. To this day he has difficulty cracking the code to ordinary daily stuff. He once exclaimed: "Everything in this life is flawed" – hey, Johnny guess what!

In his declining years, you didn't need to be a psychologist to conceive his dismay at being overtaken by younger climbers – he would tell you straight, agonising over his forced abdication. He sometimes wept like a grown man.

Johnny wanted nothing new. He simply felt the need to put all his energies into a purposeful mission. He wanted the age-old scare, the fight, and the kudos which comes with the successful hunting of wild beasts. Several of us were similarly engaged – it's just that he picked on much bigger ones than we did. And he regularly netted these metaphorical mammoths, going that bit further, employing superior skills, putting himself in great danger. Then he'd victoriously parade the tamed monsters past the rest of us on his way to Pete's

Eat's New Routes Book, where their fate would be sealed into neat, smug little entries, describing the events succinctly. Afterwards, for a few short hours you would see a man truly alive; a little piece of greatness. "There!" he'd titter. His grin would light up the whole café.

Yes – there are strange bits in this book. Because that is how he is. This is a man who can see the value of traverses on drawing pins and skirting board – has climbed hands-free as well as bound in boxing gloves. A route setter for spiders!

And yes – there is a close and serious interaction with a grounded bee. Perhaps beauty is in the eye of the bee-holder after all!

I

*

Professor Whittaker

Loaded, ready to shoot up from the base of the cliff, is a luminous, black lichen lubricated slab, so inclined as to cut my legs clean out from under me if I trigger a fall. The sheer force with which the slab will rip my legs out from under me gives me a frightening sensation; my head feels delicate as an egg.

I've no children of my own, which is something, but I don't want to end it here.

I have a rope, but a rope is only of use to a climber if it is above them, or, if on your way up, you can jam something in the rock to hold you as you fall back past. Fifty foot up, ground to a halt under an overhang, there are no cracks to fix protection and the smooth bulge above me is set in an icing of shale, too flimsy to hold anything.

His name echoes: Ray...Kay... The unfamiliar, largely scavenged rack of gear I sift through to fix in the cliff is his. I'd never climbed on the spooky cliffs of Gwynedd's Lleyn Peninsula before, or with Ray Kay. Wished I'd known then what a couple of market gardeners told me two decades later, when picking up my landlady's vegetable box, about the man who now holds the ropes. Trained with the Special Forces, he'd once lodged in an outhouse at their farm. One night, catching sight of his door slightly ajar, they called in on him. Apparently he often borrowed the shop's heaviest weight, used to bag up the spuds. Nearly invisible apart from his head, hardly lit by a solitary candle, Ray Kay sat pumping out curls in front of the single remaining adornment on the wall, a mirror. He had painted the whole of his room black.

Now, by the sea, from the back of the amphitheatre, amplified, Ray Kay chants rhythmically to the Earth Goddess – not helpful *at all!*

* Ray Kay. Photo: Dave Jones.

Hampered, unfamiliar, struggling to find a single placement and me 'off the couch fit' made what to focus on – gear, just staying in contact with the rock, or deciding what to do next to survive – feel lethal all of a sudden. Head pressed into shoulder muscle to assist bicep, using the fresher muscle of the neck, the ungodly stench of whisky reminds me of how I find myself in this predicament.

Last night over a game of pool in The Padarn Lake Hotel bar, Ray, a cockney, had touted Vatican Zawn as a cliff of gritstone; a solid, rough sandstone he knew to be my favourite – on which, fighting fit, I'd made my name as a pioneer. What had been conjured up in my mind had been a steady affair, tinkering with the run of the ropes not to unseat protection, uncovering hidden slots, solving moves patiently, figuring, if I didn't like what we came across the next day I'd simply climb down. So how is it I find myself facing the end? Ray you've sold me a pup.

The slope down to Vatican steepens alarmingly. You barely see the cliff until you almost trip over the top. I should have trusted the tell-tale churn in my stomach then and there, but the thought of the wearing walk back up the slope without even trying the unclimbed line had proved too much for my pride.

Birds can sound pretty, or eternal and frightening. Here, now, the birds weren't heard at all. Fifty foot, rounding the uppermost of a series of ledges that have spirited me high quickly, this last *ledge* is anything but. Holds are absent, the terrain unnervingly steeper than expected and features that appeared from below as if they would offer places to lodge protection are too wide or flared.

Concentration fractures beating up my heart. A break from fear by trying to relax by looking at the curious twists in the rock isn't working, nor does singing softly. The pain flooding freely into my body threatens to drown out any sense of peace and induce runaway panic. Pulsing colours of pain offer no option but to learn to tolerate, try to accept or transcend them.

What shape did the cliff have me in now? Well, imagine being in the corner of your living room, toes perched on opposing skirting boards. Then warp the whole corner towards you, make the floor disappear and you'll see you're four storeys up.

Out here above the Irish Sea my left foot is on a slick tablespoon notch, placed hurriedly while committing to the only obvious shape. Now blinded to the foothold, my leg gently shakes, threatening to dislodge itself or even break the notch. In this state one might want to reposition the foot, but you can't move it anyway, and even if you could it wouldn't rest it for long…my right foot lies on a slanting shale ramp and only resists the left's opposition by a scud friction like that of ski boot against sandpaper. One hand is redundant, resting on a flat greasy sill. It's only the heel of the left hand pressed into the edge of a poor dish that keeps the bridge effective.

Splayed, unprotected and insecure, unable to chalk, sweat seeps on to the dish. How near is the heel of my hand to sliding off? Any attempt to climb down feels doomed; sequence forgotten. Though leaning out further on my left arm makes the dish feel more reliable it is much more strenuous. To give myself any margin above I have to go for it sooner rather than later. But is there a way out above? I can see one hold. Soon I'd be forced to hang off it. If it snaps, my body will slam on to the slab.

Why do we climbers climb? I can only say for myself. There's the thrill of doing well, the company, the wonderful places one would otherwise not find oneself in, but the true reason is that it has shown me the animal I was born into. When your animal works completely, as it was evolved to, the human can show itself clear. Soon fear only comes from real threat, and when you understand yourself that threat is easier dealt with. Some get their kicks from a rush at goal, others from a tussle on a Saturday night but for me climbing is a voyage into the universe's innermost rhythm. It can show us how rock and we are kin and make us at the end good friends.

That is all well and good, but *this* situation is not good and I don't feel well. I'm petrified as the rock moves around me. Leaning out at full stretch for the only hold, it proves better than I could have hoped for. But *where* it is and by having to pull on it straightaway I've upset the tension in the bridge. Right foot poisoned, about to ping off, I feel my body start to sag, the drop feels near.

No…

Must… maul over the bulge…

Clamp legs around it…

With the last embers of strength and determination, grabbing the hold with the other hand as well, I attempt to wrap loose jeans around the bulge. Only by sliding back off the roundness again, then, pulling, lifting my body up again... and then again, does the roll of jean around leg finally leave me sat on the friction of cotton on rock. Barely perched there, perfectly still, unprotected, afraid to slip, the tautness in my arms and dangerous adrenalin level recede a little and I can safely hear myself think what to do.

Above, a solid crack accepts big gear. Strapped into a comfortable niche, cooling now able to shake, body rocks violently. Like the body's animal wisdom not to sneeze from hay fever on a bold sunny May arête it'd known not to play up below.

Cold, stiff from holding the ropes, Ray falls off coming out of the corner. Rope above him, we can even laugh at that. The last pitch is butch but not scary, the cord between us no longer telegraphs the jagged shudder of a creature in fear of death.

Soon Ray and I are walking through the tourists in Abersoch. Looking ahead at the slender soldier weave, an alien grinning between mewling kids and portly visitors is to remember that mortal combat has been normal to Ray. Just a climber trying to have fun I vow to handle beer goggles with devout care in future. Black had rattled sinisterly in the jaws but instead we've arrived at the chippy to cover ourselves in glory.

We climbers get to name climbs if we do a new one. The queer horror of the climb with Ray smacked of an atmosphere I'd felt hitching up into the Llanberis Pass the week before. The driver of the car had said, pointing his knife at me, but kindly:

> "Would you like a piece of *cheese?*"

Strange, but not as strange as *how* he had lingered on the word "*cheese...*". A dry pregnant atmosphere persisted until he slowed for the 30mph sign in Nant Peris when I heard a painfully quiet breath from behind – turning I see a young girl carrying a stuck, startled expression pressed into the corner of the back seat, quite silent.

The driver, the climb: *Professor Whittaker* 1989, E7 6b, 5c.

Providence

I was born a human on the 9th of May 1964, in Birmingham Maternity Hospital, already on drugs.

Events long before we even exist hold all our futures in the balance. Our planet has to be just the right distance from the sun to be the right temperature, needs a moon to kill the wobble so plants can take a consistent hold etcetera etc et. The circumstances that flocked together to allow my particular future were no less precarious. The sperm that helped make me had to outrace a billion others, negotiating a maze of dead ends resisting chemical warfare from Mum's body then burrow its way into the egg. In an instant interdependence could have spun, can spin, a totally different web.

For example Dad told me a story about his father's trip to Germany in 1938.

'Pop' was in Leipzig to assess a new machine for laying concrete. On a day off, walking on the fringes of woodland, he came across considerable stockpiles of military vehicles and artillery under tarpaulin.

The storm clouds of war in Europe threatened the very future of British climbing!

On return to Birmingham, he immediately sold the family house because of its proximity to potential industrial targets. He found a cottage in the wilds of Worcestershire and, at the end of the garden, built an air raid shelter. Sure enough, within the year the high wail of sirens interrupted a pint with friends in Birmingham. Without delay he said goodbye and headed home while they stayed to finish their drinks. The pub received a direct hit.

Again, my brother and I may never have even seen the light of day were it not for my father's love of racing cars. One day in a Black Country pub, Dad, simply Mike Dawes then, was waiting for a young lady he was courting to arrive. He was sitting at the bar nursing a scotch, when he recognised a man who came in, clearly looking for someone.

"Are you Peter Collins?" (the grand prix ace) Dad asks him.

"I am", he replies (famous and blond).

Collins is there to meet a young lady too. Conversation reveals her to be the

The Chief on his Indian.

very same young lady that Dad has arranged to meet. Just as my potential future Dad gallantly starts to back out to avoid embarrassment, Collins pulls something swinging to and fro from his breast pocket. It has a *DB* insignia and fits a car parked outside. Gleaming in British Racing Green stands a works Aston Martin DB2. Dad gets to take her out instead, for a drive in the Staffordshire Peak…

Sperm finally neared egg at the Roger Williams Hospital in Providence, Rhode Island, where my father – now Dr Michael Dawes – was an intern.

Dr Dawes had already been out with most of the nurses on the intensive care ward when a colleague took him to one side and said: "Wait till you see Nurse Medici". But possible future mother was in quarantine fighting for her life against a *staph* infection.

Again, climbing history teeters on the brink…

Lollobrigida good looks, dark eyes under jet locks and a solid refusal to be another of Doctor Dawes' tally steels Dad to visit her ward repeatedly. Fortune shines on us again when eventually Nurse Medici is persuaded. Off they go to a private party; Dad on 'Manhattans', Mum on whisky, ice and water, Errol Garners' jazz piano sounding them out till dawn and the start of the next shift.

The Medici had come over to America in 1890. When my grandfather John Medici's parents died, he joined The Force to support his brothers and sisters. He rose to become the Chief of Police – quite something for a wop[1] in WASP[2] Barrington, Rhode Island – just as well as Dr Dawes, his daughter's new boyfriend, was forever getting tickets for speeding. 'The Chief' was a powerful blocky man, little more than five feet tall, still driving at 101 until he had his car keys forcibly removed from him. His sprightly sister Annie lived to 102.

I can see him now, walking back towards his modest white wooden slat house, greenhouse harvest in his arms. His zucchini and pomodoro gave him great pleasure – not a fool amongst them. He could be a bit of a handful himself in my reckoning and we occasionally locked horns, which I think he enjoyed.

[1] Wop is a U.S. pejorative slur for people from Italy.
[2] Western Anglo-Saxon protestant.

My Mum was always very insistent with me when I was a nipper. When I resisted her instructions about dressing smartly or some other aspect of behaviour she would say: "You know I am always right". This, of course, did not leave much room for manoeuvre, but it did set a wide frame for rebellion. Now I can see where she got it from; I'm not sure my grandfather was always appreciative of my mum's qualities, nor she mine, nor me hers. Looking back at photos of me aged sixteen, pierced ear and blonde '*Le Bon*' quiff, I have to concede she was sometimes right.

The Chief's wife Helen was a district nurse, a sweet, devout Welsh woman with a dry sense of humour, who made the best spaghetti and meatballs. They were difficult days back then and Helen ran an essential, informal clinic for the less well-off Italians.

My mother said it was difficult to leave the close-knit Italian community and come to live among the starched English. However, she did find a good friend in my father's father George. Pop naturally had a soft spot for the mother of his first grandson, treating her like a daughter. Respecting her sharp intellect and counsel, he gifted her shares in his company simply so she could attend the annual board meeting.

Grandpa Dawes checking the roster.

Grandpa Dawes went on to make the not inconsiderable family fortune floating Black Country companies on the virgin Birmingham Stock Exchange he helped to establish. After the war he enabled munitions and engineering company owners to realise their capital. It was around then that he bought Birtsmorton Court, a dilapidated, 14th century, moated manor house in the lee of the Malvern Hills. A county tennis player and British bridge champion, George Dawes was a man of many talents and interests. He wasn't trying to be flash – in fact he was concerned that the 250 GT Ferrari he had bought, the first in England, might make him appear frivolous to his 1950s clients, yet it had quite the opposite effect. He was a motor racing enthusiast and enjoyed nothing more than to fly the whole family to European Grand Prix rounds in his De Havilland Dove.

Grandma Dawes was a soft, sensitive soul who would sometimes go missing, only to be found by Peter Cleverly their gentle gentleman butler, in the loo, at loggerheads with the last clue in The Times crossword. She was a Conservatoire-trained pianist, although circumstances meant she never played professionally. I have fond memories of sitting in the window seat watching the swans on the moat, soothed by her playing Chopin. In common with many people and their grans I felt she knew me as I was.

When Grandpa George developed pancreatic cancer, my father knew of a treatment newly available in America. My brother went with them to the States but my parents thought it best to leave me behind with a nanny as I was only two. I have sometimes wondered if a certain remoteness I feel stems from then.

I grew up, as you can now tell, in a high performance environment. Born into a dynasty, one side with the Medici for ancestors (who, they'd have you understand, invented science and art), whilst the other side owned a tidy slice of Worcestershire. As a consequence, my parents had their ideas of what a young man should be, and I had mine.

Nanny and I, Mum and Michael across the moat at Grandma and Grandpa's house, Birtsmorton Court.

Hitler's Bedroom

Inspired by *Escape from Colditz* or the cunning ploy of a gym horse to disguise the entrance to an escape tunnel, a diet of Second World War P.O.W. films encouraged me to cast life as a madcap game of adventure.

Christmas. Harrod's toy department. A *Green Devil* pedal kart has caught my eye, demanding a half hour test drive around the store's ground floor. Least traffic is on the polished stone floor of the neighbouring food hall – combined with the carpet in the toy department, the twin surfaces made it a great Rallycross circuit. Silent and low, it was tricky for the staff to see, let alone catch the devil amongst the pyramids of Foie Gras and Gentleman's Relish.

In 1975, while John Allen and fellow gritstone pioneers are hard at play in the Peak District, the Dawes family are touring Germany en route to the Austrian Grand Prix at the Österreichring. It's incredibly hot and the black vinyl seats of the BMW 2002 burn stickily. My head is stuck between the front seats, chatting incessantly about cars, driving my brother Mike to scream: "Why don't you just shut up..!"

Deep in the Black Forest we stop at a wooden inn. Shockingly, below a signed photograph of Adolf Hitler, reclines a vast Bavarian, ticking off the number of Steins he has drunk on a beer mat – just one corner remains blank.

Finally we arrive in Vienna but hotel after hotel is fully booked. Our last resort is *The Hotel Imperial*, a former Hapsburg Palace. Giant portraits hang high in the entrance hall. The huge marble staircase is cool. Not cool like wearing jeans half way down your arse, but cool to the touch, so I lie down on the big steps: "Embarrassing myself and my parents..."

"Zee hotel eez full", we're told. However further interrogation reveals there is one possibility – one rarely available – The Royal Suite. We were soon stood looking at the carnival wheel in the Plata from the very balcony where Hitler had addressed the baying crowd after the invasion of the Sudetenland. As children we knew none of this, we were just thrilled the carpet was long enough to get up to full running speed in socks before transferring full tilt to polished wood.

The Prince's penthouse, seemingly untouched since the Austro-Hungarian Empire, was full to the brim with gilded mirrors, huge oil paintings, ornate tables and carved chests. The folks off shopping, leaving us alone, soon heavy portraits of long dead monarchs and gaudy mirrors form a long straight section. The tunnel snaked all over, through wardrobes, under a bed, in and out of the bath (roofed in by towels) and down a gorge of intricately painted chests pulled away from the wall. In places it was impossible to turn or back up but it was cosy in there and took at least a couple of minutes to follow it all the way through.

Mum and Dad confess: "We didn't know what to do with you..." I suppose I did take things too far sometimes. In retrospect, perhaps I was on a quest to escape right from the beginning. The photograph of me looking like Mussolini gripping the bars of my cot seems to suggest that.

Prep

*"Don't let schooling interfere with
your education". Mark Twain*

Wells House School on the Malvern Hills was an old-school boys'
preparatory where physical resilience and sentimental qualities like honesty
were still encouraged. It was also a suitable place to cut loose.

British Bulldog is great fun. The whole year lines up at one end of a field
and charges at a boy who must tackle one of them, who then joins in to
tackle for the next go. Once, last on, I found a weakness in the line where
one chocolate enthusiast could be used to advantage as an obstacle. A
fainting dodge and I was through the lot of them.

It wasn't all rough and tumble, there were times of easy affection. My first
experience of physical intimacy was with a boy. Interestingly our physical
closeness was not an issue for others in the open dormitory – no one batted
an eyelid. We were both 11 years old and simply lay on each other and
cuddled. Pre-puberty no climax, sensation just ran, no low-energy aftermath
or confusion, feeling close was simple.

There were gangs. Ours came up with some lucrative schemes. For a few
terms we 'ran' sweets for the other kids. A friend's father was the ambassador
to Hong Kong and while he handed in a parcel to be weighed, distracting
the postmaster, at the other end of the shop I filled my satchel with the
sweet order. We distributed all the booty the same day so we couldn't be
caught red handed.

Knowing the run of the undulations in the oval gutter by Chip's carpentry
workshop intimately made betting on model car races lucrative. By making
a slow car outrun a quick one, not only could you pocket the winnings, you
could raise the odds. The overrated winners sold at a premium. At home

I modified some cars by jacking them up or swapping wheels, felt-tipping then varnishing them with a new livery. They sold well.

There was a cracking season for conkers too. A clear winner emerged when I kicked over a stone on the drive that looked exactly like a conker. It was patiently drilled out in the garage and did very well. However, the real kings of capitalism are bankers.

It was a chance encounter. Tearing up a steep slope, a friend's foot levered something white out of the hill. A casual rummage in the undergrowth revealed more... chalk. In class demand was spontaneous for the 70s Home Counties' bling and The Great Chalk Rush was on. Chalk's appeal proved to rest not just in its strange whiteness, but also in each piece's unique shape and, used to write on a blackboard, it left what was written nearly indelible. Others started to offer money in exchange for our new currency of chalk. Like diamonds, the largest, purest pieces went for the most.

Beneath a large root left to support the roof, I set about carefully locating the run of the vein. The inclination of the chalk gave away where best to dig next. Before, I used to read The Koran with an Arabian mate, play table tennis, five-a-side or climb trees, but now every spare moment was spent at the mine.

Rocks were set out to dry slowly in the breeze to avoid costly cracking. Fresh earth from the burrow, able in an instant to give away the mine's location, we carried downhill to spread out under a vast yew tree where the earth was already barren and broken. However we had a problem; each morning at 6.30 a bell announced a run up the hill to Holy Well[3] and back. Lazy, we normally jumped over a wall halfway up, waited, then joined the pack on their way back down, but that was precisely where the mine was. I didn't trust our improvised camouflage so did the whole run.

The best new seams our gang worked, while less hopeful prospects went to rival outfits. All activity was beneficial only adding to the popularity of the fad. Why chalk was to be found in 680 million-year-old metamorphic rock I don't know, but aged 12 our gang had uncovered the true fundamentals of capitalism from the raw: create demand, control supply.

In our best term in 1977, these various enterprises grossed £200 plus. But to join *the* gang wasn't pain free. The first trial was to drop each of the school's

---

[3] Malvern spring water was first bottled for sale there.

four piano lids down on your knuckles. The last of the four and one with the heaviest lid was a mahogany monster in the Head's study. The initiated knew that distinctive thunk well; nothing quite as amusing as hearing the victim try not to cry out. The final trial presented itself after climbing four flights of heavily waxed stairs to a small antechamber with a large window with openings at either end. You had to climb out on to a wide sloping sill, cling there facing outwards, looking down at the tarmac until the gang were convinced you weren't scared and allowed you back in. It was quite tough I'm afraid.

Our P.E. master was Pym Hall. Like me he was short. He had been with the first landings in Italy at Monte Casino. Legend has it he avoided the Germans by hiding in the bottom of a well. He also taught French and coached the excellent Wells House 1st Rugby team. It had a happy mix of brain and brawn, the scrum was a well-drilled engine room of farmers' and doctors' sons – Richards our prize ripper and thug could even catch me by the arms when I jumped across the yawning gap to the science block. The backline was strong: Mahler was clever at fly half, tough with a good kick, at full back was the Right Hon. John Packington and on the wing John Dawes (not the Welsh International). No one got past us – like JPR Williams we would suffer contact. But our secret weapon was 'prep school obligatory early adult' Michael Parffrey; super-fast knee-lift swerver extraordinaire.

Once the Headmaster arrived at practice and decided to join in; all fifteen stone of him. I didn't like him, nor him me. So when he ran at me with the ball I was going to tackle him whatever it took. Coming to in the Sanitorium, my first words were: "You know Mr ….. is not a gentleman, daddy..!" I took comfort from finding out I *had* taken him down. It was no surprise to us when he was later alleged to have embezzled money from the board of governors.

Pym Hall cared about us and would have made a true headmaster. When he was denied the post, it rubbed it in that things are not always just.

In gym on the last day of term, Mr Hall always treated us to a game of 'Coastguards and Pirates' a game of tag where gym apparatus serves as ship's rigging, the floor as sea. I still love this game more than almost anything. You could avoid the coastguards by speeding along benches in and out of control, but on the wall bars was where you could make up most time. Using hands and feet simultaneously, springing, even diagonally if in rhythm, it became possible to actually accelerate upwards.

The last time I'd ever see Pym, in Colwall, he recalled he often had to tell me to come down from the roof beams where I'd hang out of reach. He lent my brother Heinrich Harrer's *The White Spider*. Soon I could project myself into the compelling hell of the North Face of the Eiger before bed.

Half-boarders went home at the weekend. After prayers in the green corrugated metal chapel, far up in a dorm high on the Malvern Hills, I'd listen out for Dad far out on the Severn plain below and try to guess what car he was in by the engine note. Was it the flat 4 Porsche or Ferrari V12? Wow, it *was* the GT40. Sometimes Pads allowed me to warm it up. It had so much torque that when the throttle was blipped the 4.7 litre V8 would twist the whole body around it. Geared for English short circuit racing sometimes we'd do over 165mph on the way home from school.

Above: The venue for the end of term 'Coastguards and Pirates' games. The wall bars that were pulled out perpendicular from the wall.

Eastington

We lived on an estate. If you picture youths with weak necks, a brown Mondeo with one red wing sat on bricks, a lazy Quaver packet knocking about, you'd be off the mark. Our estate was not like that. It had three cottages, the homes of the Yearsleys, Roberts and Freemantles, a tennis pavilion, swimming pool, garage buildings and at its heart, Eastington Hall.

The hall was big, a Baron's manor, but not posh. Living there was like living in a lovely old tree. The 12th century great hall was of base cruck construction, tarred beams dowelled together, limed wattle and daub between. Beyond a carved oak door, rarely heated, the cold of the hall accentuated a peculiar sensation that even though you were inside the outside remained there nevertheless. Fresh cut flowers, hops, whatever Mum, Mrs Freemantle or Mrs Roberts had brought in and arranged, made it beautiful.

It was enjoyable to search for priest holes and hidden passageways. When friends visited I was often the one who took the role of tour guide.
…In the medieval dining room:
    "Here is the Brueghel…"
In the great hall I lift a flagstone pointing out:
    "That is the original clay floor"
But on the way to the study, diverting attention by pointing out a lifeless brass clock on a walnut table with a little trot, ahead I could enter the room with some seconds in hand. On entering the study, a buttoned velour cul-de-sac with nowhere to hide, my charges would find me gone. There is no sign of anyone, even behind the floor-length curtains.

"SSSssscoooooooobeeEEEE…!"

…behind a wood panel, a spiral stair winds up a tower to my parents' bedroom. Dashing up this then sprinting downstairs to the study I mysteriously reappear at their shoulder.

A big hall is not a home, so in the winter we retreated to a small, warm room in the newer Lutjens wing, where each of us engaged in our own pursuit. My brother Michael devoured Tolkein determined not to be disturbed, Mummy, a Dick Francis with a Silk Cut, 'Pads', guillotine on lap, stapled tight-cropped photos of race cars into albums. I was lost on the floor in a scree of Lego, attempting the transmogrification of straight into curved. Old Lego made you roam diligently through all possibilities.

Life at the Hall sometimes felt like a long eternal present that only the passing tone of the seasons changed. At Christmas, the big house became fully alive. One winter, conditions proved spot on for the use of our 'patent' slurry of snow and water mixed in a bucket to sculpt. Drawing up the already stiffening sludge to the top of the curve, the traditional shape could be accomplished without making blocks from packed snow. Impressively thin, the igloo glowed like an orange with a candle lit inside.

Back at the fireside Mike and I warm our numb hands, snow glinting outside. The Baron's big fireplace had an oak seat nestled in the right wall bounded by a mullion-windowed alcove. When it became too hot you had to retreat into the alcove, not quite big enough to escape the heat of the fire on full chat. When the pig on the spit spat fat into the heart of the flaming trunk of elm, the only relief was to rotate your body slowly in the recess, soothing your most roasted flank against the coldest diamonds of glass.

Mum taught me how to bake flapjacks then lemon cake. In season, in front of McEnroe/Borg, Ovett/Coe, we shelled endless peas and broad beans from the kitchen garden. I really liked to watch movies munching buttery popcorn, often painted or drew, studied *Vogue*, read Roald Dahl over and over, (*Danny, Champion Of The World* was my favourite). Often I played *Colditz, Monopoly*, or *Buccaneer* with the Freemantles' cheery rosy-cheeked daughter Anne. I usually won, which was just as well. Our den was in an ancient hollow elm, unfortunately felled by the Dutch disease.

Come summer we were all outside a lot. We ran a loud little blue two-stroke Italjet on sweet Castrol R. Paul Roberts could wheelie but sometimes looped it over backwards which made me grumpy. At night if you were quick you'd catch glimpses of the Freemantles, Roberts and Dawes kids playing 'searchlight' in the front gardens. The one 'on' has to catch you in the beam among the warren of hedges, walls and dips and identify you. I liked to sneak right around the back of the house and wait for my moment. When the searchlight moved away momentarily, hilarious sounds of scuffed gravel, panting and owl hoots followed… then I'd creep up and tap the one on, PC Plod-like on the shoulder, to win.

I cycled all the time around the hall, sometimes even on it. The flat lead roof provided a spectacular challenge – to skid around on the algae at the narrow end without putting a foot down. Had I caught the square lip and gone over the edge, I doubt I'd have stopped on the mossy pottery tiles. Last chance not to fall 40 feet to luminous green flags below would've been to grab a square lead gutter.

When there was nothing to do, a visit to the Lodge was in order. Mrs Yearsley made great pies. Teddy Yearsley liked to play pontoon or gin rummy – it wouldn't be long before he'd try his new batch of sweet homebrew out on me. Dusk would see me happily weaving back up the drive to bed.

It may seem I was a hyperactive child but an early experience I recall most vividly illustrates a more reflective side. It was when Mum shared her love of plants to help me to feel at home in our new big house. When she told me the tiny dots in my hand were carrots I looked at her then down at the seeds confused. She read out the instructions, leaving me to sow them in a narrow bed beside the Freemantles' cottage. Afterwards I sat on my haunches waiting to see what would happen.

"Ding, **Ding**…ding". Supper's ready.

At one point engrossed in eating, unexpected, an unmistakeable feeling bursts out:

We carrots now know we are in the ground… we are starting to grow.

When you're young you don't know this would be considered fanciful, whatever you feel is real – if anything this feeling felt more real than normal life to me then.

"Can I leave the table Mummy?"

Food bolted down, dish in sink, I sped off to the patch – but surprise – bare earth, no carrot tops to be seen. I didn't give up hope though and sure enough all my prayers came true. One exciting day there they were, curly leaves poking up through the soil. Every day I visited them I wondered what was going on below ground. Later, when we pulled them up, even though knobbly from giving best to stones, not one snapped. Their sheen and crease, sweet Worcestershire flavour and the distinctive lilt of voice with which they had roused me all went together, confirming that it *was* the carrots that had spoken.

It's not surprising that they knew my language. Later I learned I was born Imix in Mayan, wooden dragon in Chinese, and Taurus, all three earth signs. The carrots had been brilliant company and teachers.

Mum and Dad put on some grand splashes; pirate parties, gatherings around the pool. But when family friends and others would dance and joke I often felt at sea. Sometimes I heard guests say disingenuous things…but I remember fondly 'Pads'' prodigious DJ activity – Dudley Moore, Oscar Peterson, Burt Bacharach, George Harrison and Mozart inhabiting the house. They all emanated from a huge late Tudor chest on legs. Nested inside were 8 track, Thorens deck, Technics cassette deck all feeding a reel to reel master routed to the swimming pool, annex and to Cambridge monitors, almost as tall as me, in the great hall. If Dad was not to be found mastering four-hour party tapes, including bossa nova bought while ship's doctor off Rio de Janeiro, he'd be beavering away in the office or down at the garage.

Craig Smith showing how one should spot, 6b lines littered these walls, each making its way to the pipe - just one finishing onto the apex of the roof.

Nurse Medici at The Roger Williams Hospital in Providence, Rhode Island.

Mike Dawes, intern at the Roger Williams glamorizing a Chevy. Eastington Hall, in the lea of The Malverns. Birmingham greengrocers done good – The Dawes at Christmas.

Top left clockwise: Dr and Mrs
Dawes en route to Le Touquet.
Mum about to do 170mph on the
autostrada on the way back to
Maranello in the works Ferrari
GTO - earlier that day Aston
Martin beat Ferrari for the first
time at Monza.
Mum in '63, in Surtees' Ferrari.
The Ferrari owners club at
Eastington.
Mike and I in a Type 35 Bugatti.

Top left clockwise: Lock...pull...
pinch...
One of my best moves.
Mike on an unknown climb at
Stanage Edge. Stubai, Whillans, Joe
Brown, Golden Wonder.
My first lead. *Scratch Arête* HVS.
The day I got my colours.
The mantel and stand up were harder.
Sprayed with water after dusk the
next day its possible to get full air.

Having a sit down on the 5th ascent of
Lord of the Flies E6.
'The Bridge' at Slawston. The iron
pipes got more polished each year.
Mike on *Vulture*, Sean Myles below.

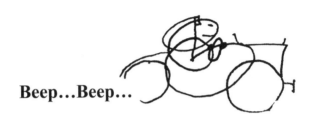

Beep…Beep…

After a number of pleasant afternoons having picnics and spending time on the river, Mole and Ratty decide to visit one of Ratty's friends, Toad who--when they arrive--explains to them his latest obsession, a horse and cart. They go for a ride with Toad, but whilst on the road they are tipped over by a speeding motorcar (which completely breaks Toad's little cart).

Far from being upset by the loss of his favourite toy, Toad's first thought is that he, too, wants one of those incredible automobiles. This obsession leads him to trouble, however. Much to Mole, Ratty and their old and wise friend Badger's sadness, Toad is soon arrested and sent to prison for stealing a motor car. However, within the gaol, one of the guard's daughters soon feels sorry for the poor Toad (who certainly wasn't made for prison life), and gives him some old washerwoman's clothes and helps him to escape.

Wind in The Willows: Kenneth Grahame.

The Dawes brothers were all keen on cars. Dad's collection included a Dino and Daytona Ferrari, Allard J2X, MG TC, lightweight E-type Jag, Facel Vega and a Bentley R-type Continental with a pale alloy body that came up a treat, capable of cruising at a ton without rippling the scotch in the crystal decanter in the back. Uncle Howard had an SS100 Jag but Uncle Nigel was a well-known collector of Jags and Astons, most notably Project 215, which achieved the fastest recorded time of 198.6 mph on the Mulsanne Straight, the quickest Aston ever made with this set up. He also kept a Monza Alfa and a Blower Bentley.

It was great when Uncle Nigel and cousin Simon came to visit. Whether in Jaguar C type, D, lightweight E, or DB3S it meant cousin Simon and I had to share the tiny passenger seat with the hamper. We'd be off to Prescott or Shelsley Walsh Hill Climb to watch short 5-litre Pilbeams scare their drivers witless.

I first learnt to drive in Mum's Mini Cooper S in the field, then later in her Carrera RS lightweight; a car prepared for the RAC Rally. It was arguably the quickest tarmac rally car in England at the time. On one occasion, which I've only just shared with my parents, I nearly came unstuck. Hairless, left to my own devices, I'd hit on the idea of breaking 100mph down the drive!

It's a long open left, down a slight hill. Just before it straightens out there's a dip and then, where it runs alongside a beech hedge, the tarmac polishes up. Not to worry the Carrera had amazing Le Mans 917 brakes.

…Three cushions behind, two underneath, I was ready. Third through the top gate, a brief pause to see if anybody was coming – recalling Dad in the GT40 nearly meeting Mrs Yearsley there in her Morris Traveller – clear, downhill, Stuttgart's finest wide open, the magic ton wasn't hard. At the dip it's possible to get extra compression for a moment so shed speed dramatically, but overnight a mist had settled and the front tyres locked up almost instantly on the damp... *Whoops*…release…brake again but at the end of the drive, the precious 911 is still going. Only by taking a dogleg to the left through a rarely opened gate do I lurch on to a bumpy field, surprising the farmer at work. My head barely visible, I rack my brain for an explanation.

The Ferrari Owners' Club sometimes descended upon Eastington, upwards of two hundred prancing horses spread out around the lawns, sunglasses on heads, champagne. In the hum of twilight, the vivid thralp of a Tasmin F2 rises and falls at the foot of the Great Hall's steps. One year, the police pulled four for speeding.

I knew *all* about Ferraris. Once we went to the Ferrari factory in Maranello to pick up a red 512 Berlinetta Boxer that ran in at over a ton. I remember the enthusiasm of a family in a Fiat Cinquecento, mama in black at the wheel winding down the bambinos' window for them to hear the guttural flat 12 yaw past. It was reputedly capable of 190mph yet above 140mph would wander around like a drunken pig, the dark art of aerodynamics still in need of illumination back then.

The factory was painstakingly elegant like a film studio, colours subtle like a plush handbag. Although there were no oompa-loompas, everyone wore white coats and everything was immaculate. By the Daytona production line, below a 40s tin plaque with the words **'Scuderia Competizione'**, waiting their turn by a canary yellow door were a string of engineers, protective headphones on. Beyond it screamed the unforgettable wail of a Grand Prix V12 being revved to destruction. Every four minutes the door opened, letting an intoxicating blend of heaven and hell out, another Paganini-tuned engineer in. In 1979, human ears were still the best tool for the job: as if listening for the slightest off note at rehearsal, the instant an engineer heard a change in pitch he would immediately shut off the engine, the motor be stripped to see what had broken so in the next prototype they'd know what to beef up. Apparently Enzo would sometimes turn down a design simply because it didn't look pretty or sound fierce enough. Those were the days of automotive sculpture.

Afterwards we went to the Trattoria opposite the factory. Dad told me that when Enzo was alive he lunched every day at the same restaurant where we now sat cool under a vine, and that on a day when he wore a striped tie it meant Signor Ferrari was not to be disturbed in his office, he was to spend the afternoon with his mistress.

Dave 'Skinny' Jones and below Sean Myles leaning on my blue Rascal. Skirmish above, its demise below.

Uppingham

I've always thought that much we're taught at school is deliberately designed to stop us thinking comprehensively and frustrate our discovery of what is most useful, gentle or true. Even the three R's are lies, Reading, Writing and Arithmetic. Rearrange those letters and they spell WAR, apt for an institution conceived to gird children to stomach the machinations of empire.

Stephen Fry's *The Liar* describes the period when I was at Uppingham well. It's where Johnny Vaughan learnt to be bubbly and sarcastic, where Rick Stein developed an appetite for food other than that on offer. It fuelled the speed record-breaking Campbells and bore the boy band *Busted*. I'd been a big noise at Wells House Preparatory but nothing could've prepared me for what followed at Uppingham.

School founder Thring located his intellectual nerve centre on the crown of a windswept hill in Rutland. The land of ruts is the smallest county in England. My very own rut was to be in a house called Farleigh, presided over by a dapper little man with silver hair and matching Volkswagen Polo.

Turning onto the straight potholed drive, I remember the atmosphere immediately threatened. The slap up lunch at The Falcon Hotel with my parents had not settled. Fearful, unstable, my heart an engine either about to stall or rev to destruction, my senses are plunged into a smell of polish, sweat, carbolic and leather. No other fragrance. **John Andrew George Dawes**, you're on your own. Not strictly, as my elder brother Michael had already been boarding at Farleigh for two years in eight stretches of 13 weeks. Mike's big trunk was true blue, mine very green. Mike introduced me to his best friend, Andy Gittins, who sat at his desk under a poster of a rock climber, "*Remember Last Summer*" emblazoned on it. His younger brother Tim was a new boy too.

Strange customs awaited us new boys on our first day. We were shown our locker and then subjected to 'posting' in the dormitory. What might that be? It starts with each leg being grabbed by an older boy, your shoulders by another. I half hoped this meant I was to get the bumps, but no. Your legs are splayed, each pulled either side of the oak partition separating each

Left: *Shadows and Light* E8 7a, ground up over 30 days, bruised feet and fingertips; in retrospect possibly the hardest climb in the world in 1981.

cubicle. You couldn't say: "You've got balls" to one boy in another house any more. I hear it doesn't go on now.

I was not very confident socially and had a different way of expressing myself. Over the first weeks I fell out of favour – stilted, boring – became ostracized. On the long freezing walks to school my overtures to walk with one or other person became more forced and repellent. Soon my unintelligible comments were derided as: "Johnny classics".

At public school one absorbs a visceral grasp of hierarchy, and from 'joking', how it operates. One way or another we each find our place. Ironic too that parents pay thousands of pounds for the privilege of their sons working as 'fags' for the prefects. Fagging was a pain but no big deal, one person was manageable – it was the herd instinct I could not stand.

At public school, some boys are hairy men while others are still delicate children. A situation I lived in constant horror of was shower time. After sweaty, muddy games of rugby, I'd return to the shower block with boys confident of their manhood. Eyes shut, shampooing, my shoulder would be pulled around, and a wave of laughter from the group would take another raft of self-confidence away with it. "Dog" came to hum and not the latest tune.

My parents took me to Great Ormond Street to see a growth specialist. From a dark oak drawer, the doctor produced a rosary of graduated testicular moulds on a string. I was told to drop my trousers. My testicles compared to those on the set.
    "Was I abnormally small?"
Borderline. It is just as well I never took growth hormone treatment, as all who did so at the time have since died.

Each day, as you rotated around the dining room table towards the master or matron, you were confronted with each and every person in the house wheth-er you liked it or not. A stewing fear simmers up in me as those grinning apes approach to yet again attempt to dismantle my peace of mind. Genuine laughter triggers ridicule, answering back proves futile, escape impossible. I did attack verbally, yet on some level was prepared to believe their taunts. A part of me came to think of myself as they thought of me, the will to join in unleashing the perverse tendency to finally slag myself off as well.

Almost everyone at chapel, a sticky hand rifles through pockets in the dormi-tory for money to buy sweets and cigarettes. Later, lights out, no hugs nor privacy, and after a calculated, tense silence, their night's entertainment would begin. If they're on a roll, there's no knowing how long their exploration of weakness will last. For some reason I never thought to fight back physically. Sometimes I'm lucky though – they torment Ng, a Chinese boy instead.

In retrospect, it must've been difficult for the other boys. We were all away from home. However they were to me, they were *kind – same* as me – even if we didn't realise it. From where I am now, the "Johnny classics" seem confused but somewhat insightful. I'd been successful at prep school – full of it – ready for it to be kicked out of me. You can see the bullies as educators from that angle. It was just the way it was. My father told me he was bullied at Uppingham as well.

The smell outside the housemaster's study was always insistently beige. Be unaware of that atmosphere seeping into your heart at your peril. Unaware and the gall of its supposed superiority could remain undetected. One had to spot it early to reject its red and black innards. I did, side-stepping it in the company of the year below with B&H, toffee treats, cheese 'n' onion toasties at the buttery, drawing, compulsive *Lady Pacman* and other unspeakable habits, and naturally music, AC/DC or Joni Mitchell. Sometimes everyone in their studies off the main corridor tried to synchronise their music-centres to headbang to Led Zep's Black Dog. Pushed to their limits, the Goodman's watts/channel rating would prove unconvincing. It was also the days of music "You had to get into", like Genesis' 'Lamb Lies Down On Broadway'. I enjoyed all that.

In time I didn't wait after class hoping to walk back with someone. I enjoyed whoever was friendly, whistled my own tune.

Hilarious, the housemaster later made nearly all of my year, except me, into prefects, handing my nemeses extra powers. Year on year he was voted 'the best-dressed master' and he proved the best cloaked too, but less about that. I once laughed in his face as he caned me but he wasn't all bad – he came to turn a blind eye to my exploits up Farleigh.

One afternoon a week at Uppingham you either did Combined Cadet Force or Community Service, 'granny bashing'. I plumped for the CCF. We even got to fire a live Bren Gun once, like those used in the film *If*, but guns weren't for me, nor was marching up and down. An alternative was rock climbing…I gave that a shot instead.

Two masters took us away climbing at weekends. Jerry Rudman, squat bolshie canoeist, always pushed us hard. Jerry took circuit training on Wednesday evenings, the night Farleigh kitchens cooked my favourite, egg and chips (the eggs floating like space ships in oil). I tried really hard, eager to impress, fully appreciating the sadistic irony of Rudman's choice of Christopher Cross's *Lovely Day* to accompany the interminable final leg raise. The other master was Malcolm Campbell, who the sixth form girls all thought a real dish, he was deputy housemaster at Farleigh.

Jerry and Malc were a breath of fresh air. They drove us all over the country in a faded green army transit – the fast one with twin back tyres and flared wheel arches. I recall a novel incident on an early trip to the Peak District. Jerry was performing a normal overtaking manoeuvre, as normal as the overtaking manoeuvre the car coming towards us was making! What this meant was that our transit and the overtaking car were both on their own respective wrong sides of the road: nothing rash, just two drivers deciding to go for it at precisely the same time. Wow! We all watched to see if they would hold their nerve. Jerry and the oncoming driver thankfully did keep their cool, the whole van of boys whooping as we pulled back in.

Malc, Jerry and smiley, highly eye-browed Dickie Boston introduced us to a world of adventure and 'Lovers' Leap Café's' limp greasy bacon butties. We tried classics on classic crags. At Froggatt Edge, the blankness immediately generated a strong gravity all of its own to me. You can see us all dressed in green army sweaters and heavy canvas trousers, Andy Gittins in purple Hawkins Rockhoppers, Mike in blue EB Grattons from Alpine Sports, the rest of us shod in Dunlop Green Flash pumps. *Allen's Slab* Severe 3c was easy, and we bombed up *Green Gut* S 3c too. A decade later Dad seconded it, his first climb, dubious of his youngest holding the ropes above. Sometimes he reminds us how, with his leg shaking, he had to *"slap out* and *share!"*

It was the cracks that kicked us in the teeth. Andy Git and Mike were already storming up them, even things like Joe Brown's fabulous *Valkyrie* Hard Very Severe 4c, 5a. Ignorant of how to jam properly, the rest of us attempted to layback *Broken Crack* VS 4b, quite a feat even today. We must've looked like we were there to try to pull the rock apart, not climb it. Strenuous, awkward and polished all but one of us, can't remember his name, got spat off the slick, steep *Diamond Crack* HS 4a as well. We never drank enough, developing superb thirsts, but at least the roast chicken crisps and Penguins in the pack lunch were soggy.

Before the time of health and safety, still the time of *Health and Efficiency,* we weren't dissuaded from climbing without ropes. Once at Stanage Edge, three of us got stuck on *Z Crack, April Crack*, and *Christmas Crack* at the same time. It turned out 'O.K.'[4]. Later on my own, further down the crag, picture me sussing out *Leaning Buttress Gully Direct* VS 4c, a tricky looking crack skirting a blocky roof. Before, back at prep school when the Head was snooping around, long before I rock-climbed, I'd used a horizontal full body bridge to climb far up into a recess, looking directly down on his oblivious bald head. Here, ropeless I use it again to safely avoid the damp, *Tricouni* [5]- polished holds pressing into dry, rough gritstone.

The more experienced boys tried a climb that day with a rope from above. *Saul's Arête* was an XS, an Extremely Severe, a sword-like edge with no holds at all, just patches of white up it. The grit bug bit hard into us.

Back in Rutland, as often as possible we'd cycle 40 minutes from school to 'The Bridge' at Slawston. Two storeys high, of engineers' brick, seemingly studded intentionally for purpose with a great variety of rocks, cut through diagonally and with slabby flanks, the topless railway cutting made a perfect playground on which to cut our teeth.

The two jaws of the cutting are quite different in character. Just below the top of the dank side protrude large, bent, polished rusty pipes. Many a 'gripper' was had grappling onto them, trying not to slide off only to teeter further up and fail to find a slot, said to be somewhere under the grass on the sloping sandstone finish. Bold and technical the place encouraged you to "go for it" but there could be a pocket that still held moisture or come spring – post freeze-thaw – a new loose hold. Improvising, Mike used a 4mm washing line as a top rope. When Bakewell fell off, the washing line slid along the sloping top and snapped, spitting him onto the ground. Eager for one last climb, it was always a rush to get back up the hill in time for dinner. Just to hear the phrase "The Bridge" makes me smile.

---

[4] Sortie with zero kills.
[5] Nails placed in climbing boots pre Second World War.

Strangely, Leicestershire boy Jerry Moffatt, later to become a serious success, also climbed there. Who knows what might have happened if we'd met then? Interestingly our styles had already diverged. Jerry focused on doing the first in a long line of hard traverses while I buggered around soloing.

On some climbing trips, *girls* came along. A pretty boy of 14, the luscious sixth formers treated me like a Koala to pet. They were long trips. You know what Koalas are like. I got bolder on the rocks too. On my first trip to Snowdonia we stayed at Capel Curig Army Camp. We were fed libido-suppressing bromine in our drinks but much more than that I remember the climbing. "My Lord..."

Malc singled me out to come to a cliff called Tremadog Rocks. First we climbed *Christmas Curry*, even going direct up the *Micah Finish* VS. After struggling on polished grit cracks it seemed quite straightforward. "The others are probably sweating like pigs lumbering up Siabod by now", I thought.

Eric Jones (who'd soloed the North Face of the Eiger) served us tea and cake in his café. Malcolm looks at me, back at the green guide, then...back at me again.

We set off down the road looking for the path up. I even get to lead a short easy pitch up a gully. Malc straps me more securely to a tree, reminds me how to hold a lead fall with a sprung Sticht-plate again, then surprisingly instead of going straight up *One Step in the Clouds* VS, traverses right across a steep wall into the heart of the overhanging flagship Vector Buttress. Greek dancing, he disappears into a groove out of which unprintables echo for sometime.

Finally: "Climb when you're **ready**", rings out.

Everything untied from the belay:

"Climbing............"

Feels great, really great.

I sprint across until the ropes are above me again, rope goes slack, then too tight. It is desperate to pull into the slabby groove. Forehead dripping, sweat stinging hay-fevery eyes. There are no handholds except for one. I squeeze all my fingers along it. Malc gives no help but looks down quizzically.

The grip on the polished rock is actually quite good if I keep my feet squeaking low down. Running out of go I push down on the greasy finger ledge, twist my foot into a slippery pod and wriggle up into the cleft. Struggling to flick my foot onto the finger-ledge eventually I hit upon the idea of lifting it up with my free hand. There is a good flake in the corner, by putting my feet far out to the side, breathing quickly I'm soon up near the cave by Malc who is smiling broadly, shaking his head.

"Well done Dawes you have just done an Extremely Severe!" he says whacking me on the back. It was a Joe Brown route called *Nimbus* graded 5c.

I was a hero back at camp for an hour or so. Malc felt I was ready, we would return to Tremadog tomorrow.

It is an airy day. Pant Ifan, another crag at Tremadog is quite different to Bwlch Y Moch, sleeker and more intimidating. I was there, aged 15, about to try my first lead.

159 Scratch Arête

*HVS — 200 ft. * Ingle, Jones, 1962.*
Scratch, vs, starts as for Barbarian but after one pitch escapes R. up slabs to find an easier line up the R. hand area of slabs. This route, as its name implies, climbs the arête on the R. of these slabs. Start about 15 ft. R. of the step in the path. A weakness leads to a T-shaped crack.

1 **90 ft.** Go up the rib tending R. to reach the foot of the crack. Climb it, quite interesting, then via a chimney on the L., get onto a final rib and so to a stance in trees below the arête. (The crux of Scratch, a layback corner, lies 20 ft. L. and traverses in to join the arête at the top.)

2 **90 ft.** Delicately up the slab to the overhang. Step R. onto a small ledge, then using a piton, get onto the upper slab. Climb this on good holds.

3 **20 ft.** Easily up the ridge to the top.

I had a Whillans harness but it was terrible, without leg loops, just a sling up your crotch – it was not something to fall off on. Tapes with steel screwgates slung around the neck, stoppers and hexcentrics on rope, I clipped in at my waist. Malc lent me a chalk bag to keep my hands dry.

The only gear is far off to the right – an old peg and a sling on a spike on the arête. From there a traverse leads leftwards across a thin slab until under a jutting bulge. I find nowhere for a hex or nut to go in but spot a big jug above the bulge. Going for it too early, as in immediately, I'm suddenly aware of the huge swing around the rough arête into space I'll take if I fluff it. Can't reach the jug but there are two dinks below it. Foot very high, push hard on a snappy looking quartz bump a lurch for the most likely sharp bit of what looked like a bomber jug comes up trumps… Hang around there for ages beaming.

Looking out over the plain towards the sea, I give it what a fellow climbing teacher at Mile End Climbing Wall three decades later would call "Charlie Big Ones" to anyone in treble earshot. Malc tells me to do something for the camera. I'd done my first lead. It had a harder move on it than *Nimbus*, I thought.

At school on sports day all us climbers gathered below the clock tower, including all the occasional signees to trips away. It felt super cool to strut across the quad past the sixth form girls not in school uniform or khaki but now in climbing kit wearing track suits just like Fawcett and Livesey.

The clock tower was fashioned from an easily shaped shelly limestone. It gave an entertaining ramble up louvred ledges, petal carvings in a corner, with a gargoyle crux at the top (5c) to round it off. But the most excitement was when we did the big abseil off the top. Not with a belay device but with a classic wrap around the body system able to deal with the intense heat generated from a speedy descent. It therefore involved hefty steel army screwgate carabiners and multiple layers of carpet to protect shoulders and back. One boy my brother's age who rarely came along on trips was not just easily the most natural climber among us but decided he could descend the 50ft tower in just two giant leaps. Each leap had to be timed to perfection for that to work. Viewed in silhouette he actually appeared to fly, each leap away from the tower in essence a free fall where maintaining good poise in the air could only ever burn gloves and carpet. After a few practice runs he did make it in two; happily breaking the record… and his ankle.

I couldn't wait to go climbing again. One Friday, double Geography meant climbing in the Peak District with the 6th formers was off; *really* unfair. Long scheming hatched a plan, one possible to accomplish even before 'the fags' delivered the morning papers to the houses.

While everyone is asleep, EBs in hand a drowsy boy slips quietly out of a study window. Street lamps are still on. No Hallelujah chorus, frost on the ground, the quad is deserted. Torn notices do laps around the pillars of the colonnade.

The Arts Block had 12 classrooms on three floors. Each classroom had a podium, a fortunate coincidence was that the wooden desks were exactly the right size to chock against the podium to brace against the door, rendering the room un-enterable …any classes impossible. In each identical room, desk slotted as chock between podium and door he escapes out of each window, looping a string carefully on just the spindle of the latch, pulling that shut before climbing down the drainpipe from each of the classrooms. Well before breakfast he was back in his study with a cup of tea.

Sweet music to my ears when a master tells me, "Afternoon classes are cancelled Dawes".

Christmas Drinks

Over mulled wine to the soundtrack of Mel Tormé crooning out: "Chestnuts roasting on an open fire… Jack Frost nipping at your nose…" "What do *you* do?" jumpstarts the typical Christmas conversation. The question tempts me to cut the conversation short like an aristocratic patient of my father's once did. When dada asked him: "What do *you* do?" he simply answered: "I don't".

"You're the climber…?" is almost as bad.
People don't really know what rock climbing is. "Have you climbed Everest?" is the usual one.
"No…" I say (already losing patience) to the Christmas conversationalist. "I'm not like Chris Bonnington", and explain: "What we do – my brother and I – *rock* climbing – is entirely different".
I like the tone of Bristol hotshot Chris Savage's reply to a tourist who asked him how do you get down: "Oh I just jump down!"

Conversationalists can look disappointed if one is not careful, disorientated even, they can fall strangely inward, running the risk of moving on to a mental picture of Tom Cruise hanging off by his fingertips having leaped across a chasm or of Stallone bravely shooting in a bolt, from where the conversation rarely survives.

But this time my partner reloads. His eyes point up, one is squinting a little. It suggests he's got a winner in the chamber: "What about that Frenchman who climbs buildings?"

Above: Edgar, George and Mr. Yearsley.

"Alain Robert...?" I suggest, tone of voice rising at the end.
The default inevitably follows:
"*How can* he do that when he has a wife and kids?"
Then later:
 "What about the French girl who climbs without a rope?"

"More mulled wine?"
"Yes…yes…**please!"**

…Ahhh, Catherine Destivelle has come up. Finally someone to discuss with gusto, someone I've… "I've actually met", I gush.

"Miss Destivelle and I once *bouldered* together, (*climbing on tiny climbs* – I clarify).

"While *spotting* her, (*protecting her back from a rock*) Catherine fell. Protecting her I ended up embracing two things more than I'd intended..!"

Finally, inevitably, *Touching The Void* comes up:

"How *could* he have cut the rope?"…tum tee tum… "What choice did he have?"…tum tee tum… Failing is a good way to succeed these days.

Mercifully common ground is finally exhausted. In its place silence may ripen or the conversation turn philosophical, perhaps peppered with the three 'hardy perennials':

"*Have* you got a death wish?"
"How do you cling on *upside down*?"
"Why *do* you do it?"

Pre-Turkey and trimmings, unknowingly, acquaintance's forehead is slowly coming to resemble *Wrinkled Wall* on Bamford Edge.

1st – "Have you got a death wish?"

My brother Mike once said about me when I was at my height: "There is a sense about John, it wouldn't matter if it all went wrong." Perhaps that was true to an extent but it can be safer to have some distance from reflecting on danger like a doctor engaged in emergency treatment cares more efficiently by exercising triage, emotion free. In the same way a climber focusing on the rock allays the fear of falling by simply *per*-**form-**ing the most appropriate movements. It can look lackadaisical, like a death wish, but isn't.

2nd – "How do you cling on *upside down*?"

"Imagine holding on under a horizontal ladder moving sideways by hooking your heels…" I explain. My new friend's head tilts in an effort to catch their thoughts on gravity. "Given time, you could do that", I assure the by now hungry accountant.

3rd – "Why *do* you do it?"

…I love the way it calms and excites all at once. Crags are curious, enjoyable to touch, holding configurations with surprise choreography. I ape some wild moves nearly falling over.

"Dinner is served…" father announces to everyone's relief.

Summer Holidays

Christmas 1980, Mike gave me '*Hard Rock*', Ken Wilson's compendium of different climbers' essays on the best middle grade climbs in Britain. A habit grew to scan the photos for faint weaknesses on adjacent rock. Looking at the rope blown upward by the wind on one route in the Hebrides fired up a strong will to explore the cliff.

Mike had recently got a red Escort XR3i so now we could go to Snowdonia, Avon Gorge, Wintours Leap or The Peak under our own steam. Once we went to an awesome sea cliff called Craig Gogarth that put the fear of God into us. Mike's partner was Andy Gittins, so naturally mine ended up being Andy's brother, Tim. At school we got on terribly but seemed to get on alright at the crag.

At big overhanging Main Cliff we decide to try *Cordon Bleu*, the only VS, easy enough but not entirely suitable as it's a traverse. It seemed to be a series of ledges and bushes so enthusiasm encouraged me to read the guide's "make a tricky traverse" a little too freely. Arms had never known pain like it. Deserted failed nuts bounce on crossed up ropes running horizontally to Tim. Eventually, in failing light, overhung territory is escaped, up in a lichen-encrusted groove. It takes an age to fiddle in a reasonable belay but then Timmy refused to follow. There was nothing for it but to leave a runner behind to backrope and reverse the pitch. Our brothers had done *Aardvark* E2 6a without hiccup.

Years later, a look in the guide revealed the traverse done that day was in fact across *Mammoth* and *Dinosaur,* E5 territory. Next day more sensibly we try going up *Wen* S. Fifty foot off the belay, perched on laybacks and smears, moacs refuse to lodge in hairline cracks. Unbeknownst to me I was mid-crux on Livesey's 70s test-piece *High Pressure* E4. Again we make a retreat.

It was good to get back home to Eastington, onto *George's Wall* so named since it was next to the Old Holborn balmed room where gardeners Edgar Bateman and George Cam brewed up – grumbling or laughing – *what* a couple of characters. The image of Edgar's Orinoco veins forking in relief under his transparent skin will never fade, nor his 'Yoda' kindnesses, while George's loathing of "*Them bloody warrrsps*" remains a family legend. When George found a nest he'd swiftly disappear into the garage loft returning dressed in homemade Victorian regalia. Complete with mesh helmet he looked like he was testing Da Vinci's diving equipment. George and Edgar made that wall special, sometimes they brought me out a mug of 'Mellow Birds' to nurse whilst sat in the gravel dreaming up a harder move.

Mike and I watched cassettes taped off the Trinitron. One was a live broadcast of Joe Brown and daughter Zoë on the *Old Man of Hoy*. Wish we'd recorded the first in the series of *Rock Athlete* with Alan Manson trying an unclimbed high bald arête on Caley Crag in Yorkshire he'd never practised. But we did have the last episode, which was put on most days, eventually to parental groans.

> …Chris Gibb's gold Opel Manta jounces across cropped green grass to a halt opposite Dinas Cromlech in the Llanberis Pass. Fawcett lopes out, slings a big rock away from where they'll pitch a tent, grabs a boot, bends the detached sole back, saying in a Skipton drawl: "GrrrreaaaT".

Big Troll chalk bags, tracksuit bottoms and running tops the order of the day, Mike secured Dad's permission to make a traverse along one wall of the garages…

> "Come on arms… do your stuff"
> "Don't let me down, don't let me down…"

We hacksaw metal for tiny footholds, drill shallow finger pockets. I cut placements, hang gear by them so that we can practise placing protection mid-crux:

> "Get in you… Rat!"

Fawcett's climb in *Rock Athlete*, *Lord of the Flies* E6 6b was our fuel. Sustained 5c with a 6a/b crux, the traverse soon grew to take in two further (un-agreed) walls. Mike even used a belt with lead diving weights that bruised your hips if you fell. Competition soon upped the record to four 150ft circuits in one go.

Later when Mike became president of Oxford University Mountaineering Club, we, with physics brainboxes Alex Renshaw and Sean Myles (who'd later pip me to some corking new UK lines[6]) did hideous problems on

---

[6] *Rodney Mullen*, Ogwen Crack, Cidwm Roof for a start.

the shiny pebbles of Iffley Road Climbing Wall (within earshot of where Bannister ran the first 4-minute mile). Mike had a horrendously long 6c hand traverse, me a collection of tenuous slaps and multi-move dynos. Sean could often repeat them both. Then we'd all go for a pint before one of Mike's "ring-stinging" Vindaloos was ready.

Sometimes Mike took us all to Derbyshire: quantum weirdness to pass Middleton Stoney only to arrive at Stoney Middleton. Graffiti on the flaky white walls of the outside of the café's loo read: *Pull chain hard, long way to café canteen"*, and more famously: *"Oedipus ring your mother"*. Limestone dust from the quarry across the road slickened the lino, passing trucks shook your tea into a squall.

Behind their pints of tea were the local hard lads, one with his round specs misted up. Didn't know then they were there thawing out after a freezing night *up t'dale* in the woodshed. Apparently if you got there after last orders at *The Moon*, the wood racks occupied, a large wheelbarrow was the only doss. One of them had probably had their cheque that week as a cheerful woman brought them a large plate of generously buttered toasted teacakes.

Wild garlic for starters, bilberries for afters, we did what my brother called 'real climbing' in the morning – on limestone – and in the afternoon, if I'd not been a pain, we'd go to grit: Stoney/Curbar, High Tor/Black Rocks, Chee Dale/Cratcliff Tor, or Manifold Valley/Beeston/Dovedale/Roaches.

One typical day, High Tor, Mike, elbows up, grunted boldly up *Supersonic*… Was it the country's first 6c? No. Then I get to try Rick Graham's harder test piece *Bastille.* Afterwards we go to a Victorian café by Willersley Crags, octagonal like the musical box on *Watch with Mother,* for tea in cups and saucers and tarts. I'd lacked the stamina to go much beyond the crux but had managed the moves.

We go to the frightening roundness of Black Rocks afterwards. Don't solo around willy-nilly; one VS, a bald bulging bold arête sports a 6b move with a 20ft fall on! *Demon Rib* E4 5c went in the sun… seconded Mike up the reachy *Firebird* E2 5c in the gloom of the Promontory Left gully[7] and tried the scary hanging start of *Curving Arête* XS 5c. *Curving...* is a blunt powerful chest-high layback onto a hanging arête, a tenuous toe-hook essential to oppose it to share hands, horrendous for the short.

[7] Twelve years later I'll lasso the spike on Prom Traverse and leap across the gully to hit a sloping pocket to give *The Bounder* E5 6c.

One day I find myself successful, standing cosily on the big notch of *Curving*... beyond all difficulty I take the opportunity to peer around at the raw dimple-rent folds of the pinnacle's tantalisingly unclimbable groove. Sole protection would be in a baby's rattle flair at its base. Guarded by an unusable 60° sloper and violently undercut, you could see why Woodward had faltered.

I hadn't done any new climbs yet but I'd come close early on at Avon on *Gymslip*. At Millstone Mike and Andy were wrestling with *Twicker* E3 5c, a testing roof crack out of a cave. Left to my own devices I'd soloed John Allen's *Technical Master* 6b, the first flake of what in 1984 became my *Monopoly* E5 6b, as usual had soloed 40ft up to the scoop below the crux of *Edge Lane* E5 5c, then bouldered out the arête right of *Green Death* until standing on a big foothold. I walk back past *Twicker* again to take a look at the 80ft high barrel-shaped *Great Slab*. Its slick 60° unclimbed centre had a big untouched pocket at 50ft. Was the notion the slab could be safely slid and rolled off before that reasonable?

…Climbing up, then down greasy penny thick rugosities, eventually I trust a smaller one not to snap or grease me off before eyeballing the hole … lurch, grab, *squirt* – it's full of water – Champagne! From the ground chalk and water streak spell outrageous. The feeling of doing this new climb was unsurpassed. I can't wait to show Andy and Mike.

Later, I spot the climb written up at E5 6a, *The Snivelling Shit*.

Gabriel Regan's classic celebratory article 'Grit Between Your Toes' in *Crags* magazine cracked open the atom of my obsession: black and whites of Choe Brooks high up on *Archangel*[8] rope arced way off to the side, Pete O'Donovan teetering up the flared groove of *Profit of Doom*, Bancroft poised feline on *Heartless Hare*. At home at Eastington, magazine put down, the arêtes of the Hall now dry outside call out to be climbed, curiously 'well-appointed' to crystallize the enthusiasm born from what I've just read.

One oft-tried wall on eroded serrated brick above a window involved the use of the sloping gloss-painted putty of a window frame as a foothold. A slip would result in a nasty tumble into a mangling gap between jutting concrete lintel and upturned oil tank slick with algae. It was under a significant bulge. However it dawned on me that sucking waist out as far as it would go from the wall then flicking it back in to create a bespoke

[8] The other name for *Saul's Arête*.

Mexican wave down the body, the toe's grip on the sloping putty would be enhanced at exactly the moment I reached up for the unfamiliar edge. If the hold above did prove poorer than necessary this way it would be possible to jump back in time flat onto the oil tank.

Approaching climbs by learning to down climb, working out the sequence carefully by sight and sortie, practising landing well, all these technical experiments stood me in good stead for the grit.

There were also possibilities for what later became branded as *Parkour*, which helped me to speed up and trust my movement. When we first got to Eastington Dad installed a playground. The 25ft slide's handrails were good for no hands balance practice and grinds, the steel slide itself for smearing. Best of all though was a scary heavy oak beam swing, basically a medieval battering ram, and not safe at all. Articulated on two 'A' frames with six square metal hoops for us kids to hang on tight, when we gave it full bananas the down bars would almost go horizontal. Alone, running on the spot to move the beam, the challenge was to run over all six hoops as the beam went back and forth, hurdling the hoops as they hurtled past. Beam rising and falling, at its highest point you had to bend your knees, at its lowest ebb your feet almost coming off the beam completely. It required a feeling for the Rolls Royce rhythm of the giant cue. You couldn't look both ways either. Blind in the reverse phase you had to learn to trust your body knew where the hoops were. It took time to build up to that.[9] As Simon Jones, Wharncliffe pioneer might've said in 'Barnsley' were he there then: "*It could get messy*".

With hard carbon EBs, $Mg\ CO_2\ 5\ H_2O$ powder bought by the kilo from bemused chemists accustomed to selling it to the constipated, Axminster offcut as bouldering mat, I'd always finish on the garage traverse but only after scoping the same lines on the house over and over again. With potential new climbs facing every point of the compass, the punch of weather became something to reckon with; in any given mood which line to give a wide berth to, which to try. Ace to add another climb to Eastington's repertoire once in awhile.

At the back of the hall, open at ground level was a sheltered area resembling an Elizabethan market used by the BBC for a London street scene in *Twm*

---

[9] Tiger Woods used to chip a golf ball off a putter onto a cylindrical wall.

Sion Cati. I played an urchin who eyes and pilfers an apple. Having to run slow for the camera pan but look fast took some doing. Twenty apples later I was sick. One possible line went up from here. It'd finish in Dad's office directly above, if I could do it.

Dad is optimism in a tin, visible at a glance into his office: a photo of a Jojoba, a revolutionary oil-producing desert plant on the wall, a tin of new environmentally friendly paint on the floor; a layered 3D acrylic display device on a side desk; all investment concerns of his, and something Mum was concerned about as well.

The line wasn't a rock climb at all being on wood and lead. Dowels could prove loose, rotten or bomber, or when absent left a pocket you had to be careful not to leave a finger in. Flagstones dry today, oak dowel checked and seated like a mid 80s hand-placed peg with the heel of a hand, the move is a footless mantel off it and another to its left. This attempt I've sufficient confidence in my and the dowel's strength to invert my body by locking out mantled, crowding fingers over thumb, wrist to cheek, heel-hooking a flat lead lip off left, and roll up to poke my head into the open office window.

"Hi Pads."
"Hey Spud."

Like I often felt, it was as though the line had become familiar with me, thought it over and simply decided to let me do it that day, E5 6c. It was as if any line would go with enough familiarity, in time.

Another line, another day, an attempt on a sandstone arête by the kitchen leads to a traverse right above pea gravel and stone trough to the window of Dr Dawes' surgery. It was here Dad treated patients including Led Zeppelin's John Bonham, whom Dad cautioned not to drink too much! Folks out, I've climbed 30ft up into a cul-de-sac. The window not open enough to reach the latch, no one about to let me in, all that consoles me is the violet blue of the sunlit apothecary bottles. I could try and reverse but there *was* a possible finish above that would involve monkeying up questionable clay roof tiles, feet still on the sandstone and mortar wall. I can't resist. An unlikely find, a good long edge, makes it possible to clear loose grit off yet higher edges. Soon the section where I cannot chalk up goes quickly enough from the window for grip to remain laybacking up the 35° edge of the hot red roof. E6 6b.

At 45ft, the highest line was up a twin chimneystack above the study. It had a hefty Wisteria at the base, a one off 'Get out of jail card', but nevertheless a pest to find holds under. The brick line had no particularly hard move but was very sustained, finishing gingerly up a flimsy zig-zag lingerie of bricks to the stack's summit. It got the name *Poland* for some reason, E7 6b.

At the other side of the house was the Music Room, bright, calm and contemplative, lined in rare splendid oak panelling. Nearby were the swimming pool arêtes, superb Millstone Edge-like 'highballs' with spongy flowerbeds at their base. One rounded a flagstone ramp by a swoop rock up on just adequate dimples then stormed up a well-pointed brick chimney by a once and for all bear hug.

But the most outrageous line, Eastington's last great problem, was the gently overhanging *Snooker Room Arête*. Just like Millstone's *Master's Edge* it encourages you high quickly. The crux revolves around a curious four finger tip incut in a beautiful kiln warped brick. Stepping high on a just adequate edge, a pinch stabilises you, then, having originally spied it from another angle, I knew there was a tip side pull around the arête, allowing a layback to reach an improving nest of triangular notches. What I would do if I got higher I didn't know, it was too high to finish. It might be possible to traverse off into my bedroom…

George Cam on his gardening rounds was at a loss to explain the growing divot in the lawn.

One day I was really taking it on, frustratingly close. Upstairs for a bath…
too hot… Steve Hackett's *Voyage Of The Acolyte* skips cold tap on …I
clean the Ortofon VMS20E needle… "Eureka!" – There's another way to
do it. I return for just one last go. The sequence almost works. I try twice
more, Tips screaming, peering up, a queasy feeling comes over me. "Oh
my God!" Niagara.

…There're just two examples of panelling like it in England…My parents
are sweet about it but the days that went by waiting for the panels to dry
were excruciating. Thankfully they didn't warp.

It seemed every time I did something great I'd have to do something terrible.
I worried a lot really and for years had a recurring nightmare:

… a winding colonial avenue, Brazil perhaps or India. Deserted, heavy in
the overcast heat decaying palatial villas hum, slowly overcome by jungle.
Suddenly, I'm flung deep into a villa's innards, dropped into a dizzying
motion, impossible to stop. Forced to run around corners to keep from falling,
mushroom plaster and damp rotten apple wood beams tumble, rotating slowly
into the darkness of the void. My body lands in a solid but flared alcove. It
provides nothing more than a temporary lull. A flaking meat-like beam below
is the only place left to go. Feet first, full weight, the beam holds…then
suddenly high up on a giant baroque cathedral to an unknown religion I'm
hanging on unfastened blocks that teeter out into space. Huge wind rises and
falls so I don't know if I cling on too hard or not enough. The block's huge
weight scares me but is my only reassurance. Closing my eyes, hands on, the
stones and I whirl together. If I can only just relax, hold on gently, that's what
makes the looseness solidify in my mind.

Jolt…bolt upright stuck to the sheets, I feel no relief on waking, for
throughout the dream there's a feeling that my doppelganger is actually
experiencing this too; and that if it does go wrong in this world he'd not
wake up in that.

It was a wonderful aspect of my childhood to have lived in an impromptu
cliffscape and to have grown up outside in a place where the world was able
to do things at its own pace – appreciating vegetables emerge mysteriously
from the ground, seeing clouds tumble slowly overhead through an afternoon.
It'd be easier to accept later: unclimbed stone may take time to know you.

Anything Goes

In term time I climbed all over Uppingham. Ropeless, eyes peeled constantly for 'objecting' danger. I improved a lot, became physically stronger too, by doing pull-ups, experimenting in the gym with wrist rolls, dips and rings. In 'The Book' I kept cut-out photos and made lists of prospective new climbs on both brick and cliff.

One major challenge was up the outside of the sports hall, its thinnest section was 30ft above flat tarmac. It consisted of two vertical brick ribs, a foot apart, protruding either side of a concrete stanchion. A mere single digit deep, these barely allowed a precise and very strenuous layback that had to be taken at a sprint. It put me just within reach of the concrete lintel at the brick rib's thinnest just as the only foothold, a round structural plate, fell out of use.

I'd tried this 35ft line repeatedly but had never quite gone for it. This time past my highpoint I find myself marooned, pumping out, hanging strenuously on a sloping concrete lintel with only a tenuous scissor bridge for feet. The situation is far worse than it might've been since I find the lintel is simply sitting unfastened on sandy cement.

Through tilting glass slats, the sharp backs of which scrape my arms, I see boys in their gym togs blithely playing badminton inside. The only way is up, and now. Holding on, elbows up, forced to press down precisely on the very middle of the lintel, throwing a foot out to the side, rocking and making sure to press gently only on the screws above batons, I manage to roll over onto the mossy asbestos roof spreading my weight as evenly as possible. Sliding down a plastic drainpipe back to the sports centre car park Uppingham's boldest climb is in the bag. E7 6b.

Mike and And larking about.

Everything done pleased me, everything almost done excited me, and the things I couldn't do, far from being frustrating only spurred me on to continually practise conjuring up the easiest way they might be done.

Amazingly, in Farleigh House's very own grounds, under the ivy cloak of the deserted Fives court, existed the perfect laboratory. Jumping the fence to try its main arête of reliable handmade engineer's brick was as pregnant a leap as it would've been to turn the cover of *Crags* magazine and actually jump in. Over the fence John Allen was on a cairn, confident below Proctor's *Green Death*, Bancroft smiled, scaring me with the prospect of trying his *Narcissus*. Even the waxy rouge of the building itself held a special atmosphere for me, its silence and smell grounding me happily in the damp grass beneath a big tree, birds and bees cruising around.

Aged 17, I loved pull ups – a record of 77 on a thick scaffold bar without getting off, 48 in one go, shaking out on one arm to continue – but something about training didn't appeal. The point was to climb rock by deep intention, experiment and invention, not just grunt. To make it come alive.

I heard about Baguazhang later, a martial art whose expert practitioners could reputedly float on air. Even though that would nullify the game fundamentally, it hinted at the mystery. What the mystery was I was not sure, that was part of the mystery.

In the 80s movement was taking off, coming away from its surfaces in a revolutionary way. Bodies lightened speeded up: breakdancers' heads became feet to spin on, skaters *ollied* the board they stood on top of, opening up a whole new wave of moves. BMX. Laird Hamilton rode the big waves looking like a God. Freddie Spencer slid GP bikes on tarmac as if he was still on grass. Vatannen in Group B *left foot-braking* the T16, Senna in F1, Oh...my...God! All this was a fresh kinaesthetic mandala, a quickening expression of our inner urge to fly.

As much as Fosbury's Flop changed high jump forever I could sense climbing would be transformed by new ways of spinning together body and mind. Years before at preparatory school on the gym wall bars something had begun to bubble up. Start, feet on the bottom rung, hands three rungs up...first pulse, feet go where hands have just left – a position your body knows already so you don't have to look. Then using synchronised movements of hands and feet all limbs could generate movement as one – like a gibbon. Strangely, using this mode of movement the steeper it gets the easier, as the body naturally peels away increasingly from the vertical as it accelerates. With each pulse it is possible to miss out more and more rungs as momentum builds.

Of course this approach works easier on a regular format like wall bars, but on Plas Y Brenin's greasy wall we would experiment at unlocking this innovatory scamper on the assymetrical by a variety of limb combinations including flik-flaks, simultaneous hooks, arm whirling etc.

Master Of Rock John Gill had performed amazing dynos in 50s America, but I sensed momentum still hid potential. I love high grades but I wasn't interested merely in the pursuit of difficulty. What are the lost sounds of karate!?…'Hung', 'ha' and 'hai' remain, but three have reputedly been lost. Can we find them again?

Paul Pritchard, Trevor Hodgson and many others came along but it was Bobby Drury who most got caught up in the kinaesthetic web we were spinning. Enthusiasm and belief caught holds you would never suspect were possible. Using holds one after the other without stopping, by *knowing* where holds were rather than *looking* at them it became possible to fly past sections impossible to climb in any other way.

When the Wright brothers left earth there must have been a sense that the fragile plane flew not with just a person aboard but with the whole of humanity. The sky wasn't even the limit. Into the blank of mind came the unmistakeable sense that this was a new thread for the fabric of motion to weave with. The great climbing library in the sky would have to find a new shelf for these moves.

All this was a continuation of the search for what lay at the heart of the profound mystery radiating out from the photograph of Andy Barker on John Allen's *Above and Beyond the Kinaesthetic Barrier.* Embedded somewhere in its name and the quality of the light in that image of Burbage South was the absolute sense of something I longed for. Moves that dropped into mind, or I dreamt up I scoured the physical world to find.

One recurrent daydream at Uppingham was that somewhere out on a moor was a stone. Pick *that* one, *your* one up, and the secret character of rock would reveal itself. Aborigines feel ancestors all about. Rudolf Steiner considered the rock conscious, even the *only true mind*. That is the strange inkling I felt coloured with. Of course this animist leaning was ripe to be picked on as a 'Johnny Classic'.

No compensations on the horizon, arriving back at Farleigh one bleak black evening, wet collared after trudging back from double Biology I pass the magazine pile. *Dawes J* is handwritten on the cover of *Climber and Rambler*. The magazine I'd ordered had come. Inside is a photomontage of Jonny Woodward, bespectacled, employing what must surely be magic on an amazing blunt arête. The crux of the E7 7b 'used a solitary crystal'. In another shot he had left foot and left hand out in space, three ropes dangling. Yet the climb's name *Beau Geste* communicated most, it opened a place in my mind outside time.

That talisman came with me over the fence each time I tried the centre of the Fives Court's back wall. The base of the wall sported two shiny horizontal ramps. Parallel, four feet apart sloping at 45°, they lent the line a slippery slab aspect, classy for an Uppingham climb. With familiarity you could skip the first move, pointed toe still for a gentle hop for a high edge. Everything had to land just so, one foot tapped crucially on the shine of the first ramp for the position to deliver. Above were quite good fingertip edges, useful until perched upon the upper shiny ramp, when bodyweight returns, trying to peel itself off.

Above was dread-fingery, slightly outward leaning – biting crimp...toes face the same way, right toe pulling out...body left low, left toe across into crease, two finger tip way up, and share, left foot rip...20ft fall *sting*-ing feet...roll... woman bringing in washing turns around amazed, sees me hopping, silently swearing. Warm red rugby shirt.

A new level of excitement comes...in the scent of the impossible.

Two weeks later there is a fresh sense of purpose as I vault the fence for this latest "last go" of perhaps 50. The start sequence goes by cleaner than ever. Side on diagonally inclined jabbing off feet to snatch a razor incut left foot comes off, body unbalanced rotates out slowly; fall and success *ablend;* at last the 'unclimbed zone' arrives feather-bold with rich momentum. Before checking the distance, hand snatches again to a decorative tile row. Stomach strong, floating precariously the edging foot askew, fingers skate to suit on the shine. Stood motionless in a new way atop the narrow wall, each moment's balance now sampled at a new higher frequency, even though I've just climbed this wall it still seems impossible. A look across into the first branches of the big tree has me indescribably happy.

So far the hardest climbs on rock looked covered in holds to me. None seemed truly impossible but at Millstone Edge in the holidays I'd tried to solo a 60s aid line between Embankment 2 and 3 ground up. That faint old peg seam did look wildly impossible; natty, blank, and, at 75°, a good angle for me.

…Once stones on the run up were cleared away, the grab for the first pocket 15ft up was slowly perfected. Then you had to pull one hand out, put the other in. A few more moves led up to where there was an old bolt stud. Climbed down, jumped off.

On abseil, cleaning ancient grit out of the peg scars higher up, a Stopper slot is revealed to compliment the bolt, making it feasible to lead – if the moves will go.

EB Grattons had perhaps 20% less grip than Firés. On this short man's crux, delicate, brutal, and turbulent: right toe went on a shiny shallow triangular ramp forcing the ill suited right hand to oppose it at only one angle, a horizontal edge for your left hand holding that precise angle. This made the key shape very fierce, to move from it fiercer still. At some point the left hand had to come off to make room for a super high left foot. To do this extra grip had to be conjured up from the ramp mid-move. Even to set up for it the bunched laybacks and foot swaps involved a maelstrom of conundrums. Eventually steeling up on the crimp at just the right time to make extra grip a single leg press up on the edge gives a hands-off reward. Thirty goes and the ten moves to cover the crux five feet were solved.

Unfortunately, investigating a potentially easier sequence yanking hard on a higher sharp flake I rip the tip of my finger clean off. But I was very excited. Awareness fizzing smoothly, body somehow feeling less dense, driving down the sump breaking quarry track in the Honda the powdered seam looked incredible.

Words are too furry to carve this out cleanly but the experience freed a private recognition. All everywhere felt where it was by matching body so keenly to the rock, all points in space had become space. It felt like an undulating porcelain sheet, my body on it a porcelain ball. Separate, inseparable, now with each tilt and roll of the ball the new porcelain land runs silent.

The sense of magic the unclimbed set off in me then was huge, precise and naïve. I felt all climbers felt like me. I'd elevated climbers to an antiauthoritarian priesthood that projected themselves up increasingly reflective mirrors escaping the captivity of capitalist dronery.

Late 1982 returning to the Peak to try to lead it, it was a slap in the face to read the Stoney new routes book. There was a new route at Millstone, *Scritto's Republic* E6 6c/7a, by none other than Ron Fawcett, the first 7a in England. I was bewildered but proud. It *was* the same line.

At Millstone, immediately from a long way off I sense there is something different about the line. Stomp across the quarry floor. Right where the flake that'd been solid enough to rip my tip off, what had ended the previous visit's efforts, was now a 3-finger first digit side-pull. Climbing up the hillock right of *London Wall* shock furiously moves young legs beyond me. Don't know where I'm going. And suddenly there he is…FAWCETT.

"You should have left that for someone better than you… someone like me", I say.

Fawcett's wife Gill scowls at me, eyes seeming to say: "*Who is this public school brat to speak to my husband like that?*" She chases me around but she cannot even touch me. Throughout her pursuit remaining perfectly parallel to, and facing Ron, head on like a gimballed tank's cannon, the separate reality I thought I shared was forever ripped to shreds.

That was that. What had been a dreamlike collective experiment to push the limit had become – inevitably – a lethal stone-faced competition.[10]

However there was one last climb still to do back at school. The Headmaster was leaving. I had a surprise for him: some bed sheets from Farleigh, an indelible marker from carpentry. Dawn on the last day of school, scaling the assembly hall by a long drainpipe, traversing the roof ridge, I abseil to place a banner. It was out of reach of school maintenance's longest ladder, impossible to remove before parents arrived, and read: "THANK YOU SO MUCH FOR ALL YOU HAVE DONE FOR US OVER THE YEARS!"

Sundays at chapel was for contemplating Paul Nunn's guide to *Climbing in the Peak District*. As the gaps on the crags had drawn Johnny in so it was he drew new lines in 'The Book'. When we all finally sang Jerusalem for the last time before leaving Uppingham the book according to Johnny was full. It was time to see what was in it.

[10] With hindsight it seems far-fetched that Ron altered *Scrittos*. See Note A at back.

Top clockwise: *Fives Court Arête* E5 6b, crux at the
top, the side wall had a hard layback rib, inside was
a running problem across from corner to corner.
Powerful tenuous E7 laybacking up Uppingham
School sports centre.
By the Chemistry block *Epée* 6c, was a devilishly
thin, long arête; blind slappy to hit holds, pre-sight-
ed, around the corner.

"Manchester... so much to answer for". Problem 5. Photo: Craig Smith (in green).

Above: The arête in Stone Monkey.
Right: *Midnight Oil* 6c. A hold found
pressing nail into blank concrete is just
enough to kill the barndoor.

Unclimbed problem 8.

The Veil 6c. Fantastic problem pressing off a poor crease to a twisting dyno.

Breakdance E3 6a. On a cold day the Cowperstone is as close as you'll get to Club Tropicana as it faces in a different direction to the main edge. Photo: Neil Foster

Above: I first did this wall at Millstone left of *White Wall* in '84 with a side runner in the pod of *Bond Street*. Going back in '86 I did it with a low peg. *Monopoly* E7 6b is a brilliant climb. Photo: Bill McKee.
Right: *Hot Knives* E4 6c second ascent. Massively hot day. 1984 was hot. Photo: Neil Foster.

Facing page, top left clockwise:
The Fingertip Phenomenon E5 6a.
Twin Cam E4 6c.
Onsight optimism... I'd spotted a runner slot high up. And attemped the line of *Knocking on Heaven's Door* direct from the ground. The genial and kind Phil Parker, sadly no longer with us, on the ropes. The runner in the flake pulled breaking the rock. Take a look next time you are there.
The beautiful *Weather Report* E6 6c. It does not go up the wall, but goes left to the arête.

Grit 'N: Small particles of stone or sand, esp as causing discomfort, or clogging machinery (also ~ Stone)

Coarse Sandstone. Grain or texture of stone.

Colloq: Strength of character, pluck, endurance

Concise Oxford Dictionary

Top right clockwise: *Non-Stick Vicar* E5 6c. Ground up first ascent with falls. The mantel is the crux.

Silk E6 6c. On sight first ascent half an hour before doing *Ulysses'* second ascent. See note a. Photo: Neil Foster.

Untoward E5 6b. Photo: Neil Foster. An exciting prospect to do ground up, first ascent, no falls. Note shirt and wire brush in the break.

Old Rubber

Surprised waking up on an iced gritstone bench in Froggatt barn, with no feeling in one slept-on leg, I knew I could cut what I'd come for. We were off to Froggatt Edge, a place one bespectacled blond perceptively calls 'The Beach'. If gritstone edges were characterised as chocolate assortments it might be considered a box of mint thins. By that token, Black Rocks might be Grandma's liqueurs. Many of the essential steppingstones to competent cragsmanship are there but that was not all.

Previously in super EB Grattons, a hasty apprenticeship on *Great Slab*, the neighbouring *Heartless Hare*, and *Joe's Slab* traverse had peaked with a new 6c direct start to Livesey's *Downhill Racer* XS 6a. (Pete brought an athleticism to climbing and had an irreverent sense of humour. One party piece of his was to emerge magically out of Malham Tarn on crowded Sundays to alarm tourists, having dropped a heavy rock, used to keep himself hidden under the water.) Funny but chipping is sad. *Downhill Racer* – supposedly brushed with a *'brush of 6 inch nails'* remains chipped, but an unclimbed prospect of his left of Allen's *Hairless Heart* had had a new hold too until filled in by Steve Bancroft. It lay up the very centre of Great Slab finishing up the unclimbed steep central headwall.

Teetering over the sloping edge thick cotton drags around my shoulders. A peek down with young eyes for more holds is a disappointment. It takes a frustrating hour to fix a tricky belay to inspect the climb. The steep headwall is on poor slopers but fortunately there is a Stopper 2 placement side on in the break that marks the change of angle. (The fashion then, dumb just to copy, was to extend the plastic sleeved wire using a sling, saving the weight and length of the extra crab!)

The slab is a tease. Easy to 30ft, it then turns to a ramp that pinches up, finally disappearing in an unappealing volley of ripples. They must be trod up on blind, till edging very precariously on a dime-sized edge, fingertips can walk up onto a natural crimp to the side of the filled-in chiselling. Hard carbon rubber took a precise determined approach to get the most from but on this move they are even more unnerving. At my height, to pull into a crimp on the tiny hold pulls the boot up, threatening to peel it back, off the ripple.

Side runner far to the side was academic, a 40ft ground fall unavoidable unless you somehow grab the slanting ledge down left of the crux. Naively, the side runner would merely have ensured my hips got a medieval battering shortly after legs.

I was said to have problems concentrating at school, though that was on dull things. Here, focus sharp the moves pass as imagined. Though pumping dangerously on the slappy headwall, I mantel out to an amazing tangle of elation. A palpable lightness finds its place in my body again.

Mrs Yearsley's *Jugged Hare* was favourite tucker and an apt pun for the slab. E5 6c – routes didn't get E6 then. Seeing the photo of it in *Climber and Rambler* was a validation. Prone to pop off, to have driven old rubber that hard was impressive. Has anyone else done it in EBs?[11] Was it 6c like that? Looking back it was trickier, more dangerous, if shorter lived than contemporary E7s like *The Bells, The Bells* and *The Master's Edge*.

It was a major new line on *Great Slab*. Only Joe Brown, John Allen, Steve Bancroft had routes here. John Dawes had arrived.

What did you do in your year off?

---

[11] I'd love to get hold of a mint pair of size six originals.

"Avon calling…"

I got a job in a fancy box factory in Upton on (often in) Severn, where Nigel Mansell comes from, to earn the money to fuel car and obsession. Getting my bum pinched by busty middle-aged women, I mostly burned waste out the back on a big bonfire in the sun.

Climbed a great deal that year, a lot with Mike and Andy. There was quite a rivalry between us, and precious little patience. We climbed regularly at subtle Avon Gorge. Bold, intricate of line, technically tricksome yet often sustained as well, it was a great place to develop strength of purpose and body.

Once on Suspension Bridge Buttress, I'd just led *GT Special* E3/4 6a. Mike didn't want to do it, had done it before and went off to the car. I'd managed to jam Mike's favourite Hex 2 on orange rope in the mid-height bulge and – God forbid – failed to get it when lowering off on lead. I was expected to get it out at any cost. Normally the second's job, for some reason probably my impatience, I ended up truly 'hexed' attempting to retrieve the gear from below.

It's an easy solo to 40ft. There, locking off a jug on easy ground the piece in the bulge was not quite retrievable. It had rotated. To twiddle it out I sat crouched, one foot pulling on a ledge, the other pressing in below it. With this cantilever it was possible to reach his Hex 2 with either hand. It moved around but I couldn't see how to manoeuvre it.

…figuring I need to see it better to unseat it means having to grab the Clog 2200 with both hands! Pulling up on it reveals how to twist the Hex…when it comes out I'll just grab the ledge at my feet.

It made sense!

It starts well – the piece comes out, but with a surprise jolt the cantilever on the ledge fails suddenly… grab for the ledge…werrr…slip on shiny polish somehow makes me catch it with my chin and nose! …Falling… 35ft in a blink, steep scree collects one foot twanging the other leg into a split.

A staggering crawl has me back at the car, not much blood spilt. Mike's precious Hex 2 safely back on his rack. I said I was fine apparently, didn't want to go to hospital, not wanting to cause trouble.

Next day, off climbing at Wintours' Leap, Mike parks in a cul-de-sac opposite the pub. I can't walk. When Mike catches sight of me crawling on all fours back across the road he can't resist laughing out loud. A week on, the pain persists. The doctor scanning the x-ray overlooks a crack in my pelvis. I walk around with a broken pelvis for a further week before it is spotted.

I was dissuaded from doing the A levels I wanted to do, Art and English, ("they'd not form the basis for a secure future") so my subjects were decided for me. Suddenly incapacitated by my pelvic injury, with three weeks left until exams, I revise hard for once, getting C in Chemistry, D in Biology and A with distinction in Geology. I wanted to live in the Peak and Manchester University accepts me to read Geography and Geology.

Heart Stew

On one rare occasion when I find myself looking into an oak drawer of the palaeontology room, I hear a voice at my shoulder. It's my tutor who asks me: "And you are?"

But the regularity with which I missed lectures seemed a sensible waywardness to try and pull myself together. It felt like my bones were splintered throughout the national park. Somehow I had to collect them back together.

My sympathy worthy housemates at 20 Clarke Road, Julian and Catherine, were trendy lefties. Durutti Column slunk under their door past long wool coats toward a party a long way off. Freezing like only Manchester can be, no ice in sight but with a ripping wet wind that tore the heart out of you to no-one's benefit, a kebab from Abdul's in Rusholme often felt like necessary first aid.

I'd already decided I wasn't going to stay at University but I had no clue what I wanted to do in '*the real world*' as mother called it. One morning the deep tones of my father were audible in the hall outside my room. Father in blazer and tie appears at the door, clearly horrified to see me buried in a single mattress on the floor. Fellow Geology student Julian reminds me: "Johnny…don't forget you've got an exam". I'd forgotten the exam and that my parents were coming as well.

At one pinched party my lack of interest and contempt for 'normal' – cheery stupid – people left an unforgivable calling card on the floor, for which I apologise. Insecure as well as angry I don't think I realised I was shy then, a rock face still expressed me more clearly than my flesh face. To talk, be heard as well, meant to shout, something that must be heard. Self-centred, I was where my world started and finished. With The Hacienda, The Smiths and Joy Division Manchester was on fire with dour cool that suited my melancholy 1000 yard stare perfectly.

While waiting for the bus, precise body shapes track through my mind, thin tips preserving the tactile sense of hold on shape. Then I remember again, the night before – Oh no – I'd made improper, and looking back sensibly, doomed advances to Julian's girlfriend; not the most amazing move I've ever made.

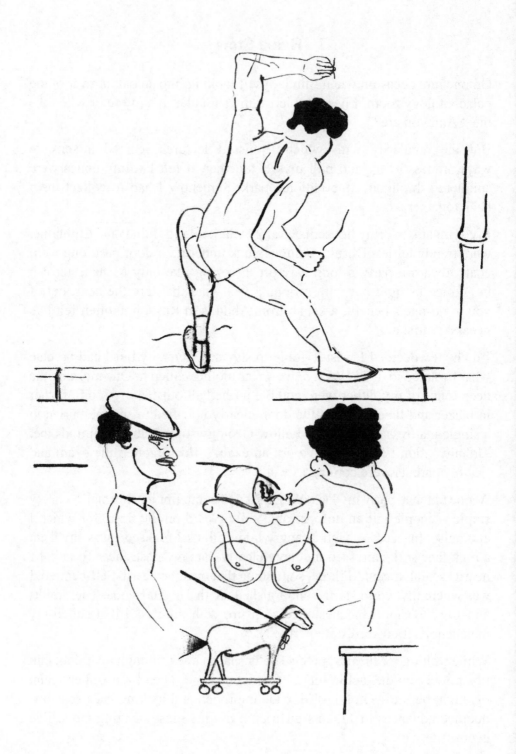

In 1984 Manchester University's climbers all met at MacDougal Climbing Wall. It was in a single room, one amongst many used by other clubs on the corridor. The windows were stuck fast with gloss paint which ensured it suffered from condensation that sometimes froze to the wall.

While skint, toe through boot wit, Dave Abbey huffed efficiently around yet another circuit, Big Nige quietly locked off, solid on the next small scraped hole or inset rock. I was more into new problems, sparring with the ever enthusiastic Bill McKee or patient friendly Doctor Clark or winding up squeaky Mark with a brilliant opinion. Oh dear…

Most of the MUMC hardmen climbed E4/5. Bill was the main person to indulge me chatting about new climbs in the Peak, with a reach on him and strong fingers he did problems that tried me. For ages we vied to repeat Jonny Woodward's English 7a *Pinch of Salt*. The Pinch was an impossibly flared vertical inset slate. Married to a gloss edge, using a foothold in an awkward position the idea was to strike for a distant edge. It took me two terms. Jonny told me when I later met him making my Peak climbing history video, '*Best Forgotten Art*', that he'd never actually done it, but leaving myself no option but to succeed, I'd finally done just that.

Sometimes a visit to Crispin and Hugh's flat in Mosside was in order. My dress suggested I wasn't worth robbing, but I was still careful to keep plum in mouth on the way there. Crispin cooked a mean heart stew which we'd eat watching Danger Mouse. "Don't be so ridiculous DM". We all loved Stanage, Crispin did a new route in *A Thousand Natural Shocks,* I *Weather Report* E6 6c up either side of the same arête, but *The Cool Curl* was more respectable commemorating our good friend's death.

Success on the MacDougal gave some inoculation against gravity on the dynamic new grit and slate lines but even more so did the concrete challenges of the Mancunian Way. Almost all of the concrete underpass stays dry even in rain, but the hardest possibilities on concrete only came feasible on bitter days when the grit would have been in perfect nick.

…Black ice lethal underfoot, Cola frozen inside a crumpled bottle, itself stuck fast to invisible grime, all around are the hardest looking problems, and just as exciting, impossible lines; so hard they encouraged one to practise wondering how they *would* be climbed rather than if they *could*, all exercising the crucial invisible muscle of imagination.

Doing even a single new move was a big buzz. Over a year I slowly made the venue a rich one; with a taut crucifix bulge, dynamic layback, numerous superb arêtes, limit hangs on traverses – most never quite linked, and dynos, big and snatchy small. Soon there were 20 problems including three 7as and six 6cs, there was even a 100ft 5a traverse on jugs finishing, fear and loathing, on the busy summit flyover.

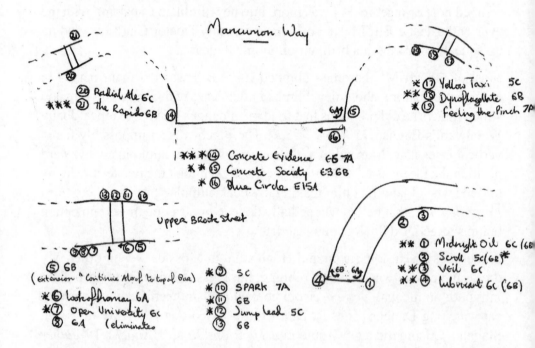

After I repeated Quentin Fischer's huge *George's Wall Dyno* at Stoney on my first visit, a problem the 6ft 4in boulderer had tried for two years, Quent visited the concrete to add a monster jump of his own. Tony Ryan, a meticulous over-talented climber from Longsight, was the main person to repeat any of the hard problems – without getting a hair out of place. He used to give me a good going over on visits to Altrincham Wall too, where the Lancashire, Liverpool and Manc scene met up. John Hartley's 7as at Wilton were sitting ducks.

None of this was where my mind was. It was at Mesmer's[12] playground, the ball and lightning impossible grit that I, clueless with clarity, was bent

[12] Franz Mesmer might have recognised the natural energetic transference at Burbage that he believed happened between all animated and inanimate objects.

on the trail of something impregnable, unstoppably on target. Homing instinct itself, but without journey or destination or home even. There were hushes though; engine stilled cooling, the alloys' bright twang fades slowly. Manchester, and school and home behind in the same direction, somehow I could hear my quarry over the hill. A hopelessly detailed dead pool, not free of hope, but knowing nothing of hope, nothing to hope, all satisfaction, policy or ploy all clearly unnecessary and extra.

Quartz healing, a stout oblong Magritte-tuned gritstone water trough on the top path to Burbage South always struck a chord with Jules and I. Pebble stuck out beyond its geometry, right square, allowed my mind to drop away. Julian had inevitably caught the greatest bug as well, so contagious is it. He cut left to solo around the right hand end of the crag. I'd a wonder to explore further along the edge. Excited but embodied steps take me to where my eyes can see a tremulous symphony of ached green dishes, just so dimples, sinuous nothing rivulets. Cold clean air rips at my face.

Perspective enriched, years later on a summer's dusk, closer again to satisfaction, the last Lancaster bomber will fly – seemingly slow enough to fall out of the sky – from the ancient fort of Higgar Tor passing right over me on the top of Brook's Buttress[13]. But on this clear crystal spring morning Julian will join me just as I finish brushing off the lichen. He has just soloed *Pebble Mill* E4 6b clean (his hardest previous climb was E1!) We were strong if strained friends but the rock eclipsed our awkwardness, a lightness, a brightness lit up my mood trying that rich dark green slab. It wouldn't go straight up the arête, (or so I thought then Pete) no-one had entertained the teetery lesser traverse, though when you do, it is all it needs to be and no more. Feeling, as though finding your dancing way by a strangely sound sound, on this line holds *were* where I felt in my mind they should be. It was unlike any climb on grit at the time and close to the fantastical lines peopling my mind. A slab climb but embedded in a wall, each twist swing and pop was crucial to link each semaphor of fragile grip back in. Working beautifully the climb exudes a tense rhythm. Halfway through what, energizingly I already knew I'd call *The Braille Trail*, I look down off the mid-height hands-off shake and smile at Jules in celebration. Thanks for being there, you two, then.

[13] One 90s winter, taking thaw-released ice mushrooms from the cliff top pot-holes and turning them upside down, they gleamed in the icy sunlight.

The car park for Burbage South was in a different place in those days, just after the hairpin bend. You would never suspect it was ever there now. It had a stream at one end by a comely boulder. The boulder was a way of enjoying the day after it had passed by. Once back at the car the natural warmth in it would draw you over to sit down. That is where I digested the day and built my grade.

I didn't last much longer in Manchester. It was just possible to be earnest there, but when in Sheffield, by then I didn't always have to be. I alternated for a while between the cities but finally moved across the Pennines. Manchester was the hub of British rock climbing when I was there, now it would be Sheffield.

Neil and I

Toasty, a touch greasy, Stanage Edge that June '83 evening was as comely as an AGA stove. As a nipper I sometimes lay curled up in front of ours till hot granary buns were taken out to be buttered. Tonight on my own I'm just happy to graze my way along bombing up each route in turn having a whale of a time. Up to 600 odd in an epic 'tick Stanage odyssey' I've found there are lesser climbs here and there but even they have an interesting hold, quirky flake or some curiosity or other. John Allen said there was a great little new route he'd recently done – *So Many Lines, So Little Time* – on the far left.

Heading for that, thinking myself alone, on rounding an arête a fellow enthusiast comes into view. The sun's glow warming us both is slowly swinging out of view behind Bamford Edge. By way of introduction I offer him a toffee treat, saying before thinking: "Wonder what it's like now on Cloggy? Have you ever been?"

"No", he says.
"Shall we go…?" I suggest.

Neil McAdie climbs into my silver Honda Accord, off to North Wales. Everything goes well until long after dark, pulling out to overtake a car. A car I've already pointed out is going, "…*Ridiculously slowly!*" But half way through the manoeuvre it starts to turn right[14]. Braking hard…by the time the other car rounds the junction in slow motion my car is leaning over familiarly on his. Eventually this mess grinds to a halt. The other driver rolls out of his car followed by alcoholic vapour encouraging the suggestion: "Shall we call that knock for knock then?"

We camp out under rhyolite boulders beneath Dinas Cromlech. So hot and sticky, so midgy was it that we rise before dawn and go down to Llanberis. (Too late and too early for Rosie's 50p camping charge). What sweet relief it is to slip into the chill water of the Padarn Lake and swim our bodies free of insects and itches.

We make our way up to Clog. A long walk, excitement has license to run. There is no wind, the previous day's heat still communicating yesterday's

---

[14] 70% of accidents happen like this. (Johnny's fictional driving statistics.)

warmth from the path. Too early for Half-way House to be open so no delicious 5p homemade barley lemonade in little cups this time.

Bit by bit the black cliff comes around the brow. The lake, which gives you a feeling of vertigo when you swim across its pitch depths, as if you could fall into it at any moment, has a tent by it. It is light but the sun has not yet given away where it will appear.

I can recall what we climbed but not in what order. No routes we tried were so hard for us at the time to give us the fear, but they were *go-ey*: brilliantly glorious, just to hear their names makes me pine. Banner's *Troach* impressed; just three runners solid and easy to place in 100ft, a sling on a big spike and big nuts in a flake. Steep climbing between good rests is punctuated by committing chunky laybacks and lock-offs on jugs.

As the morning sun starts to light the pinnacle we're finishing *Silhouette*, a rewarding tenuous face climb with good obvious gear.

On the comfy *Great Wall* belay, leaning back on a rum tangle of ancient slings, bound for *The Arête Finish* above, it was thrilling to stare across and easily recognize the familiar blind flakes and angles I'd scanned in *Hard Rock* laid stretched out in front of us. I looked in vain in the sea of extraordinary frozen lava for the bolt that was the belay of Redhead's incredible *Tormented Ejaculation* E8 7a.

By the time other climbers arrive we are slowing a little. Down below us, a hot day has drawn ten or more parties to the cliff. The hubbub grows, my excitement too, as I realise a serious attempt is going to be made on what was known as *The Master's Wall*, the obvious subtle depression that runs up the right flank of the Great Wall of the Lower East Buttress. What *The Tormented*...had failed to complete.

Chesters, a Stoney Café regular looks on from *Great Wall*, Geraldine and Big John Conn look down from *Jelly Roll* above. Serendipitous, Neil and I find ourselves in the ideal place to gawp. *Curving Arête* sits out in space above and to the side. Years later I'd solo *Curving*... one time muddling the sequence I'm forced to launch into a full *Archangel* layback but today it is a tingling promontory. I used to get the same flutter at home as the Welsh team fanned out onto the hallowed turf of Cardiff Arms Park and even more when late onto the pitch came JPR sprinting at full pelt. The whole place would erupt.

The day with Neil had been so very enjoyable already, to share those climbs and then to have the Royal Box for the finale was extraordinary. To watch the future slip into the present before our eyes would have been unimaginable yesterday at Stanage yet in the hum of the morning here it was unfolding.

We had all heard of Redhead, how he had extended his neck like a giraffe, seen the picture taken before he cartwheeled 80ft down the face onto a Chouinard 1, so I knew this figure wasn't John Redhead.

Where *had* I seen those socks before?

Tremadog. Eager, straight out of the car, even before a brew at Eric's we often stared up at Vector Buttress. Looking up on that occasion my heart missed a beat. Off to the right a climber soloing *Meshach Direct* was wobbling badly. Suddenly his arms and feet came off the rock, but instead of falling he floated inexplicably, suspended in mid-air. Even more surprisingly he began to revolve about his waist like the human target in a knife-throwing act! What he'd done was clip the crux peg into his harness hidden under his clothes. Later I heard he often performed this comedy burlesque. Who was this joker? Jerry Moffatt.

There was a fierce rivalry between Fawcett, Redhead and Moffatt. Remember..? Fawcett limbs out like a cat, peeling far out off *Strawberries* E6 7a, Redhead going *Bananas* at E5 7a, look how far the crucial peg on Moffatt's *Psyche and Burn* E6 6c sticks out.

Fawcett's mentor Livesey's classic *Crags* article *The Shape of Things to Come* categorized the different styles into:
 1.Boulders.
 2.Sustained, safe and technical.
 3.Sustained, technical and bold.
He presented the 3rd as the ultimate and Clogwyn Du'r Arrddu's last great problem as its epitome. All the test pieces of the period were creative bold solutions requiring hands, head, *and* heart but in Wales in 1983, they were all simply preludes to the prize of *The Master's Wall*.

…We all look down at the scoop from our vantage points as the late Paul Williams pays out rope to Moffatt who is not only wearing white socks like his Californian hero John Bachar but strange white boots rumoured to be able to stick to each other. Paul was often at the helm of significant events. He had encouraged all three of the main protagonists at different times. Paul if you met him at Pen Trywn would march up, clench his vast forearm and utter the words: "On patrol youth". It added something to have the consummate enthusiast cheer on his man.

Moffatt climbs fast. He gets high but then starts to slow as if he's strayed into a patch of treacle, a runner few had seen, perched between thin flanges of rock, the soon to be famous lilac Simond 7 is clipped. It occurs to me he is almost dangerously careful. After a further 25ft that look thin, precise and reachy, gear went in sequence into a seam on Mick Fowler's ground up endeavour *Spreadeagle*, surprisingly some way off what was then known as *The Master's Wall*.

Later at the base of the cliff I ask Moffatt what he'll call the climb and starry eyed enquire, "What grade are you going to give it?"[15] Jerry had succeeded in climbing a line on the wall without the bolt Redhead had placed. We had witnessed the latest episode in the wall's history.

Whatever, the main line of the scoop remained. On the dusk walk down I tell Neil that I wondered why Moffatt hadn't done the direct line and said I would do it.

---

[15] It later became clear that Moffatt had already chopped the bolt by this point. Much later Jerry shared with me he had held John Redhead's top rope. That was all supposed to have been on sight.

II

Lover's Leap

When Stoney Middleton's Lover's Leap Café was shut the new routes book (honour wrested from the crags serendipitously mummified in water repellent chip fat) sat resting off to the side of the till on a ledge, the corner of which had been cut off to spare the waitresses' hips. It was a blue lined A4 account pad identical to the café's daily takings book. They were kept on the same shelf. If you reached down without looking, butty and brew balanced precariously in the other hand, you'd notice if you'd confused them by their different feel. One book was clean and crisp, the other bursting with grease and frazzled energy. It's as if at some point in rock climbing's evolution these blue books mated and professional climbing was the unholy bastard child.

It was quieter in the 80s on the grit. Mohicans bobbed above dry-stone walls; punks patiently looking for magic mushrooms. You could hear yourself think. Sometimes when you got really lucky you could hear yourself not think. 'Haircut 100', lurid 'Flashdance' tights and 'The Birdie Song' remind one of the period. Boots clumpy, chalk bags huge, the climbs now seem almost quaint.

He was a true gentleman and a gritty climber on any rock. Derek Hersey. Photo: Mark Pretty.

While the White Peak dead-hangers turned right out of Stoney Café, went 'up t' dale' or to Raven Tor (which even they themselves called *The Snore*) a few of us still turned left. You had to make sure the grease was wiped off your hands before touching the crag. That small detail could make a big difference. Seldom was I without a distinct sense of trepidation dipping under that low door since I knew I was off to try a line with mortal consequences.

At the time there was a sense that the best lines on grit had been done. Unprotected, grit had become a backwater as far as the pack was concerned. But while Rotpunkt[16] was on the march making the limestone super-accessible, the Dark Peak lay ready, awash with bold bald arêtes, roofs, unflattering scoops and slabs that deep down I knew would go.

But climbing into the Honda, July '84, I'm still smarting from local activist Paul Mitchell's words in the new routes book: "*Will Mr Dawes please remove the mattress left at the base of Burbage South*" used to pad out the unclimbed wall left of *The Knock* for a ground up attempt. (Square mats doubling as companies' advertising hoardings didn't exist then.)

Quent, Pollitt, Zipps and company on Windy Ledge, Stoney 1984. Photo: Mark Pretty.

[16] Flipper Fietz was a boulderer in The Frankenjura who liked to do the moves on unclimbed cliffs but seldom returned to climb the routes in one push. He left a red circle painted on the rock at the base. Kurt Albert led one of these lines and filling the red circle in, leaving a red point, created the climbing style Rotpunkt.

Earlier in the year, eager to push the outcome in my favour on another line without altering the rock, I'd collected black bags full of grass clippings from Manchester hall of residence lawns, but as flatmate Julian and I approached Gardoms it was clear the grass was rotten. We reeked to high heaven by the time we'd walked the full length of the crag. The grass was laid out over the rocks under the amazing ramp spotted through the trees in the winter, but in truth all it did was disguise where the most dangerous gaps between blocks were! It was a brilliant feature but escapable as Steve Bancroft with relish pointed out to me at a party – *Charlotte Rampling* E6 6b.

Rain or shine, the café was always balm and encouragement. Sue the owner was like a mum to us. She sometimes gave you Parkin[17] for nowt. We had a delightful surprise emotional meeting years later at Heathrow.

Geraldine, sole female regular would ask: "Been up to much?" ...off I'd go waxing lyrical about forays on the rock. On crowded hopeless days, even *Minus Ten* wet, crouched on the tiled window ledge, hot chocolate misting up the window, the bogie man kept at bay, there was always the *Many Sided Queer Thing* to play. Could a continuous line be found all the way across the zigzag Formica table top? Apparently two did exist, but the prospective line hoped for always gave out, like new lines on the crag. In some places where the lines didn't meet some cheat drew them in.

After, a walk along a drying Burbage South did its healing trick. As the basis of this, or a bonus I don't know, but in the tilting evening light, sitting just out of the insistent breeze, I loved to pick out otherwise invisible undulations on the unclimbed rock, imaging the motion they made, committing it to memory.

When it really pissed down it was time to go off to Sheffield Collegiate Wall where climbers capable of almost anything, The White Peak, used to hang. Tights – gold, purple and yellow – dangle visibly under a board covering a stone-broken window. It's impressive to see Jerry or Ben, Basher or Quent attempt one arm pull ups or almost lock off side lever like John Gill on a first digit edge.

People treated me as an irritant so that was the role I took on. I did it very well. I liked to play on the big pebble-peppered climbing wall doing

[17] A delicious sweet ginger cake indigenous to Derbyshire.

complex breakneck dynos, but before I did, I'd go over to the blocks to remind them… .

For maximum effect, rucksack stuffed with a down jacket still on my back, I'd hang off both hands on the finger edges on the beam. Pulling up on the block, I'd flick one hand then the other into a mantel then stand up on it, as if the prospect of my trainer slipping off the half-inch edge had not occurred to me. To press out this straight on mantel on the finger blocks was powerful as hell, brutal and scary, but it was my forte and I could do it cold every time.

In time we'd all become good friends. They just had a different way of being arseholes. But the bottom line was that they were making a big song and dance out of artificially safe climbs with basic if powerful moves: no use of momentum from one move essential to do another as far as one could see. Don't get me wrong, in Fontainebleau and Tom's Roof they were doing things that fatty boom boom here would always struggle on but could they physically do the mantel? No, and I don't remember them even trying it, or the multi-move dynos on the wall beyond.

Sometimes I'd walk up the hill to 124 Hunter House Road to see them! Quent's 2CV was parked on its side again. The rolling cast of inhabitants included Jerry Moffatt and Chris Gore. Each bigged up the other in *High*: "Jerry, you're the best", "No, NO, No, Chris you're the best" …but neither was. Tim Freeman was the strongest of them or was it the mule strong poet Pete Kirton whose problem on the pinches on the lip of Tom's Roof no one could do? Zoë Brown, Joe's daughter, thought I was obnoxious after giving her constructive feedback on her dyed hair. She strung along on ITV's 'Razzmattaz'. Earth Mother Mandy, Ben, Chipper, Smeg, bright red-dyed haired proddy bike racer Julian Taylor, et al, etc, all shared the house with smelly dogs, overflowing pub ashtrays, and singed knives. "Thus Spoke Zarathustra" and eventually the Environmental Services were called in to clear an infestation, evicting them all.

…powerful weak-framed motorbikes sit out on the street. If you went out right now, you could see as I do aged just 20, tips weeping on this hot day post *Benign Lives*, two men walk up the hill, baking in bulging duvets; one very short in stained light blue, one very tall, purple haired in brown. Trickledown economics in South Yorkshire Nuclear Free State was working somewhat, if not as Maggie intended. In 124 Gore unwraps ropes from sponsors, early Beal 'snappers' (before they became great ropes!) destined to travel down the pecking order from Pollitt/Atkinson/Moffatt to Zippy/Plant Pot, then finally to the Stoney woodshed boys by which time their core would be visible, the rope's original colour a mystery. It was a great place to ruin your throat, depress your will to live, but also womb to some of the physically hardest routes in the world.

Ulysses or Bust

Two of the triptych[18] of arêtes at Stanage I'd done without rehearsal. Now an eye was on a ground up of *Ulysses' Bow*. People hadn't climbed that kind of route then, unrepeated unprotected holdless, E6 straight off. To do so your understanding of friction had to be exact. You had to be able to glance at a smear and see grip.

Surely many must have slung a rope down the rough cracked toffee arête of *Ulysses' Bow* but only John Allen in 1975 had climbed it on a slack rope. He said, seemingly holdless, in EBs the arête had a distinct sequence on specific small holds – at British 7a.

1983. Jerry Moffatt took delivery of unique boots with sticky rubber developed by Boeing – Firés. Climbing would never be the same again. Footholds grew like mushrooms all over the Peak. Moffatt top-roped then soloed *Ulysses' Bow* renaming it *Ulysses* E6 6b.

Some prospective lines I practised on a rope too but some I climbed in the style of those at Eastington and Uppingham, straight off. At Curbar two routes bear this out. Only precise practice on a rope would unlock the blank looking sidewall of *Insanity* buttress for me, *Committed* E6 6c. It was a hard challenge for a short man, where a capricious press up into a seam were it to fail would fire you unpredictably into space. While *White Water* E6 6c was climbed from the floor involving successive commando roll ground falls.

Sloping subtly dimpled concrete, handless practice on grit, one chance only fast dynamic moves on buildings had all developed an acuter sense for how to eke out friction from a shape to move, and when to go for it. Deciding on what day to try a particular line comes more easily with those eyes too, but raw bloody mindedness and bottle was always going to count as well. Climbing in poor conditions in the damp, on hot or cold rock were additional avenues of learning how to conserve or conjure grip.

---

[18] 1972 *Archangel* XS 5c Ed-ward Drummond (originally called *Saul's Arête*).
1975 *White Wand* E5 6a John Allen solos after top roping – Drummond solos it three days later claiming it as *Wind*. In 1984 the rightmost of the three arêtes still had cachet… One night in the Porter's Cottage, asking Basher Atkinson (who was to do the first 8b+ in England, *Mecca* in 1988) if he'd like a drink, he blurts out: "*White Wand*…" Even *me* offering *him* a drink failed to distract him, so eager was he to share his ground up experience. And so he should've been.

Starting to feel the crag's pulse cleanly was very exciting.

The second ascent of Moffatt's *Hot Knives* was pushed through ground up in the heat. Then hotter still, when it was so hot the wardens actually closed Froggatt Edge for fear of forest fire, I found myself hiding from the Peak Park Warden. Eager to complete a new slab line near *Strapadictomy*, the only way to avoid him is to back into a rank sheep's corpse at the back of a little cave, hold my breath and listen to him pass.

Emerging, eager to complete challenges quickly to move on to more, even with the stench of death in my nostrils, I'm as good as committed just peering at the baking hot slab. The crux, already practised, undercuts a slippery chunky black pebble for a bluff share in a crease. It's a steep little killer, only 25ft high, but perched above an unavoidable boulder-choked gully. Solo, it is a race; precision against what seems like milk seeping from my fingers. Powered by the momentum of necessity I slither over the top of my first new E7, *Benign Lives* 6c.

Mercury at the other end of the glass the blitzkrieg was kept up by trying climbs in the snow. On an on-sight attempt on Fawcett's unrepeated *The Mint 400* E6 6b, a 30ft super thin blank wall, I find myself not above the encouraging cushion of snow the wind had blown at its base but above gently angled sheet ice just to the side. "*No problemo…*" Fawcett's albatross reach is dispensed with by a crimp on a painful intermediate using a waist-flick assisted slap for the sandy break.

The high edges in the winter of 1984 became impassable, valley roads nearly so. That didn't stop 'the disillusioned brew machine' Zippy and I teaming up for a visit to the obscure, but very impressive, south facing Wildgoose Quarry. There was an overhanging unclimbed 75ft seamed wall reminiscent of *Billy Whizz* at Lawrencefield Quarry. Thick snow lay under it, over the scramble up to inspect it from above, but it was in sun and out of the wind. So while Zippy aka '5c' Mark (who regularly did 6c) lays the rope out, dry as possible on a sack in the snow, the sound of a brand new Firé squeak blesses the quarry.

Gear at 50ft, a vertical blade peg and Rock 1. Sunlit rock disappointingly still cold, no feeling in fingers is soon replaced by the gnawing pain of *hot aches*.

Do my frozen fingers know how to work unsupervised?

My stumpy paws can take it. No warm up for the arms, I only climb on happily since having previously abseiled to place a peg what's to come is clear: a long series of pods and cracks, off balance laybacks leading to a narrow plinth shake out, 6a crux, then a hefty crank to the top.

The top out looks relatively easy, a rolling press onto a slightly inclined shelf, fortunate since you face a 30ft fall onto the gear. But grabbing the flat top I find it covered in ice. Marooned mid-move, locked down hard on a low flat waist hold un-warmed bicep spasms.

I must *cut a step*.

That's what Bonners would do. I use my nails to carve a crimp in the *verglas*. Rolling over gently, quickly before the crimp has time to think amazingly works, but even once up on top the ice still threatens to spit me back off the ledge. Unlike skin or rubber, cotton grabs the ice initially, so I teeter on knees, short stilts, toward a tree root poking out of the snow. Phew!

Freezing hands from belaying a snowy rope prove treacherous for Zips when he seconds the pitch. When he bones off the move up to the peg it strips out, just from the torsion of the swinging rope. Whoops!

The Fingertip Phenomenon E5 6a. (Quarried away now unfortunately).

No EasyJet or EasyWall, most climbed on whatever the weather. Jerry would be up in Tom's, feet off, others holed up in some cave waiting for the rain to pass. Rock rather than outright standard was still the hub for some – those I term the 'Dark Peak', for whom affinity with rock rather than power was still central. To spend treasured times with grit luminaries of the 70s was ace. John Allen, the amazing Stokes brothers and I shared brilliant days on the crag, warm conversations about 'The Tyranny of Finish' and the meaning of life.

One frosty evening back at Chippinghouse Road after we'd done *Conan The Librarian* at Mother Cap and *Traverse Of The Gritstone Gods* at the Cowperstone, I prepare a mushroom pasta to make up for a long sofa surf, putting a good bottle of Pinot Grigio out to chill in the snow of the front garden. Later, olive oil, basil and tomato rolling nicely I go out to collect the Vino. I come straight back in empty-handed and draw back the curtains for all to see. The living room lights illuminate another's tracks in the snow…but no bloody bottle. I enjoy it when they roar with laughter.

It was fun to pretend to curb crawl with John Allen in his hideous green automatic Vauxhall Commodore, or sit in seasoned Lycra nursing a pint of Tetleys at *The Porter Cottage* stared at by locals. After we might go to a nightclub, *The Limit* or if Johnny was feeling lucky to Barry Noble's *Roxy*. "How's that for yerz?" Barry bellowed on Hallam Radio. Pre-Raphaelite beauty Nicky, the laziest, if most talented of the Stokes – or was that Mark or Neil – put me in the cricket nets they'd hobbled together in the car park of a disused factory and bowled bouncers at me. I recall a friend of theirs ate Bancroft's passport.

Throughout these festivities however my constant secret friend was *Ulysses,* It was always in the back of my mind.

A drying Stanage Edge…soloing around all morning the grit had flowed by on countless old favourites. *It* was not in mind. Just as a pianist having played many pieces by a particular composer might eventually accomplish a difficult piece of theirs with ease, one they never felt they could before, something in me had come to a silent accommodation. But this something had not really told me as such, as a good teacher might hold back, eager to not unsettle their student.

Instead of *Fern Groove* again, I let my enthusiasm guide me and take a look at the steep slab left of *Fern Crack*. A chunky layback press start leads to a stand. I suss how to get right foot super high onto a chest high smear, side on onto an exacting limit dish lower leg kept still. I thread my way to flash *Silk*[19] a new E6 6c ground up.

Working further along the crag, starting without decision if noting a mild surprise, body rolls smoothly up the lower flank of *Ulysses'Bow*. Unsurprised, the lichen vibrates, neither hard nor easy. Lust for success, enthusiasm for shape has shot me onto the rock where the body – the inner body – takes me up, my mind suspended, all about me was more apparent, the impetus to move limbs arose spontaneously, any dread held in the height and hardness had dissolved. Perception was of climbing *all the rock*, knowing what *it* was. Just as affectionately slapping an elephant's haunch you would be greeting the whole creature, the surface of the rock became the skin of all the rock beneath. The sense of separateness that always lingered had suddenly disappeared.

[19] It was strange I called it *Silk* as I found out later that the silk road from port to buyer reputedly came over the edge past this buttress.

A sense of *me* unplugged, gone, the rock had a vibration that struck such a chord with my own that my heart opened to a strangely familiar satisfaction of which the whole Hope Valley remained a wondrous part for some hours.

One Step Beyond

The diminutive but brutal Cowperstone is unique. Facing south it will be out of the wind and dry. I make three visits in all to try the central line of the block left of Llehctim's[20] stonking *Snug as a Thug on a Jug.*

Experiment reveals shared knee-locks, a hands-off strangely the solution to the crux. A few more goes gets past it. Each time I try to jump off accurately onto a rucksack stuffed with rope and clothes. The key to the blind section above is to know where one disguised hold will be when you're below it. Looking up from the ground, at a similar angle as I'll be in on the climb, plots it as twice the distance past one pebble, in line with a distinct patch of lichen. Catch it and you arrive below a strange gothic horn barring entry to a sloping top. The powerful mantel is too high to fall off unlike the boulder problem beneath. Nice if you like that sort of thing. *Sad Amongst Friends* E6 7a. (It gets E7 6c now.)

Finally Curbar Edge dries. A frightening display of murderous blank walls, the majority unclimbed at that point, greets pretenders with a smirk. Not me, I'd come to climb the hardest route there: *One Step Beyond Direct* E6/7 6c. Rather than top rope it, I threw a 9mm down to the side reasoning if I was about to die I could traverse off to it. It was *the* big route of the crag, a top five Peak test-piece and one of the fiercest of those. After my run-in with Ron this was it; used to high ground falls, able to see plenty to hang on to here and there, I was determined to climb this as clean as I could.

Just off vertical, 60ft high, a visible weakness weaves up the wall to an obvious slanting stepped sloping finger ledge at 40ft. Stood on that things would need to calm right down.

…20ft up, placing a toe half an inch too far left, a hideous press for a sloping/slanting fingertip edge rips foot off without warning – just miss obligatory starting spike boulder.

…The feel of the waxy slanting edge accompanies me on the climb down; that's all wired now. Sack with rope, sweater, tweed, jeans stuffed inside, placed where decided previously, from looking down from below the crux.

…Up again weighting a smear wrongly, pushing on, in a second the move

[20] Mitchell backwards.

White Lines E7 6c. 1st ascent. 1985. Photo: Ian Smith.

above is sussed but next adjustment, spat off, I'm in the air, missing the sack, whizzing down the hill hurdling sharp boulders hidden in the bracken.

…This time waiting longer than it takes for my feet to stop smarting, I sit musing until little tweaks in sequence are unmistaken, tangy enough *in here* to allow my body to go for it *out there*. A look from a buttress off to the side confirms it; this slowly gathered A-line tunnel that my body will travel through, where speed will help or hinder, now cossets the route with a trustworthy rhythm able to unwind itself.

…Last try… 'hopefully not of any route'.

Shoes laced a little differently, climbing effortlessly to a crouched twist rest at 15ft, I pause to take one hand off to pat chalk on the heel of the other ready for a mantle spotted high above the crux – too high to fall off even if hitting the bulls-eye of the sack.

Ah ha..! I tag a smear with chalk that'll be invisible from above.

Sombre. A party looks on from the side.

Wiped dry on my shirt cuff, fingertips immediately bead fluid slowly. Late on, there's briefly time to think, 'should've left it for another day' but it passes…

The egg timer turns. Chalk cannot stem the tide forever, rate of finger slickening set scary, body is on the link. Now each known move gifts me a touch of extra oomph for the next. Into the death zone – what Curbar does really well – finally committed totally that familiar curious joy of 'going for it' at last kicks in. But at the edge of awareness a dangerous thought lingers, *the wish to be back on the ground.* More pungent, queued up behind it, the splintering force the body would hit the ground with winks up.

I know I just used the holds correctly but also notice a rushing weakness encroach, feel glad to have extra momentum, if only *just* right now. I feel eyes press into my back, the sloping slanting inch mantel must be held not just with a straight pressure down but with a little outward pull. Leftward movement gives some time for a foot to flick up high and land next to the heel of the hand that supports my whole body. It's new territory for me, for pure boltless climbing worldwide. I've never pushed so deep into the rewarding tangle of excitement and worry before.

Skill lifts its foot and watches it all unfold, then stops to feast eyes on the killer height, open space about, an elegant lace of white holds cool below. The last move of *One Step Beyond* is a handless pendulum onto a foothold far off to the side, at mild 6b it's enjoyable. People will start to climb like this now I thought…?

Two years later in 1986 I'll link it into visiting American Pete Beal's direct finish dubbing the combination *Slab and Crack*. Some now consider it E8[21].

[21] E7 + E6 = E8?

Ulysses E6 6b. A climb with a great rhythm that soothes while it scares. *Ulysses Bow* was a special experience, coming at the climax of many trust establishing solos, like *White Wand*, which I thought on sight was on a par with *Narcissus*. All the crux section was on sight, although Ed Douglas has a photo from a school trip that shows me on the start on a rope in EB's. Photo: Neil Foster.

Adam Smith's Invisible Hand E6 6b. See note b. Photo: Neil Foster.

This page: *The Braille Trail.*
I gave E5 at the time when
E5 was E5. See note c.

Velvet Silence E6 6c. Woodward was rumoured to have done it first, Regan too, some thought neither had, maybe I did. It's good to share. Effortless nancy boy moves follow a rock up that requires the right knack. Photo: Neil Foster

Sad Amongst Friends E7 6c. Neil Foster's brilliant cover shot for The Spinach Guidebook reminds me of how much climbing the Cowperstone packs in. It is a strange climb in that on the crux both hands are off using powerful knee locks. See note d. Photo: Neil Foster.

Top left clockwise: Neil Foster, Andy Pollitt
& catch, Pete Kirton, Martin Veale, Sean
Myles, Zippy, John Allen and I.
Opposite: Good effort Lucy, *Slab and Crack* E8 6c.
Photo: Tim Glasby

Above: *Kaluza-Klein* E7 6c. See note e. Photo:Neil Foster.

Left: *End of the affair* E8 6c. An early attempt in 1985 on *'The Sorrel's Sorrow* arête'. See note f. Photo: Bill McKee.

Dharma E7 6c. See note g. Right: *Janus* E6 6b. See note h. Photos: Neil Foster.

Beau Geste. Originally given E7 7b by Jonny Woodward in 1980. In EB's the arête itself must have been more powerful. On the quiet it was quite competitive between Mark Leach and I for the 2nd ascent.

Left: A luxury death route, although all the falls off *Gaia* have rebranded it as safe, at the time I was not convinced that, like the Burbage South prow, the gear would hold. Photo: Simon Nadin

Remnants from
'The Book' of
unclimbed lines

Opposite: *Perplexity* E6 6c, incomprehensibly
chipped. Photo: Neil Foster

Dawes of Perception E7 6c, April '85, day before *Windows of Perception*, was the first climb I'd considered giving E8. Here's Paul Pritchard on the 2nd ascent. Photo: Paul Pritchard

Teenage Menopause

Summer 1984, bouffey blond Bob Drury and I hung out in Tremadog barn a lot, getting on Eric Jones' nerves. What a Baltic rat hive that was then. Bob had deffed out his 'O' levels, ran away from home aged 16, robbed a car and got pulled. He was lying low.

Our first taste of action together was repeating a bold arête called *Emotional Crisis*, very prescient that was. We shared a studied unimpressed attitude, a clear grasp of how dynamics would take climbing further and an appetite for the madcap. Before we realized we didn't particularly like each other, we had a wild time.

One day in Llanberis we jumped on the back of Dick Griffith's VW camper as it cruised past. Dick refused to stop. He deliberately would not slow down enough for us to get off at junctions. Little did we know he was off to the Orme 20 miles away. By the time we reached the dual carriageway to Llandudno we had to do something. Roof covered in algae and rounded, the only option was to finger traverse along the rain gutters smearing on the wheel arches and louvres in the bodywork until we could slide into the front windows, Bob on his side hilariously right into Dick's lap. Most would baulk at this sort of thing but Drury loved a drama.

Once, we'd gone together to a frighteningly hairy party in Sheffield for Class A mountaineers: Mark Miller, Sean Smith and company. They were off to the Himalayas. Afterwards we'd spirited two lovelies out to Curbar for the sunrise, where I let Bobby drive since he was: *"Really good at driving..."* He'd rounded the hairpin below the crag well, but the challenge of the following straight proved too much. The steering remained turned which led us directly into a wall.

Back in the Welsh mother lode we'd just done the pleasant *Poacher* on Clogwyn Y Wenallt. Bob had his feet out of the car window, the B52s' 'Bouncing off the Satellites' upsetting the speakers and anyone else who'd listen. Before dropping down Llanberis Pass, Bob waves a pair of cheery German climbers in purple tights into the back. Immediately accelerating to avoid being overtaken by a train of slow tourists launches our guests into their seats. Had they spotted Bob's handiwork on the nearside front?

Years from then, a fettled 205 Mi16, keeping to the legal side of the road will hit 116 before the Cromlech Bridge, but in those days my driving could never have competed with someone who could do that. Just after the famous rescued[22] boulders there's a bump on a slight bend where the car takes off, demanding you pre-rotate it in the air to land.

That day, even with the weight of German hitchers, it got air. Then there's a hump where experience would teach me it's good to ride the brake, and lift off a little on the gas to settle the car on the road without bouncing. It's a mark of how on the ball Bobby can be that as the slide really set in, he turned the stereo down to help me concentrate – but not off mind! Mid-slide I remember reflecting: "Wow…all that weight does make quite a difference". It may seem strange to floor the throttle but with front wheel drive that's all that stops the skid delivering a proper crash. By the time wall greets car it's down to 25mph and angled to glance. As we get busy pulling hard on slings attached to a crab on the bent wheel arch I catch Bobby grinning – the car had struck the same side Bob had smacked in the Peak.

We drive off after a bit. Two hitchhikers with their thumbs out suddenly pull them in as we approach.

At Pete's Eats Jackie with the proudest bum in Beris takes our order…we'll go cragging again in a bit. "Two pints of tea and an apple pie and ice cream please." Watching the door for pretty girls, the action stills for a moment, sweat stretched like cellophane across our faces the buzz of muscles and steaming tea urn disappears the walls.

The anticipation then was unbelievable. SH Wall in Crafnant Valley, Sexual Salami Buttress, Clog, the Wenallt, Bustach and Craig Gogarth, were new to us boasting piping hot new climbs from the houses of Redhead, Fawcett, Littlejohn, Haston, Moran, Cathcart and Whillance.

[22] For some years the council tried to knock away the boulders but a famous revolt saved them.

92

Car wounded, things had gone a bit Demolition Derby. Yesterday we'd done *The Long Run* – Whillance at his boltless best. We'd gone there in convoy with Johnny Redhead in his van. We'd both vied to get our 'heaps' to the top of North Stack Wall by the old dirt track at the back of the quarry. We almost did. I managed to round the first of two switchbacks but had started to roll over the side into the quarry.

Young, improving noticeably every day, Wales was a heady crucible where anything seemed within our reach. Parched, friendship was forged in evenings in the Vaynol Inn in Nant Peris under wind hot faces. We met Nick Dixon and fellow Western grit activist Andy Popp in that first roasting summer. Nick used to migrate on a Friday night from Redcar near the North York Moors[23] on his Honda C70 scooter, picking up Popp, purple Alpinist on his back, in Cheshire on the way. Nick, short like me, enjoyed the same style of climbing. We became barometers for each other.

[23] Where his *Magic in the Air* now gets E7.

Nick and Andy. Photos: Al Williams

The reputation of the Cromlech Wall routes was crumbling. It felt like the new order had finally arrived. Nick did the 4th ascent of *Lord of the Flies* E6 6b. Desperate to have a bash, but up there without any gear, I had to scrounge a belayer and put together a motley rack from almost everyone on the crag to try for the 5th.

It felt easy. Halfway up you could sit down for heaven's sake. Thinking: "*there must be a hard bit somewhere…*" I went up to the right. Just after seeing a huge chalked jug en route off to my left, I took a 50ft whipper.

I even did the 2nd ascent of Fawcett's much harder *Ivory Madonna* swinging leads with the Orme limestone expert Andy Pollitt. Then later in the week I did the first repeat of his *Carousel Waltz*, a bold exposed arête in Crafnant Valley, downgrading it from E6 6c to E5 6b, a sure way of making oneself stick out. This is what it must be like I imagine getting the odd fastest lap before figuring on the GP podium. I was there or thereabouts.

The 'climb up from the bottom of the cliff' style was still standard then. Occasionally one tried moves on an unclimbed line to know what to clean, but, significantly, the lead was usually left 'unprofessionally' in doubt. We weren't into making 6c holds into 5c holds by training. That could go on forever. We were into pitting our skills against fabulous climbs that were at our limit.

Andy Popp's style could be a touch more radical still. Technically adept but slim limbed, sometimes he would become too fatigued placing gear on the lead. It was a worry to see him, back on the ground untie his harness, forgo the rope, and attempt to solo the climb you'd just seen him fail to lead.

A fun game of the time, which Andy and Nick enjoyed, were running races up Idwal Slabs. Hundreds of feet up they shot by weekend teams clinging to *Hope* or *Faith*. Inevitably they bungled the odd hold, slides only averted by grabbing whatever slithered past. One day on the slabs Nick hands me a tiny runner crucial to a recent climb of his left of *Demetrius Wall*. I make the second ascent of his *Teenage Menopause* E7 6b without practice. Now even the direct line on Clog's *Great Wall* didn't seem out of the question.

It was a cracking hot summer. Swims in the lakes, sarnies and tins of beer secreted in your mate's sack à la *The Eiger Sanction*…and local girls… Andrew Ridgely peers earnestly from a pillow, her parents watching Brucie in the next room. Snogging a gorgeous girl from the chemist at the bus stop, sheltering from the pouring rain.

There were always great parties. Dai Lampard, rock hard cragsman/alpinist, had some belters at his cottage at the old village where a rope swing was one of the many notorious attractions. Drunk or worse, you could take your turn on 'Stone Right Hand' or the feared 'Swallow's Nest'.

'Stone Right Hand' was the wiser choice if you were drunk. Run down a slick boulder, leap off its right edge and at the same time lift your knees onto the cross bar before swinging far out over the house. The surprise for first timers was that halfway through the swing the rope would catch a notch on a branch above, making it swing in a tighter faster arc, at the top of which the rope flicked off the notch dumping you violently down. The 'Swallow's Nest', was less tricky but properly lethal: 60ft up a Scots pine, all you had to do was jump out a little and slot the bar underneath you. At the end of a 20ft free fall, followed by a long swing, was a trapeze to pull up into the canopy. It is sobering to note that the crossbar broke on one hapless party-goer, luckily low down.

There were two schools then: Yorkshire/Lakes and Peak/North Wales. When those venues were shot folk went to Pembroke, Avon or the South West. I was most definitely from the second school, driving between them on the best roads in the world.

Over the years I've had a dodgy over-powered Dutton/7 look-alike that used to wander around above a ton, a very rapid Wessex-engined Mini van with one red backdoor, a blue Rascal van and a series of 205's, but not all were that hot.

At 4 o'clock in the morning, at one of Dai's dos, I needed to get back to the Peak so I bought a red Mini 850. One crook I'd met sold it to me for a fiver. A good deal? Well no actually, having no tax, *no* brakes, though suspiciously an MOT. It would do for a middle of the night romp. You could grind the barriers to brake. By keeping to the back roads police and public were avoided, even if at one junction it was necessary to actually hold the car on the foot break – my right foot that is – out the door.

I often stayed with illustrious mountaineer and cragsman Alan Rouse in Sheffield in those days and by the time the milk was being delivered I pulled up outside a well-kept three storey house in Wayland Road. It was never locked. Alan had got some new prints of the Alps and a new teapot. Kettle on, brew made, I quietly climb the stairs, put the mugs down on the side, take a run up and jump onto the bed. The faces of two people I have never met in my life shoot out from beneath the covers.

"I've brought you a cup of tea," I say by way of introduction.

Alan had sold the house, Tom and Wendy had moved in.

Alan had moved to *Rupert Road* in S7. He and his lodger Neil Foster were tearing it up on the grit. Neil's fierce *Make it Snappy* E6 6b, Alan's *Blind Date*, (now V8 with a rarely done E5 above it) were impressive. Rouse *was* a master of dangerous climbs and did the first 6c on British rock: *Technicolour Yawn* at Helsby in '72.

The action then turned again to Millstone Edge. I did first ascents of the unlikely *Monopoly* and the technical gem *Wall Street Crash,* bold and hard respectively.

Hard climbing is often a competitive activity – it's funny when people say it isn't. It's a secretive business. There was one rival's vehicle in the Peak I'd always keep a special lookout for – KAK 192 – a Renault 5 GTI owned by one Ron Fawcett. The flip side of that paranoia was I'd park untraceably myself.

Rouse was after an unclimbed slim groove near *Great North Road.* Off to K2 he'd blagged a marketing deal with a brewery so a moraine of K2 lager boxes blocked his hallway. Who his sources were I'm not sure but he knew Fawcett was after the same line. Ron arrived early the next morning to find Al and party bivvied below what became his *Quality Street,* dozing among cairns of K2 empties.

Death a real possibility, pioneers duelled remotely with other activists with their climbs. The Lees, Daniel and Dominic, did hard stuff and John Allen was still a threat, keeping tabs on him on our trips out was a good idea – as the Medici's employee Machiavelli advised: "Keep your friends close but your enemies closer."

You could ask others about a route they'd done, get 'The Numbers'[24] but finally it was down to you alone. Neil Foster had done a beautiful new arête at Curbar which I repeated without top-roping but not without a 20ft ground fall. Neil wanted to do the second on sight of *Ulysses*… I'd said that

[24] Beta.

96

it was comparable to his Curbar climb. But when he tried *Ulysses* he fell off the crux 25 feet up, snapping his femur. The doctors told him the odds of amputation were 50/50. Neil named his new Curbar arête *Ulysses or Bust*.

Ulysses or Bust E5 6b on sight second ascent. John Allen caught me when I fell off the route from the crux landing on a rucksack. It felt similar to me to Moffatt's *Ulysses* on Stanage, I said as much to Neil Foster who nearly lost his leg when he fell off *Ulysses*. Hence the name. Be careful who you get the numbers from.

Mellow Yellow

Ulysses' Bow had flung me farther than I'd bargained. It was a remarkable coincidence to me that its title celebrated an epic voyage of exploration. My experience on *Ulysses* inspired me often over the years. In some company the experience sometimes swore itself to secrecy, but I know I can trust you. The temptation to try and replicate it felt like a problem. The tremendous simplicity of the ascent also came with a pleasant sense of accomplishment, but more insidious, a wanted but rattling praise that felt at odds with it.

What remained solid was that it had taught me a healthy satisfaction can be found when you cease to be yourself and are just there, whether the increased performance this can unleash is revelled in or not. I wonder how many of us have experienced this on the crags?

It took a while to forget, to not copy, or trade in the experience. Something akin, a deep sense of contentment, did come again when it was good and ready. Each time the mystery was left alone some fear also left me. The search around for what it might have been all about though continued. One book winked from the shelves at me to pick it up – Bruce Holbrook's '*Stone Monkey'*.

Thinking this state of being was not something one got better at – something that was always there beyond time – did not stop my searching for ways to learn to live in such a state of satisfaction. For example it was one of the things that led me to accept an invitation to join Joe Simpson, Bobby Drury and Pritch on an expedition to Gangotri, the base of the Ganges in the Garwhal Himalaya. Cheesely it was there that I had another experience when it felt a peek behind the physical scenery happened.

…Deep inside a down cocoon the call of nature wakes me. I unzip the fly of the tent, step out into a clear night onto fresh snow. Windless, heat bellows off my naked body, exactly silencing the steady cold. High full moon, Tapovan Meadow shines titanium. Above the meadow the giant pyramid of Shivling booms back platinum at the coal blue of deep space. With nothing but space around – stars louder than absent thought – a strangely hued yellowing hole is all that reminds me of me.

This consciousness was undeniable joy. This background radiation of satisfaction: why had no one pointed this out to me? It didn't dull out like lust, throttle like consumption. It wasn't English, white or tall, didn't come up short. How to live like that?

In the Himalaya I'd left it under a full moon. 1990, in Harris I settled into a deep contentment again:

…Far off from the only light on this moonless cloudless night, heather, deer and golden eagle were all silent, the air about them still. In a cave, rare, a total absence of wind allowed the candle flame to burn right down. Mature, the tiny flame had become a perfect sphere. Clearly visible on the tiny planetisimal's surface were gyres, and these meshed like gears so the orb remained still and stable. With watching came delight. The same satisfaction felt in my heart appeared in front of my eyes.

Mini 850 outside Pete's Eats Photo: Martin Crook

2CV's

It is far from middle England to the ancient land of Gwynedd. There had been signs, Tolkeins, Mr Ewings, even my mother's moniker, all start with a J, finish with an R. Now I find *it* materialised in the flesh alongside me – "The Beast" – **JR**.

We're both racing flat out, neither making an impression on the other, as JR has control of the pedals, me, in the driver's seat, the steering wheel. At full pelt, our mount kettles merrily alongside a recreational vehicle with people making a holiday inside - but our *left* turn is fast approaching. As we pull level with the holiday makers, who peer across at us in the 2CV, JR grinning, covers my eyes. Time passes, then suddenly JR whips his hands away roaring "turn left!"

...I'm treated to my first view of the turn. Glee dissolves, I kick his feet away. 2CV leans over one way, tyres the other as I wrestle with the pedals. Car tries to go straight on, tyres want to go left. Just in time, not quite, 2CV claws in and is on her way. Phew!

Obviously neither of us could win that race. I don't suppose it was big but it was cleverly done and that had made all the difference. There'd be friction with this ludicrous artistic rake but it was good to find a worthy foil.

Another time with JR at the wheel of a near brakeless Mini Clubman we took the off camber right by Galt y Glyn only to find a policeman stood in the middle of the road waving us down. All Johnny could do was to grab the near brakeless Mini's handbrake sending the car spinning, forcing the policeman to leap out of the way. My failure to stop laughing did little for Johnny's licence.

Another time in grockle-rich mid-summer, with JR in a big Volvo Estate, we were halfway up the Llanberis Pass when he decided to do a three-point turn in the middle of the road. Once he'd turned around, he turned his head at me and decided, "that no" maybe, after all he had been right the first time. By this time an enormous queue of bemused tourists and God knows who else twisted up and down the Pass. This is all just to give you the background.

I loved his mysterious brooding paintings of forests, appreciated the *Poetry Pink* of *Raped by Affection*, marvelled at the image of him lethally high, flat to the ancient rhyolite, on the hallow line of the unclimbed 'Master's Wall'.

He talked about 'seeing' in such a way that **you** would know you'd missed it, but his climbs gleamed; *The Bells...The Bells, Margins of the Mind, Barbarossa, Dried Voices,* with the clean lines of Italian sports cars.

*

1985, arriving at the business end of the game the posturing had evolved a lethal edge. Although I'd never skank lesser climbers, for the likes of JR the trick was quick, clustered repeats, downgrading where possible. Bolts had **no** place in the mountains and I didn't appreciate his chipping in Vivian Quarry.

Like a game of chess moves would come through the Pete's Eats new routes book letterbox. *Margins of the Mind* with crucial blind placements had me pinned. Reachy, it was a game best left alone till I'd worked out all possible sequences. Johnny would have to take my moves seriously if he wanted the limelight. Redhead, hair pitch black not red at all, skinny with a Condor's span, sported an artful madness. I was dynamic, good on the tiniest holds and like Clark Gable…didn't "give a damn."

The Rainbow

The other climbs on the magnificent Rainbow Slab I'd managed without inspection, including a new 6c direct on Dave Towse's sinuous seam *Naked Before The Beast* E6. But right up the centre of the incomparably smooth 70° slab was *Raped by Affection*. A lively clip-up for the continentals this, with two bolts in 150ft but ideal for accustoming me to the sustained worry a ground up attempt on the true master's wall on the black cliff would involve.

Straight off the floor the climbing is comically thin to a break and good nuts, lulling me into thinking I'd done the hard bit. The gear then becomes pointlessly distant as a 50ft run out unravels past a poor skyhook to the intermission at 100ft of the splendid ramp of *The Rainbow of Recalcitrance* and a ludicrously welcome RP1. Above the ramp, off to the left, is a Troll 8mm bolt with a straight-drilled tight hole that is tricky to clip.

E6, tricky a year ago, had become on sight bread and butter. You get to know a climber's canon. I'd done most of Redhead's from the ground.

I was approaching this the same way. Little did I know the bolt (placed understandably so as not to interfere with *The Rainbow*...) had previously had a sling on it to allow the considerably taller Redhead to clip it without drama. Not only was the sling missing but also two tiny RURPS of which I'd heard nothing.

Quite a lot of this kind of 'jiggery-pokery' went on. On *Cobalt Dream,* an E5 in the Ogwen Valley across a roof, there is a crucial Friend 3 on the lip, the sole protection. I'd heard a story that a climber had asked what went in and had been told by Johnny (by mistake?) that it was a 2.5, effectively rendering it a solo. Getting the numbers and staying on the right side of folk was all important.

...I clip the bolt off an edge the width of a baked bean with just enough room for two feet, left inner toe righter-most leaves room to extend the right through inside, facing in. Like this it seemed possible to reach the bolt by gently placing left toe on a penny edge an unnerving distance out in the blankness. To use it meant leaning flat, parallel with the 70° angle. Will it creep off?

Unusually Bobby is completely silent. Miss the clip and I'll pass a narrow ledge. If I failed to grasp that, would the RP1 below it slow me enough to grab an edge somewhere on the slab?

Stretched onto the penny edge it doesn't pop, but...neither can I reach to clip. Only a thumb press and a nail flake maintain geometry. Nothing to grab at I stretch out again...again I **cannot** reach. So long as I don't move I'll be Ok but I must make my move to hit the chess clock's plunger. Can Bobby see that my position is subtly eroding? Retreat now feels crazy, more likely to spill the migrated edge of my boot past the point of no return than going for it. It's Zugswang...[25].

I was chased once by a wild boar protecting its young. Unfortunately I chose the smaller of two saplings to avoid her. I learned later the sow butting the tree would've probably eaten my liver first had the shallow sandy soil given way.

... In the flurry of action I have to get this right. The crab I need to clip with is orientated wrongly in my hand. Readying it to hit the straight-drilled eye

---

[25] A situation in chess where although you start in a safe position whatever move you make will result in your opponent benefiting.

I must toss the crab up – a once only chance to catch and turn it 180°. I toss and catch, boot jabbed into the 2mm edge for an instant buys a little time, swinging the hook of the carabiner at the bolt it pierces the eye like butter. Grab, clip, I stare down at Bob, small below.

I name my alternative sideways double dynamo, *Draped in Affectation* (6c). A draw..?

Vivian Quarry

Being bullied meant I'd been groomed to deal with panic. On climbs the panic was different from that felt in social situations when others seemed to be able to relax and I not, tongue-tied. The static panic locked into the cliffs' shape could be kept under control. New climbs left held that flair for fear potentially putting any mentally healthy mortal into a spin.

…It would make a beautiful setting in which to die. Chartreuse, the pool below, slate, a peculiar blue pleated into vast inclined panels, black water looms slippery.

Beyond the diver's fence sits a triangular trophy slab, unmolested: zero denier smooth, a Zorro seamed 75° plane: steep enough to have to pull really hard when footholds fade to smears, low angled enough for fear to fan out leisurely into the body.

I loved the way it could exist in such a magnetic drama: the divine roar of the surface, the sombre air of the water spun a dazzling hum of atmosphere able to extract the calm violence that is needed from me.

The movie *The Iron Horse* made a deep impression as a child. A warrior queen honours a soldier by choosing him to ride an iron horse – a slide that gradually sharpens along its length till it slices him in two!

The slab presents a two pronged defence: a medieval run-out off tic-tac size offsets in a flare followed by a fierce bolted crux. A cloaked danger is that the bolt at the end of the run-out is safest to clip at your knee, when the potential fall is at its most grim. A slip approaching the bolt, or faltering to clip it, will throw you 30ft down onto slate teeth, the size of a prehistoric shark's. The teeth are an inch proud. Lose contact and your only hope is to immediately crouch, briefly ride the slide, then push off at right angles to the plane just before to avoid losing a leg.

Redhead scared of getting too high had apparently tapped in the poor offsets in the flare, and taller was trying to clip from low down from the boundary of easier ground.

…Fingerhold to one side, left foot daggered down into a skatey triangular pod, see Redhead *st..retch.. . …*I know that pod well – the angle you chose to place your boot at had better be right. Redhead's feet are bigger than mine. One side of the pod is no problem, the boot will stay parallel and give support, but the other side is its jealous twin. Raise your heel and the edge will pull your foot out, as surely as if meshed in an inescapable gear mechanism. Once loaded you can't move it.

…Unable…quite to reach his free hand scratches, windscreen-wiping around for redeeming detail that is just not there. Dave Towse eyeballs the boot's sole contact… sees its creep sour…ready to leap 20ft into the cold dark pool. For Redhead to retreat now and slip unexpectedly would release a flatter greasier slide, ideal to satisfy the Shark beneath. Redhead folds, his foot's gone, his position holds by the force of will or for a moment works some other way. On cue Towse leaps off into the lake.

Slide…scrabble…Redhead lurches out missing the razor gutter but flinging himself goes upside down. rope reeling him back arches his back. There's a jerk – one rope slashes clean through and a yank – a tooth cuts the sling half through but holds the force of the fall sending Redhead whipping an axe boulder, thank heavens with just his thumb. Broken, he cradles it painfully back on the ground. Dave dripping, good effort.

Dawes of Perception had nearly killed him, the technical ones like *Windows of Perception* E6 7a done the day after *Dawes*…were beyond him. The crown was stolen.

2000, outside Pete's Eats a young lad practises on his new BMX. I ask him to have a go. I try an Endo, lifting the back wheel then the front onto the curb. He says he's called Rylie. He asks me where I live.
"I don't have a place to stay", I say.
"He could come and stay with us. Couldn't he Dad?" Rylie says, turning and lifting his head.

In a familiar doorway, smile lines blazing from the corners of his eyes, is the feral figure of Johnny Redhead.

Up there the crag scarred – by whom? The new game moved on – to what? But the climb we tried, our climb, is still the standard, our standard bearer for what we both treasured in climbing.

We sit together; "Johnny be Johnny", as the technical genius of Pex[26] Joe Heeley often said to me, but equally could have been said to Redhead. One Johnny at a time, we discuss how we'd played the game. Revel in our glorious pointless psychopathologies. It is great to share finally.

He tells me: "You were gnarly you know" – praise indeed, cute even, coming from 'The Beast' himself. This time we reflect more than refract; on how life and nature at birth sent us wobbly and, pinching each other's cheeks, what a drama we spun up there... *Canyons*™ finally bridged.

---

[26] Pex Hill – a cracking little sandstone quarry near Liverpool that had some horrendously hard climbs that other areas activists liked to ignore.

Ladybirds

In the snow-dry Dolby'd air the vibe of the place rings out. Robin Hood's Stride is aglow with remnant druid radio. The only possible climb today, and the focal point of the hamlet of boulders, is a blank blunt arête proud of the snowfall.

Initially, with a rope from above, to stay on anywhere is implausible. A new future. The greatest wonder comes in these early explorations when a line, like others eventually successfully climbed, seems impossible. That delicious – *it'd be so good if it did go* – stamping the look of the 'test-piece' upon it. A quickening hunch comes that this particular type of climb doesn't exist, yet.

Knee has to stay exactly in one place in space, knee and tiptoe motionless throughout, exact on the freshly cleaned rip-tetchy smear. The other knee too, suspended in precise counterbalance, is fixed by the just-as-rigid dictates of clean air. These rigidities took hold of the rock but left little way to move. Eat using a long knife and a short fork and your meal would taste different. Me too short to simply reach round for the shallow runnel, the

Above left: Feeling smug. I'd just done the moves on the arête right of *David*, little knowing 3 days later Moffatt would do it; *Messiah* E6 6c. Right: Feeling less smug after just getting to the top of *Kaluza Klein*. photos: Neil Foster

107

rock offers up only a touch of the poorest lower part. To reach the better part the stable awkward position must collapse, slowly, in a subtle cascade of three unstable positions until you straddle the blunt bow itself. While right hand whirls to catch the base of the runnel, left leg swings up left, almost counterbalancing, but as soon as hand snags the runnel a barn-door is irreversibly set in motion. The fall starts slow but accelerates quickly as your body swings onto the steeper side of the bow. If you react quickly enough, free left hand (that was waving in space counterbalancing during the initial starred out slap manoeuvre) can wing itself in, press into the slab, oppose the pull on runnel and change the fall's speed and arc. Done optimally half a moment later in the arc a foot can be slapped on, stilling the body for a fast hand to latch the runnel proper.

This flurry of interlaced grip felt fabulous, special in its surroundings, offering up fresh moves to the world. Seldom does such continuous movement present itself. Indeed taller climbers unfortunately miss out on this flow on *Kaluza-Klein*. It'd not hold the grade but it felt like my first E8 on lead.

On the same day a super little unclimbed bulge/pod up in Harthill Quarry fell; John Allen's cute girlfriend Sarah used to liken me to *Thumper The Rabbit* E4 6c. Later that week I did a new big bold face at Dukes Quarry without a fall *Dharma* E7 6c. I was all over it, starting to do some *great* climbs.

Mysterious climbs I'd dreamt of turning up out of the blue and unmistakable feelings of deep connection on the crags were at odds with the problems my family now contended with and the chaos of my own personal life. Around this time Dad lost money hand over fist as a Lloyds 'name'. I'd been banned from driving for impatiently overtaking a stopped bus, all four wheels on the pavement.

It was fortunate in a way, since Moira only travelled by train. On the fateful journey when we met, other travellers evaporated till our fledgling attraction was all that was left. Long silk gloves, brimmed felt hat on the seat beside her might have been ample warning but when she turned away holding *Brothers Karamazov* to one side I beamed at her, making sure before she intuitively looked back that I'd be dolefully looking at the countryside flash past. This makes a woman think you're spiritually savvy, trustworthy enough to care, good in the sack. When she went to the buffet I did some espionage, looked at her bookmark train ticket. She was getting off at the next stop.

A young schoolgirl once exclaimed to her mum, pointing straight at me: "Mummy he is insane!" Would this goddess think the same? While she was buying herself a coffee I wrote my telephone number down on the next page of her book.

It surprised me when Moira rang. She came to my 21st. John Allen, Tom Richardson and Andy Pollitt came too. I took her to 'school chum' Tim Gittin's 21st party as well. I must admit it felt good to parade the Dutch beauty past those who had plagued me at school.

Distance was soon a problem in our relationship, (Moira was at University in Hove) but not the only one. Mum put it succinctly when we broke up, "What could you offer her anyway John?" I'd no job, few social graces and my capricious depression didn't give us a chance. Moira was flexible, spoke brilliant English, buzzed like a phone but a feeling of 'love' eluded me. I was tense company. It was the world at fault. We had a final humdinger at London Zoo. A polar bear walking back and forth echoed my remoteness. When she said: "It was the way of the world" her lack of empathy for the bear's plight sealed the split. Loss and longing took up residence where love should've been. That bleak heart of mine seemed to ruin everything.

Bobby had recently split with a lass too. We weren't happy at Black Rocks that spring day. We had Ochre with us though, Redhead's Lurcher bitch. She'd proved good at leaning round corners and now she set to, digging a grave-shaped trench, strangely, right below the line I'd come to try.

In front of the main crag is a large boulder sat on another. *Curving Arête* takes its beak but running up its cheek is a shallow creased groove. Of all the unclimbed features on Peak gritstone this was the one. It surely received more beaming imagination than any other. Some have it that eyes not only receive light to create a vision in the mind but that when you look you project a tangible energy too. Perhaps this is how girls know you are looking at their bum? Had it worked on Moira? Would it on this?

On previous attempts on abseil, sticht plate at my waist in the way, I'd been unable to try the powerful undercut entry to the groove. The moves above, up onto the rib were solved but the moves right out of the shallow groove rest to escape onto the arête to summit the block were too far over to the right to try properly. Those moves would have to come to me when I was up there.

…I wasn't joyful, trying these lines was what I did, fair or foul.

Lean from not eating and angry I go with the gear in a rattling flare. A foot smeared on a bump low under in the groove, the technical problem is to yank off a big flat 70° dish with your left palm, right hand on a chunky waist height sidepull. A dry squidge of flesh pressed quickly in gives some bite by the timed 'in and out' of my waist. Falling again – cursing, clapping my hands, belting the rock, spitting – an acid intuition kicks in. I try again. Fiercely I lurch for the slap, whirling my left foot from far right under my right foot to full left; for a moment that extra motion both forces my left hand on enough to snag the gruff sloper and reduces my apparent weight – the flared undercut sidepull far up in the groove momentarily scratches into my fingertips. Unexpected, the lateral force unleashed pulls me off. Again I fall but this time an inner burst of excitement silences the shout. I point at the floor careful to log the flow of the move.

Smoking a rollie sat amongst the queer limestone gravel below the gritstone groove, pouring more chalk into my bag, Ochre licks the back of my leg. What lies in wait? Many things have almost killed me – somehow you have to notice them to stay alive. Once, climbing away from a crucial bomber stopper on Pembroke's *White Heat* an intuition came to put in another but poorer nut below. A hold above snapped. I fell. The 'good' stopper failed immediately, wire pulling free of the swage, the lower 'poorer' nut held. About to abseil down what became *Smoked Salmon*, finished chatting with a passer-by, leaning back, a feeling that something was wrong came. Thank God I froze. Looking down, one of the ropes only pokes out an inch from my hand. I'd not equalized the ropes.

I tie in small, take a pee and another shirt off, give my Calmas a final squeak.

The instant I tee up the move I feel I can set up deeper into the air behind me. Firing with knowing this time, hitting the side-pull nicely, as the lateral force kicks in both feet release automatically hopping together right, up into the groove. Oh dear! Now I've done it.

The flow out of the blind corner up onto the rib is delightful. Card tricks; dish, sharp pocket, arête in just the right spot, care on smears tight, rhythm eases the sequence dramatically. Pulling round back into the scoop to a place where a comfortable rest awaits, heels down, left hand leaning into a shallow cup, the true situation I've put myself into rises up in my mind.

Breathing changes. "Mantels are good", this angle of mantel I understand. I reach under and chalk the remainder of my weighted left hand with my right where it'll be needed on the unprotected virgin mantel above. Four minutes later, chalking again, sharing feet together out right, so it is possible to ease the right foot to a place from where I can tease the base of the sloping shelf, left foot drags unnervingly on the edge of the scoop…not yet.

I back off, tears come, foot shakes a little, Bob is freaking out as well. We discuss him running round, throwing a rope down but I'd have to untie and the rope would be off to the side. I'm slowly melting out of this big hollow. "Gone too far this time". Though I sometimes act like I don't care it shows me I do. Fifteen minutes in, stretching that bit farther, making sure to leave room to share, I ease myself out of the groove using a pockmark hole, swapping feet to shuffle the other hand in. It had been invisible from the left. A ladybird is on the hold. There is nothing to do but crush it. Its bodily juices don't help, but killing it, so opened up, throws my mind away. I rush at the mantel hell for leather, picking a good enough patch of rock that works and chuck my foot around the arête. Pulling up I feel upset. The climb is magnificent, beyond me now.

End of the Affair

Grit has to be brushed if the harder lines are to be done, just the once. Once you clean you know the sequence so the mystery of the climb is gone to an extent. One of the last truly hard lines I inspected but tried without prior knowledge of the moves first was the bald frightening edge of *Sorrel's Sorrow Buttress*. It looked tenuous but a Friend-ly break low down gave me the idea to try it without practise. In 1985 I climbed a lot with my friends from MUMC: Paul Clark, a doctor encouragingly and Matthew Gordon, the world's best hitcher. We had a secret weapon. He didn't know where it was from but Matt had brought a reassuringly stiff rope, limiting any fall. The gear in the break is bomb-proof but only 15ft up. The arête is 45ft high, on a tier above a 15ft cliff. This is what we decide they should jump off!

Nick Dixon has kindly given me a homemade chalk bag. It doesn't help, when I put my hand in I cannot get it out. On my first attempt I get to a heel-hook hands off at 30ft. Above there is a crease in the arête I reach up and pinch. It is poorer than is comfortable. To the right is a sloper, beyond it a ramp, on which I have noted the best spot from a neighbouring buttress. Grabbing the sloper, set up for it, smears are either too high or too low to slap the ramp reliably. On the pinch too long, as only Curbar can, even from chill rock, it starts to exude grease. My feet are too high. The pinch is too unreliable to lean back off now. The fall is coming. Higher above the gear than the gear is from the floor, no up, no down, this is a loaded no-man's-land. The fall is not straightforward in direction either. Off to the side is a block that you must miss. I cringe down as far as I dare, still hung off the rock. Concentrate for the landing. Take up a vertical stance in the air.

A photo of the occasion shows the two rope-men in two modes: Paul stationary, Matt already running off the cliff beneath him. During these seconds my spine's future is in doubt. Matt's heroic leap puts the weight of two onto the cam in the break. The rush into the harness tanks me up violently, the deceleration irresistibly flicking feet spanking into the flat rock platform.

"Thanks….Aawww..."

A few minutes later I'm eating a hideous ham sandwich. I'd forgotten this, but apparently I then pulled a tin of Long Life from the top of my sack, saying, "A little beer should calm me down." A little later I go up again, grind to a halt again, repeating the whole routine.

It was nearly two years before I relent, pre-empting another's claim to it and practise the move on abseil, doing the mega-line late on a warm June day. The competitive scenario made me sad at heart. It was *The End of the Affair*.

However things go wrong much more quickly at this level. The move wouldn't have worked the way I'd attempted it. Neither of the two smears I'd thought to use for the crux work. An undercut side smear between them was the subtle solution.

Nick Dixon belayed me on the first ascent then did the second ascent belayed by Andy Popp who then did the third ascent. Thus was born the curse of *The End of the Affair*.

Wings of Unreason

The first time I came here there were gibbets and other repulsive objects hanging from the trees. They almost enhanced the magic atmosphere of the place. In Queen Victoria's time there was even a zoo. When it closed the animals, including the bison, were released to fend for themselves.

Sole scooped stone steps climb to the Upper Tier where the boulders are arranged like merry food stalls for a village fête. The big climbs there are great fun. The otherworldly mood of the Lower Tier is more like you'd find within the fortune-tellers tent. Stood still among the Scots Pine, my friend could hear it too, music coming from the rocks. Piano. Mozart! It was then we saw him, looking as if day had yet to reach him. Skin, dark waxed jacket, hair, all caught with the same scary pallor. At first he seems to glare but then grins revealing higgledy Ramshaw Rocks teeth.

"Are you enjoying the music?" a rich smell partly asks us. Apparently, when you got to know Doug a little, he became friendlier. And it proved true – in time he even acted as a mole pointing out what Nadin or Nick had been trying.

Track of the Cat E5 6a. Photo: John Kirk.

The music glancing off the cliff immediately reminded me of the myth. It was her playing. Never seen, it was said she'd been horribly disfigured in an accident. Doug had made a home for him and his wife among the boulders. Now the authorities were trying to move them on, that was what the gibbets were all for, to scare them away.

The country's first E8, a shallow scoop of Nick's from '86 celebrates the Lord of the Roaches with *Doug*, and innovatively relied solely on fragile crystals for holds. Eccentric protection, a hallmark of Nick's, was this time expressed in the illusory safety net provided by two friends: Andy Popp and Allen Williams. Stretched beneath the 30ft scoop, as if catching apples – how could a blanket be expected to catch him with both holders' arms fully extended? Blinding him to the uneven hard landing beneath it, all it'd do in reality would be to neatly wrap him up, ready for convenient disposal. I'm sorry to say Doug lost his wife, shortly after his tenure, shuffled off to a Stoke estate.

The Roaches atmosphere has inspired names like: *Days of Future Passed*, *Barriers in Time, Entropy's Jaws, Commander Energy*. At the end of most crags when you go a little further to see what there might be there's seldom a surprise, but here a special treat awaits the curious – an undercut 40ft slab with an even better name *The Hard Very Far Skyline Buttress*. Legend has it, on a rope in '77, Jonny Woodward, clad in EBs, magicked 6c – the super-thin crux of what became *Wings of Unreason* – but then **lost** the hold…for a whole year! Another time thereabouts Allen Williams was soloing *Entropy's Jaws*. Face's chin perched on the flat top's edge, Popp looking on, Allen stalls mid move, has to lurch for Face's outstretched hand but misses, ending up hanging on Face's thumb.

Craig Smith and I had an entertaining winter's day on *Wings*... Craig liked to take me on limestone, gave me salads to eat, and happily tolerated me driving a car without wipers in the rain (me going manual with an ice scraper sitting on the window). He makes fresh prints squeaking beyond the skyline. Sunny…shirt off, the critical buttresses peek out through fresh taut snow. Midweek, geology lectures drone away in Manchester.

Dawes to lead: facing a slam onto a cam 5ft below, mid-crux teeter, Pudsey-born Craig lets out a stunning: *"Bloody hell, it's a kangaroo…!"* At which he drops the rope and gives chase. Everything goes silky quiet above the shiny white blanket he's dived under…at last a bush quivers and springs up as it shakes off its heavy coat. Craig dusted white hops out empty-handed. A survivor of the Victorian zoo, a hungry wallaby had come for our butties.

A special day at the Roaches came in spring '86. I'd often go over to Staffordshire to test myself on Nick Dixon's and Simon Nadin's latest routes – some on sight. Part of that was to discourage them from trying the lines on the eastern front. Nadin was tall and people talked in a hushed tone about him that rankled.

…Armed with a hit list pondered for a while, weather perfect, a bold open slab called *Bloodspeed* E6 6b was first. You couldn't hit the ground off it but you would take a screamer if you flunked where to go or what to do. It was fun to not have to clean for once, just turn up and enjoy. Not Simon's hardest, but bold and unrepeated. A firm approach, spotting the best smears, keeps it moving – it went quickly and easily.

Next, two balance solos on the left hand Lower Tier, *A Fistful Of Crystals*, Jonny Woodward's luxuriously sculpted E6 6b scoop/ramp and a lower version *Crystal Grazer,* a committing E5 6a. Further left is Dixon's unique solo *Catastrophe Internationale* E5 6c[27]. I'd backed off it before, but this time thinking it through at the half height, hands off, a determined sequence unwinds. Perching improbably on a ladder of football boot to jean stud-sized pebbles the wet streak glistening above under berried heather has left just enough dry to maul over on. Even as you do the moves they feel impossible. It looks that way too crystals invisible from afar.

Next up is Andy Woodward's dream seam *Entropy's Jaws* E5 6b, great foot crosses, quick feet poses afford a scope of a recent unrepeated Nadin line *Script For A Tear* E6 6c, tetchy, contorted ultra-thin slab above a dangerous fin of rock. In mind throughout: push out and miss it, taking whatever the bigger fall meats out. Ludicrously thin, after a toppie, it goes ok.

I get on Nadin's flamboyant *Art Nouveau* E6 6c. An unlikely undercut rib with a snaking ripple on the steep slab below. Intricately stepped so each step in the rib offers up a pinch to use differently, I look in line with the rib and spot satellite edges hidden from the left that might oppose the rib. With these little climbs, to lean over the top and suss out the flash is something

[27] The catastrophe was that Antoine Le Menestrel soloed *Revelations* 8a+ one of our hardest sport routes.

117

Art Nouveau E6 6c, 2nd ascent.

I don't avoid, even spotting a slot too. Ripples draw up crouched feet here, cross up feet there. Heels low, toes angled, reconnoitring up and down, the best combos become obvious. It suits well, with RP1 in good rock, the old Rowan below needn't worry for one gung ho last go. God this is satisfying cruising around doing all these climbs.

Feeling unstoppable, there was one more climb I'd always fancied. On the Lower Tier is a 35ft pink brown whaleback with a phrased pace all of its own, *Piece of Mind*. Ablaze on the cool rock, would there ever be a better day to give it a go? But it unnerved me.

When Woodward claimed *Piece of Mind* in 1978 it raised eyebrows. There was an air of mistrust toward the Woodwards – later he did a peerless photographed repeat of his new *Beau Geste* at E7 7b to assuage doubters. When I did the second ascent in stickies, just pipping the highly accomplished Mark Leach[28], it felt hard E6 6c. I'd done the second ascent of his *National Acrobat* at Ramshaw Rocks too, thinking it 7a not 6b (bunched up, easier for the short, it'd even stopped world lead climbing champion Simon Nadin and that takes some doing). So you weren't sure what was what.

It's got the look. It starts up twisting shallow grooves then teeters out right till a poor ramp at your waist can be invented upon to blind tickle a bald pate top. Below is a steep scoop, below that a wet narrow topped flake kneeling up against the base. It leaves a sinister, leg wide gulch.

It has a delightful rhythm, the intricate ease of which makes you feel you're doing really well; smears set to support legs at rest yet angled to forge unusually satisfying shapes. After a tense step out right, the ramp improves again – here, it's a good idea to chalk the heels of your hand ready for the press down on the waist-high scoop, making sure all the grit has been brushed off your boots.

Pressing down on the best part of the inclined scoop on tiptoes, reaching up around the top, the first hold that day to feel warm immediately worries… windscreen wiping… stretching an inch to get it better, settling for what feels barely adequate, I wonder: is my right foot creeping imperceptibly? The unplanned struggle pulls my left foot off the ramp prematurely. Body now is a little askew to place foot next to the low hand at my waist and…

---

[28] Who did the world's 1st 8c in my opinion, with *Controversy* at Malham Cove, and *The Crack* 8b at Frogatt.

Oh my God! To my disgust, I've not left enough room next to my hand. Another try, but the difference though it is no more than half an inch is critical. To attempt to use it but fail will pitch my body out, spinning into space and perhaps much further over the platform 30ft below. I can neither reach further – top hand holding me from falling back – nor shuffle the hand at my waist because it holds most of my weight on the scoop.

It's almost feasible to stay there, been here for a minute or so already. Inaudible, I hear me reprimand myself but shut that irrelevance down just as fast. There is one last possibility – put right foot above lowest hand, quickly take my hand away and accurately snagging the lip of the scoop, stand one footed.

…Hand away…foot on…it's worked…but no…rocking back ever so slowly…the fall is already released, there's a moment to log what's coming. Boot landed side on means toe is sat not on the lip of the scoop but snagged further up the scoop. It has sent my centre of gravity out too far, but the foot can still roll back around its outer edge – it stays on all the way, till knee lower than foot, eating up the first acceleration into the gruesome drop, but pitching me to face out. Once airborne the top foot wings down to join the lower. Parallel, they allow a lurch, biting into the steep scoop that jerks me out, bunny hopping over the thigh-snapping gap on to the thin platform of the flake…riding huge moguls of rock, each lurch hugely heavier than the last, crumpling into the path shoots me head first at a tree trunk. Hands jab out to protect from a brutal impact, just as my head is about to smash into the tree, my leg miraculously yanks me back.

Dazed…a jab of heat blasts up from ankle to stomach. I'm struck suddenly by the attractive patterns of bark on the pine's trunk. Trying to stand up but my foot is caught. Bootlace had hooked on a broken tree root. A broken root was all that had stopped me from head-butting the tree.[29]

Hobble… hobble happily down to the car. Just three weeks later cast off, ready to go, no matter, what an incredible day…

[29] Face says he was there but I can't remember that, sorry…

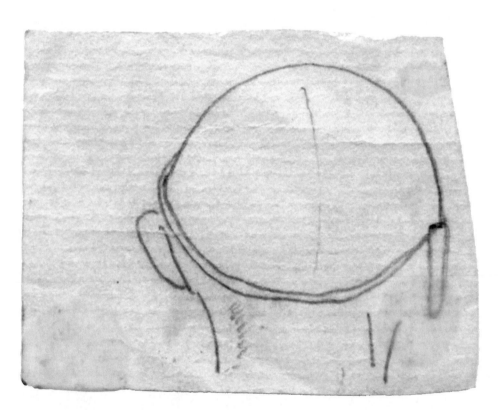

Looking at *Doug*.

From left: Mike 'Moose' Thomas, me on *Windows of Perception* E7 7a (photo: Iwan Arfon Jones), Bobby, Trev's behind, Paul with tab, plenty on it. Below: *Windows...* See note i. Photo: Unknown.

The Wonderful World of Walt
Disney E6 6b, 6b, 6b, 6a

Phils Harmonica E6 6c

The Fire Escape E7 6c

King of the Mezz E7 6c

Coeur de lion E8 6c, 6b

Blockhead E7 6c, 6a

Benqueno E5 5b, 6a

Above left: *Coeur de Lion* E8 7a, F8a+, a natural first pitch to *The Quarryman* groove
F8a & *Firé Escape* F7c. Photo Heinz Zak.
Above right: The crux crucifix. See note j. Photo: Paul Williams.

Clockwise: The Captain shaving, The Crook doing his laundry. Photos: George Smith. Ray Kay relaxed below the frightening Cilan Head. Photo: Dave Jones. Johnny Redhead. Photo Dave Towse.

Top right: *Cure for a Sick Mind* F8a. See note k. Photo:Paul Pritchard.
Middle left: Trev or Carlos and I.
Above: Vicious and precise but satisfying. *The Very Big And The Very Small* has only had 4 ascents to 2011. Manicured boots and nails de rigeur. Photo: Heinz Zak.

Moose on 2nd ascent of *The Untouchable* F8a. Photo: Glenn Robbins.

Pete Robins on the proper finish to *Bobby's Groove* F8a. Photo: Keith Sharples.

Top clockwise, right to left: The ...
Lobster, Andy Pollitt, Haston, Mark Leach
and mates in Pete's. Photo: Phil Kelly.
"On patrol youth..." Paul Williams in
Pete's Eats.
Mark 'Face' McGowan and I, 'Clockwork
Orange' outside Pete's.

Water int' dog's bowl

Have I forgotten anything at the Hall?

Plump from popcorn and Columbo, a silver 5-speed Honda Accord drives towards the mountains. From the quirky Malvern Hills and across the rich loam of Shropshire – unwittingly past the beginnings of Robert Hart's forest garden – the road slowly becomes twistier, narrower and emptier. Tape jammed yet again in the machine, speeding along a long straight. The mountains ahead swell imperceptibly – a rising flood of excitement wells up as I come to the top of the Llanberis Pass, towards what I love, scarcely a bolt within ten miles. The journey ends with a pause to relish alloy clank deep inside the engine before entering 'The Pad'.

The dour exterior of The Padarn Lake Hotel is no clue to the *hullabalooiau* tumbling along inside. Amazingly, everyone is there. All the "The's" are there; trouts, beasts, lentils and their like. Smiles, blanks and scowls.

The pool table encroaches on those on the long cushioned benches along the side. Take your shot, but be quick if you don't want a pinch or a prod. We have our table, but there is never enough room and satellite chairs hamper the delivery of shaking beer to those beyond.

The door swings open wildly and *"'ash for cash"* rings out. It's Gabwt plying his trade.

Three monkeys in a boat. Photo: Alun Hughes.

Joe's tankard shines behind the bar but outside by the fag machine – look through the murky glass panels – you can see the underage gather, peering in to share the enthusiasm amongst the smoke.

The next morning, the water in the dog's bowl is frozen solid so Pritch cannot drink it as he sometimes does to make us laugh. His giro has dried up just like the flow of stories he pedals to avoid work at the job centre. He is skint (surviving on 18p Spar bourbon creams for three weeks).

At this point in the story, many of us are living in Pwll Y Ddor. In those days it was a rough barn on the road up to Clog next to the steam mountain railway, on which we plotted our highwayman raids. It is like living inside a crag. Mike 'The Moose' finally manages a pull up on a ledge literally a nail width wide. His diet of naked white toast has worked. I reply with a hang on the 70° slick pinch on the slate lintel opposite. To count it you had to say "Archbishop Makarios, Archbishop Makarios". No heating or home comforts, some nights one would get lucky and one's hapless guest have to choose: freeze or cuddle up. Moose's younger brother Phil's music was always on, battery budget allowing, playing The Cure, Siouxsie Sue, Sisters of Mercy or Dire Straits.

Slumped at our tables in Pete's, we are all knackered today. Last night, an attempt to light a fire filled the whole barn with smoke, evicting the lodgers to a frosty night. It wasn't like life at Eastington Hall, but rock-climbing was one part of a wider existence with a freedom usually reserved for the wealthy. Admittedly, the lack of money was more of an issue for some than others. For a rich boy like myself, while sometimes *scarfing,* I didn't have to, regularly enjoying half cheese/half beans on toast, but on occasion we'd help Pritch out by distracting a tourist – whose hot meal had just arrived – in conversation. A single fork slipped in from the side came back loaded with sausage and a round of toast.

North Wales is like the corner of the room, where dust collects it's true, but interesting books too. Climbing folk and other unimpressed from all around the country blew into Llanberis in those days. The twisted *real world* where people loved to work, follow rules so they could all do the same thing wherever they were, all left behind. Here we made it up as we went along.

The George twins, the Arkless family, Pete, Robert Rat, Phil too, Nick Thomas, Ann Bierd, Steve Andy, Clint, Plums, even 'The Sex Lobster' were all part of my new life. Hitching normal, mortgages optional, athletic fervour was only half the content of our quiver. There were many other wonderful folk, most of whom I managed to interrupt frequently or forget their names. Characters included Leigh or 'Manuel' as he was known, from Birkenhead – usually up to his ears in cutlery and plates in Pete's Eats; Stevie Haston, "It's piss man" and Ray Kay ('the rhyming climber' as late beloved master of ceremonies Paul Williams, used to say) were from East London. I was warned to be careful of them. There was 'Carlos' a.k.a. Trevor Hodgson, built like a gorilla, the grinning star of Llandulas cave; Mark 'Face' McGowan, droll, bold Glaswegian run-out merchant and confident blonde bombshell Bobby Drury swelling the cast.

Many had had the bull set on them when they were halfway across the farmer's field at Castell Cidwm. Folk who visited Carreg Hylldrem on wet days would devour the excellent cakes and pies at the café on the corner. You could be amazed when she charged you a ridiculous 8p for a superb homemade lemon tart. It was the old lady's hobby to feed everyone at prices unchanged since the '50s. There was one man however, the pioneer of *Vlad the Arete*, who did not eat cake. His secret was a strict diet of pure oat. This did his guts no good at all. He eventually had to visit the doctor who prescribed a small greased cone to be *taken three times a day…*

We'd all become embroiled, for one reason or another, in the mad traditions of the North Wales climbing scene – climbing was still exciting here. Sometimes too exciting. Cliff Phillips, 'The Captain', soloing, had fallen 200ft off Dinas Mot, and then, bleeding from his ears, had crawled down and driven to the Vaynol Inn for a beer where legend has it he was told to get a round in.

I'd come more for the fun and capers I'd heard about. Take Al Harris, who on a Saturday afternoon liked to climb high up on Caernarfon Castle, reach through an arrow slit and grab a startled tourist's ankle, or try to ride a scooter up the scree to the foot of the Cromlech.

One time, early on in our halcyon days, we were all up on Cloggy. I was sleepy – I'd been with Nicky Long Legs, a chambermaid from Cobden's Hotel in Capel Curig – lying around, good for nothing in the sun watching climbers on the cliff. We had got it together at Kendal, pogo-ing around to the live band in a peculiarly narrow, jam-packed dance floor. The crazy throng heaving to a rock and roll refrain dedicated to Mr Ken Hill – you could let your legs go floppy yet still stay upright.

"For Ken Hill… for Ken Hill…*f...ing hell*…"

We retired to Plas Y Brenin director John Barry's van parked by the ticket booth. A good party sometimes gives you energy. It is difficult to tell what time of the morning it is in a dark van. Ooops – emerging, flushed we try and saunter into the film festival, jumping a long queue.

In EBs Dixon was high on Whillance's free version of Drummond's audacious *Midsummer Night's Dream* E6 6b. Nick, blind to the peg's eye, was struggling to clip it, facing a 50 footer on to the old bolt. The crab was clattering unconvincingly, up and down, occasionally tapping the eye, until eventually, leaning a touch too far, his right foot peeled away from the foothold and cliff. Slowly, irreversibly, Nick's body follows, destined to fall. In northeast monotone, loud but calm, "Barndoorey barndoorey" rings out.

I made the mountains my home. I felt part of a story, with space enough around it to write itself. For the first time I shared a life I'd chosen myself with Meeta and her canny 7-year-old son Deva. Meeta had left a violent childhood in Lausanne for an unsympathetic Coventry. In Snowdonia we found solace in each other. Our relationship was not always full of flowers, though plants always lasted a long time in the flat. Few have her capacity for unbridled mirth. Truly tickled, her head would tilt a little to the side, her hand slowly come up to her mouth to mask her gently vibrating upper lip. I enjoyed racing a towel back and forth on Deva's wet hair till it frizzed up like a gorilla's just like my dad had. One rainy day in a blue Rascal van, skilfully sold to me by my cousin Simon, circumstance cast me as Llanberis crèche. Á la "*School Of Rock*", Deva and eleven of his friends bundled into the baker's loaf on wheels to enjoy Rhyl Sun Centre. It wasn't long before two kids were missing in the heavy swell.

Not all stayed in Snowdonia, some were glad to make it back across what Big G's gruff friend Smudger used to call the *loon valve* that keeps us all here.

Take an international BMC youth meet. The previous night had been a drunken mess. Optimistically, I'd said I'd give a lift to some French climbers to Tremadog. By the time we arrived, a little shaken on roads I enjoy, they were in a bad mood. The dusky beauties Isabelle Patissier and Natalie Raybaud did not seem taken with the crag but were eager to find a safe, physically challenging climb nevertheless. An unclimbed project right of *Geireagle* up a steep wall, amply protected by four new pegs, would provide just such a climb if they would give me "un moment", je dis.

The cold sweat pouring off my temples was not a good sign as the 3rd peg was clipped. By the 4th I was in the air, stripping peg after peg after peg, tumbling down the slab towards them, fortunately coming to a stop, *akimbo*, just above their heads. On my arrival, they silently fasten their rope back into their trendy new rope bag and leave.

During the Ordovician origeny, 488 million years ago, here[30], before it was Wales, magma struggled through continental crust, baking an unrivalled spread of new kinaesthetic rockcakes: rhyolite, dolerite, quartzite. Together with limestone, sandstone, even gritstone at Rhiw, and re-baked ones left forgotten in the back of the oven, like slate, is this the greatest variety of rock in any one location on Earth?

In the mid 80s, this cauldron of rock and folk came to the boil. While the new French ethic opened up the limestone on the Orme, there were still big lines left in the mountains for when the heat arrived, and when lacking, the sunnier Lleyn peninsula offered up scary sea cliffs or a tan. Gogarth quartzite was set for renaissance and the slate boom was yet to explode. We'd sticky boots, RPs for tiny cracks and cams that worked in flares. All this: the people, the unclimbed rock and the innovation in equipment made for outrageous adventures. Climbing was undergoing a seismic shift. On the continent, expansion bolts were freely placed but in Britain the preponderance of lazy nutters on the dole was to support a fusion of the new athleticism with old style hedonism. The rock but with the roll left in.

[30] Unlike in the Lakes where there was an island arc made by unimpeded extruding magma as in Hawaii today.

Gogarth

"Friend or foe?", depends where you go and with whom. Wen Zawn I first visited in 1981 with Mike and the Gittins brothers. Andy, Tim's friendly elder brother climbed with Mike, Tim with me but we didn't get on. In mistake for *Wen*, a mere Severe, I headed 70ft up Livesey's *High Pressure*. Unable to fit moacs or hexes on rope into the tiny cracks, bickering with Tim, I down climb in a huff and we escape back out from the notch. But in common surely with many before us, we'd gawped across the void at the interlocking system of flaring grooves that skirt the colossal sea arch.

Five years later, I'm swinging in wildly to get a peg into one of those very untouched grooves. Later in 'The Pad', eyes are still bitter from lichen dust as I try to press gang someone to come to try it with me. Fresh from his success on *Vector* E2 Simon Donawho is ideal. Up at Oxford like Mike, Donawho grew up in the Malvern Hills (where quarries still hide unclimbed 800ft slabs). I assure him we can easily escape off the line at any point – *into the Irish Sea that is!*

We abseil in. The sound in the bottom of the Zawn is astounding. The fast ferry to Dublin will keep us regularly informed as to the hour, as bigger sets well under the arch, roll booming into the vestibules deep beneath the mad back wall – Wales's inner ear.

Andy Gittins above South Stack, 1982. Photo: Mike Dawes

Blithely oblivious, we learn what we've taken on as we climb. Simon's enthusiasm and courage support me 20ft up. I balance damply up the introductory blunt edge, enjoying every moment, until it is possible to swing around, incredibly into a layback on the very lip of the arch. Look right and you'd see Brown's audacious *Spider's Web* and to where Crispin Waddy and Big George will tear it up horizontally over the next decade. Look left and you can see South Stack Lighthouse. Worryingly, its light has just come on; the one that has saved post work parties on Red Walls many a time, the leaders moving feverishly as they plan their next move each time the light passes.

The open groove above the lip is blanker but less strenuous, on perfect rock with 'tasty' triangular features, crux a tricky 6b press out to a long undercut on smears that eases swiftly with a powerful grab to a long break that constitutes the top of the arch's capstone – a gap that demonstrates beyond doubt that the whole capstone of the lower arch is slowly detaching itself. Off a hanging belay on small cams and pegs, it's time to usher up stocky, cheerful mountaineer Simon, who uses 'mixed tactics'. A periodic glance up at the groove to come tells me it steepens alarmingly.

Getting darker, our drinking water finished, a slow swap on the hanging belay shows our position on the learning curve. I storm the 6b groove to its very top. Decisions, decisions: two exits – left or right. Right is across an unlikely ramp on the back wall. It's out – just too loose, in any case we've started too late. Left is a slappy number. Unfortunately I wrong foot myself, stepping blind on to a peg. Rather than attempt a nasty foot swap and risk a benighting fall, I climb on.

Donawho unknowingly training for his forthcoming adventure
deep within Wen Zawn on *Flying Buttress* Difficult.

The ground is capricious, loose and dangerous. Extenders running out I must use single crabs for the last gear, rope drag becomes extraordinary – hands and feet claw into the dry grass ramp, grateful it hasn't rained. Finally pulling up to a welcome boulder belay, jacket, lost Mars bar discovered in the hood. Simon jugs out in deepening gloom. We're blown out in his XR2 but by Beris, each of us is a shining *Conan the Librarian.*

A month later it's a shock to see where Simon and I had gone, and a bigger shock craning our heads up further to see where Craig and I intend to go this time – across a ramp that winds implausibly across the violently overhung rotten back wall. My new partner in arms is tenacious, fit, with the likes of Caley's *Great Flake* E6, Cromlech's *Rumblefish* E7, and on Gogarth's Upper Tier the nasty *Psychocandy* E6 to his name.

It is raining but we're up early this time. In any case above the lip, protected by stepped ceilings it'd be bone dry. Craig's had been a fine lead of the first pitch in the conditions. Escape problematic, with the tide now almost fully in, I lead on up the flared groove but instead of cutting left as with Simon, I explore carefully down and right, bridging on a curtain of ribs towards the start of the ramp that arcs miraculously all the way to meet *Dream of White Horses.*

Loose blocks, loose holds on them, all made out of talc. A fearless hole swallows a Warthog with five swings of the hammer. Above, below, the rock overhangs wildly. A fall will leave a man in space. Beyond the first crux, 3c, an unsafe earthy gargoyle sticks out attractively. A stretch down between my feet to place a Friend 3 deep in an empty bird's nest on the very lip of the ramp catches a glimpse of Craig, the wrong way up, across the void. He sees me see him, turns his head away, then just his eyes back to greet mine. We burst out laughing …but not too loud!

Going up and down from an unsafe sanctuary, some of the groove is cleaned away. Yet another cam is fixed. It takes 6a cunning to climb this 4b; there is one hold to trust, two that depend on each other, one looser than Sam Fox's bra straps…apologies.

One rope zig-zags around the arc, the other is in a giant loop across the zawn. Drag is significant already. Up a little more, a standing position cleared on a rubble ledge allows a reach around a corner for a sandy jam, a blessed relief, then another more fragile jam. OK, good…fuck??? Mid-pull, the rope slows under a spike. I push harder on my foot. The foot shoots straight through the hold into space taking my breath with it, but somehow I'm still there. Free foot stacks on to the other. "I'm OK…" I say, but Craig can see me clearly. Now pinned into an irreversible isometric stress position I'm already starting to pump.

Hung off the jam, drag still impossible, I can't pull up enough rope to flick it free of the spike. It surprises me when the groove I'm leaning on folds elegantly out. The spinning block's hastening moan turns to a boom as it punches the dodging sea. The updraft of sulphur from fragments hitting the slabs below the arête is invigorating, making it a welcome distraction. There's a solid break above – must be, to try and rest before down climbing…or something. Grabbing it, for a moment, even though it is an even greater strain, this new position is strangely restful until the spike below rips off… the sudden release from rope-drag hurls me up…Urrr..ghH…quickly I realise holding on is pulling me off, let go completely I stay on!

Coming to, hung on packets of sugar hurriedly stacked on a supermarket shelf, I've forgotten what gear is below and so just what the true risks are. Body draped over as much rock as possible, I go on a 'two minute holiday'.

No gear in the niche, further up a definite Friend 2 slot is visible, in better rock, just within reach but out behind me in very steep terrain. It is spooky, feet perched potentially treacherously, to lean out and trust a seemingly solid crimp. Cam ready to clip, feet jammed safely back into cracks, an unclimbed wild twin crack rippling through the bulge above distracts me nicely during the labour of clipping it.

Easy ground, Craig and I can finally let our victory giggles out. It's still raining. Precious little left on my rack, nowhere for Friend 4 or RP1 and no way to stack them together, a pleasant potter right leads to a rusty peg, pointless to clip but a reassuring proof of civilization regained. Great handles of pukka quartzite, not dubious at all, hauls what feels like a container ship's rope behind. It is a thrill to get thoroughly soaked on a sit down ledge at the end of *The Janitor Finish*.

1986 was a vintage year, full of bustle and controversy. While Redhead wrestled with his *Demons of Bosch* (Hieronymus AG?) on North Stack, setting the seals' moustaches a-twitching, many were for climbing with their heads fully in the *Helmet Boiler* like Fowler, and Crispin who'd later onsight his amazing hyper ledge shuffle *Death Trap Direct.* In fact many climbers didn't like bolts. Even situ gear lover Nick Dixon came to chop the bolt on Fawcett's *The Cad.* There was a lot of daring do going on.

After a lay off with bursitis in his shoulders, Andy Pollitt's return to the Welsh scene came with a bang. Fresh from repeating Redhead's *The Bells, The Bells,* Britain's first E7 (?), on sight, Andy set about his own direct start and finish to it. A poignant memory is bandanna'd Andy, slipping on fresh blue scarpas, passing me jumars – sole means of escape up rope hung down *Blue Peter.* Without meeting eyes he says: "You never know…" Andy sizzled up through *The Clowns* bellbottom bulges like he was back on Pen Trywn in scorching '84. Sun shone down in sheets, I cackled hysterically at the runners as they tinkled down the rope, but before I knew it he'd tied off the 'toothpick' *Bells* peg, set to do *The Hollow Man* E8 6b.

All standards of climber converged on Gogarth's welcome. Promiscuous of partner, we all sea level traversed, some of us climbed solo above the sea trying unclimbed features. One brilliant roof crack involved going footless off a hand jam 50ft up, went at E5 but it wasn't always deep water soloing. On another line, 40ft up right of Pritch and Leigh's E7 *Rubble,* I pulled a sidepull off mid-move. The strange thing was instead of falling immediately I floated on the footholds giving me time to look down. It was not a reassuring sight. A large wave had sucked out the sea leaving a view of a dry seabed. By the time I'd fallen, the wave was back in, a chest height cushion of water, leaving me lying on the floor of Wen Zawn looking up at the *Mad Brown* back wall.

Boltless, it was all about doubt being maintained, just like when Leigh McGinley freed *Ludwig* E6 6b on sight. He often partnered Haston. Leigh warned me I used to wind Steve up. Eventually, Steve put a lit cigarette out on my smiling face. I think it was probably close to the filter, burnt down, but at least it wasn't boring. He was busy on Yellow Walls finding the steepest rock. If you fell off the last pitch of his *Isis Is Angry* E7 6a, 6a, 5c, 6c, the quip went that you'd swing so far out you'd come back with an Irish accent. Did his E6 *Me* have two eggs on toast in Pete's Eats every morning? On the second ascent of *Me,* Craig turned to me puzzled saying his arms hurt.

"You're getting pumped", I inform him.
"Oh".

On another occasion, worse for wear, seeing Stevie's *Free Stonehenge* E7 7a, 5c, I was set to call it a day but Stevie in his charming way had said I'd not be able to do it. After faffing about with gear, Carlos steams up to the lip but blows it – "Bloody Karen..!" Up I go, fall, pull up, fall off, lower, trip over Trev's messy belay, *furious*…"Right. Fucking watch me Trev". Rat up a drain, knee bar, flared jam, saggy foot jam. "There!" Steve had found an edge out right apparently, rather than as Trevor delicately put it, "wrestle the arsehole of a pig*".

Each of Holyhead's cliffs is different, inspiring in its own special way. Come 'The Glorious First' of August, when the bird ban is lifted, Pritch and friends always turned their attention to his beloved Left Hand Red Wall. He was bold but his rope-boys would have to be as well. Stranded in bold fragile 6b, the mid route hanging belay of E7 *Enchanted Broccoli Garden* became notorious: RP2, downward pointing knife blade would likely rip if Paul fluffed the crux slap on the second pitch. What's surprising is that Paul had no trouble in filling the position: Moose, Gwion and Piggy all competing for their go on the seat of death. Another team later found a sound belay close by...tellingly.

A few weeks after I climbed *Indian Face,* Paul and I had a go at an easy look-ing unclimbed groove at the very base of the Walls. The rock here is more like dough than Red Wall cake. Indeed it is rumoured, in a Bolton accent: "errr…ghrr…ghrr, even monster alien spiders will not venture here".

Once I'm fixed in the base of the corner where anything falling off will cer-tainly hit me, Pritch sets off, managing to get to below an obvious weakness leading around a huge roof. Here he is presented with a block sitting on a sloping shelf, the now legendary 'Television Set'. With life-raffling gusto, he pulls up on it, at which point it slides towards him, then stops!

We chose an escape option, the more amenable looking unclimbed left arête. It leads to a girdle break on the lip of the roof. To be just 15ft up it is to realize it means trouble. Already faced with a threatening slam, big crack features above that promise protection draw me. Each possible hold has to be wrenched or tapped in turn. Few pass the test, each that does cements a profound worry. The 'rock' is no such thing; super nutritious were it not for the salty ooze. Un-warm, power pumped[31], by the time the sprint to the

---

[31] If one fails to warm up, lactic acid from exertion fails to clear in the constricted blood vessels rendering your arms near useless.

roof past beautiful efflorescent mould is over, forearms are gone, all chalk supped off by the cliff. It's a surprise not to find roses growing in the loose soil of the break at the bulge.

Canny body shapes thrown to ease the risk of feta features breaking away aren't coming off; body slowly melting to jelly, mind is all that is holding me here. The line through the bulge runs half in/half over two saggy horizontal fins. But for their fragility, a jam between them would've made for a good rest – but leaning on the thin fin it's a guess to know where it'd snap – before or after the jam? So I only use the jams to stop me peeling outward. This makes where feet are crucial: one is in a crumbling pod, the other, placed blind, sits on a break, not actually slipping – but it feels damp through the boot; can't afford to move it either for fear of picking up gunk, or worse. Above the bulge, out of reach, there looks to be a crimp in solid red rock, then the beginnings of a crack disappearing out of view.

To get here, six out of ten holds tried failed. A Friend 1 on two cams 30ft below me is the only gear masquerading as protection. Now 60ft out, the vegetation of the rake momentarily presents itself as an appealing target for a sideways leap. One part of me is down on myself for gambling a life I was really starting to enjoy, but the other is revelling in a raw buzz only a fight for survival can unleash.

One leg goes in between the fins. Deep in the woodshed gloom of the break, a 3 cam fails to bite, a 4 to fit in – what's needed is the unnecessary 3.5 left on Paul's belay below. Dirty, the leg jam is a short-lived poisoned gift, since now each boot must be cleaned ready for any small edges, hopefully likely on the solid rock above the bulge.

Panting, transferring dynamically to the upper slot before it notices, all I can do is emerge from the slot. Laying knee over what I've already clocked from below is the thickest section of the fin, mid-move, vest too sweaty to act as rag, fingertips wipe clean on red rock – impromptu towel. After a dip in dry chalk, full stretch, tips curl around a lovely, thin incut. Though body muscles are all to shit, forearm muscles being fresh as a daisy, the little hold feels really good. There's a plumper one to the right but *you'll have to stand right up on the fin to use that mate.* A test of the fin's integrity by progressively weighting a non-essential part sickens – it snaps short like a Pringle. '*Wo...*' stand onto the remaining slightly stouter part of the fin; crimping hard on the edge, standing up quickly but hopefully gently enough for it not to break, the plumper edge above comes to hand. I make sure to leave room for the other hand on it should I be forced to go footless. All fingers on the bigger, if sloping, edge, heel down, boot wipes clean on red rock rather than soiled trouser, lifts on to a thin slanting edge.

Now, thank heaven, mind gone to blancmange, muscle can be used to survive. Out of an ongoing nausea of gravity bursts silent advice to place a nut. Destiny in the form of the cliff's inscrutable waiting topography offers a side-on Rock 1 and a slung spike that only stays with a foot set against it on a ramp.

I don't say "Safe" but pull up the ropes till they swing free of the rock, swirling, incongruously pretty. Trevor Hodgson watching from the promontory overlooking it recalls the 'O my God atmosphere'. He told me Paul, later describing what it'd been like to second, said that when he looked up into my eyes: "He knew he mustn't fall". Though scarily, Paul couldn't avoid pulling off some holds I'd had to use.

Paul takes up the offer of my free leg, linking him into the unstable stance as soon as he can. A panic grab for the other leg would've undone the crucial tension, perhaps pulling us clean off the cliff like unfastened wooden legs.

Paul leads on, traversing gingerly right to escape – again, knowing not to fall under any circumstance. He nears the promontory, a steep vegetated slab. His toe reaches out like a snake's tongue toward a jutting grass tuft. I suspect he is being gung-ho with that sidepull but don't say out loud – the horror it'll unleash if it rips. He's not going to jump is he? Suddenly he's in the air…leaping across for the grass. Lands… grabs… sound of tearing doesn't come…Paul switches immediately to a secure bridge, already eyeballing a good slot, Rock 7 in hand.

Except on little crags in the Peak, it'd never happened before that I'd climbed into a position where the only escape was up through uncharted territory. It had chilled us. We gave *Come to Mother* a grade never used before: E7 6a, 6a. A death zone, *Come to Mother* was not competitive fodder, an athletic achievement laid down to be matched. Three weeks later, we're in Pete's

Eats when some pals return from Gogarth. They report the strangest thing. *Come to Mother,* all hundred plus tonnes of her, has fallen down. Had our skinny frames shaking with fear been too much for it? Was it really that loose when we climbed it? At least no one could kill themselves on it now.[32]

I finish my chicken with bamboo shoots and water chestnuts, and sit meditating on a full stomach. People in doorways finish their chips. Taoists consider rock the lowest form of reincarnation. If that *is* so, there must be many an arm and a leg in the Irish Sea that wasn't there at the beginning of '86.

In 'The Pad' say ten times a year, you'd see a certain expression – The Look – a manic but very human picture on a person's face: Gogarth. There are too many Little Chefs and bolts in this country, it is more important than ever to rail against society's burden of comfort. However futile, British climbing must survive: Cilan, The Sron, even the desert.

It was, as Sinatra often put it to Skinny in the Padarn in '86: "… a very good year".

[32] The same thing will also happen to what Paul once described as his finest climb *Oscar* E6 6b, across a sea arch at Craig Dorys, at the even more feral venue on the Lleyn Peninsula.

Quarryman

…Joe Brown has pencilled a map for me on a Post-it that leads to an old tunnel. It cuts deep into the heart of Elidir Fawr. Slates scatter music around puckered ironwork. The cry of peregrines around discarded blocks fade, through hidden shallow puddles sound merges into half-light. A recognition comes to me, invisible as gravity; humanity walked out of thin air…we look up. High above on a tower, off to the side of Joe's big adventures, flaring like a torch, is an astonishing groove. Away from it, glazed with water, a jewelled mineral array sparkles in the sun. This wall promised to be fresh territory for the world of climbing – a Schneider Trophy monoplane in sheer aluminium – tenuous seams, polished featureless shields, jagged undercut bulges way up in the sky.

Last night at a party, Nick Thomas had tried to smash my head into a basin, Steve Andy to ram my head down the bog. Today, Skinny Dave and I abseil off an un-cemented slate hut, to inspect the untouched West Wall. Usually when you inspect a wall, it doesn't quite match up to your hopes, but this did much more than that.

Where else has space-time been woven so wackily, the impossible and the easy overlapping so unpredictably? Features at a generous kinaesthetic angle: big broken toffee features coding for waist's *hippy hippy shake,* the

Slateheads: Bob, Skinny and Moose Photo: Unknown.

wall's installation of dinks angled for creative flick of limb. Look at where the hold should be and use that instead, put your foot in a position you never thought possible, on a hold that doesn't look like it'll work, setting up for a hold that looks tiny, that turns out excellent, putting you in a 'hands off' with unrivalled views of Snowdonia. That's why you can wear Lycra on slate!

You can't see gravity, nevertheless it squeezed planet Earth so hard, its stone heart melted. Earth's surface, space cooled till solid, it is only sutures in the skull-like orb that betray what goes on inside. Where sutures butt together, rocks are reworked into others. A favourite rock of mine is this squeeze-cooked mud called slate; gravity's fine bone china. There is a quiet harmony of gravity in the giant, blue grey purple pottery encouraging us to look for the crispest challenge, trusting our skills will not be squandered. It shows you that gravity is a mystery, its handiwork no less so.

Introduced to Twll Mawr, known to the quarrymen as Matilda, I found quite a gal. She even earned me money. One day Trev and I saw two waistcoated men over the fence peering into the hole. I vaulted the wire, pointing out breathlessly, that: "*right* where you are is badly undercut, it could collapse at any moment… unless you know the quarries as well as we do…" and so on, blah, blah. An hour later, one of them is clarifying another situation with Trev, "Would you like ice and lemon in that?" Trev was concluding a deal for us to be safety advisors for a Harpic advert.

"Do you know a 'boat expert'?" they ask. Funnily enough we knew just the guy, a collector of Zappa records called West. Later that summer, preparation for an explosion to mimic the dramatic effectiveness of Harpic in the bowl is not going to plan. Manoeuvring the boat to the right spot to set the explosives in Nantlle Quarry was proving too tricky for our 'boat expert'. The explosives specialist had to take the oars and West primes the explosives instead.

"Yahoo bollocks..!" Trevor roars as the lake goes up.

Sometimes the whole village got involved. A classic encounter between the outside world and Llanberis was the shooting of the movie *Willow*. When the director sent runners to secure the services of 'experienced horse-riders' the village miraculously sprouted the numbers necessary, like mushrooms after rain. The horses were dressed as 'Pigs', so come shooting day and the words: "and… ACTION", action *is* what they got. Pigs mounted with the great and the good, and the not so, charging not in one direction but in every, some just grazing the sage or heading slowly for the thirst quenching lake.

Each of the quarry faithful found their milieu one way or another. John Silvester, an international paragliding star now[33], climbed the world class *Rainbow of Recalcitrance* and *the* line of Lost World, the soaring arête *Prometheus Unbound*. His girlfriend Nicky preferred to leap off the top of the 70ft prow into Vivian pool. The Crook celebrated *The Stack of Nude Books* found in a hut, with a new climb. Captain Cliff, who made a living soloing behind hapless novices at Tremadog recovering jammed gear for sale in his Deiniolen high street house window, along with half finished cans of beans etc, soloed his dramatic *California Arête*. Ever rosy 6ft 6 inch 'Giant Redwood' Chris Dale liked to open bolt-free areas on the dolerite[34] and conchoidal slabs best, and to wear dresses to International Guide meetings.

Paul Pritchard's womanly legs looked the best in Lycra but despite clumpy boots and heavy heads, by 1986 a dozen 'slateheads' regularly on-sighted E6. Moose's E6 *Spark that set the Flame* was first repeated by Face (Mark McGowan) who romped up everything and then by five people over so many weeks, all ground up. Trevor Hodgson's impromptu solo of *Menstrual Gossip* E6 only stood out as it finished in a downpour!

Dixon's *My Ha...lo*, Towse's *Naked before the Beast*, Pritch's *I Ran the Bath* are all brilliant. Drury's E7 *Loved by a Sneer* was an impressive on sight solo first ascent, sadly cleaned up later. His *Clap Please* E7 6c expresses the showing off that was going on. I repeated it in little over five minutes on sight.

And then there was Haston, the pioneer of *Comes the Dervish*. Personally

---

[33] He has flown across the Karakoram for fun and from Snowdon to the Severn Bridge in one 7 hour flight.

[34] Where Joe Brown recorded the first rock climb in the quarries, *Gideon* VS, not all the rock is slate. Some is dolerite that someone someday, fair game to bolt, will do amazing hard climbs on. But the presence of dolerite used to be more significant than that. In the Victorian era, on land bought off local farmers, the Vaynol family instructed Quarry Masters to give each man new to the quarry a choice: where to choose their pitch to mine slate? Bearing in mind the quarryman would be paid by how much slate he brought out and could not switch to another's patch, imagine a man waking at 4am in his billet on Ynys Mon knowing that at the end of the long walk, tea and bread in his satchel, that all he had to work at was 'bastard rock', impossible to cleave into roofing slates, thus worthless.

pledged to climb anything of note I'd utter a sigh of relief if one of Haston's climbs fell down. Feral, lubricated with skating dust, the frightening smooth cracks Haston scoured the quarries to find, ideally for him were just narrower than a man, with nowhere to lodge nothing, and angled at a flock of hand hewn menhirs beneath. Everyone conveniently forgot they existed.

You can see *Comes the Dervish* from Pete's Eats in Llanberis where the butter knife to clean it famously came from. Sat outside looking on with a brew in the 80s and early 90s, seldom was there not someone on it. Two local ladies made it their business to point out over their Royals if the climbers were doing it wrong, sometimes correctly predicting where they'd fall. You don't see quite so many climbers on it these days.

Edgy stuff was soon passé, the era of smearing on slate had arrived. *Dawes of Perception* E7 6c and *Windows of Perception* E6 7a on consecutive days in April '85 heralded the future. Through the *Windows of Perception* I'd taken a peak at slate's potential. This ferment of friction sparked in Bob Drury's and my technical compendium *Wonderful World of Walt Disney* E6 6b, 6b, 6b, 6a, *The Quarryman* E8 6c, 6b, 6c, 7a, and in '87 *Coeur de Lion* † E8 7a, 6c, 6b. The left arête of the wall gave a fine back-rope[35] solo at the attractive standard of E2 5b, 6a, *Beijquiero*.

Quarryman wall is accessible, bolted, yet it's deserted. Hard Grit is popular, why not hard slate its country cousin? On both rocks motion creates the hold to a great extent but on slate the technical possibility of speeding limbs to close the gap between holds is richer. Comfy sponge, grit's a mellow fellow, where as slate whips like a flaying neon wire.

On the 7a crux of *Coeur de Lion*'s unrepeated first pitch your centre of gravity is stalled, skew whiff – foot must take your weight even though it's the wrong side of your body. A dramatic swinging leg kick is the only way to move at all: a kick that jolts you for a moment into the heart of a maelstrom where there *is* potential to move on. Watching in slow motion, you might catch a certain moment pass when left hand and left foot can move together – counterbalance-tastic, as demanding as sorting through raspberries very fast without bruising them.

---

[35]Solo, you can still make it safer by threading the rope through the belay, then as you climb un-hitch a series of knots so a loop of rope still protects you.

There are many other cool moves on the wall. *Phil's Harmonica* E6 6c, also unrepeated, only comes easily by hopping both feet up at the same time into a very unlikely tight thin bridge. Largely unsupported, impelled purely by changing shape, as you move your body it must float in the air. Does precision exposure co-exist anywhere else with so much punch and panache? Adam Wainwright's impeccable twin seam *Blockhead* E7 6c, again unrepeated, has some of the best tips laybacking in our spiral arm yet the big hole is deserted: "Calling all climbers…calling all climbers…"

There's still a lot going on: 70 and 8 year olds putting up new routes. Caff and Dobbins doing great climbs like *Serpentine Vein* 8b, *Sauron* 8b and *Tambourine Man* 8a but slate still has a way to go as a forcing ground.

A bonkers 1990 project that remains is *The Clock Face*. A steep wall with a two-and-a-half metre dyno loaded up on it; not just two moves together (2nd G) but an iterative cocktail of timing and precision (3rd G). Launch is off two opposed incuts. Below them – each angled to encode its own hip flick, small ledge footholds must be scampered up like wall bar struts, fast enough to kick off the launch incuts.

How crisp is your imagination of that flurry before launch? Can you get high enough and stay in close enough at that point to launch around the dial to snag the 30° leaning flat ramp – only usable because of a serendipitous penny deep vertical quartz rib opposing it. A kinaesthetic auspiciousness that reminds me of Dermot Somers's *The Stone Boat*[36].

It really got up my nose when the happy clappy chipping got going. Redhead started it off with *Manic Strain,* his carving up blankness but when *Dark Half* and *Gin Palace* were cleaned out hard as well I was gutted. Before this the moves on both were perhaps the hardest I ever did. The move on what became *Dark Half* involved moving three limbs at once.

---

[36] A message in the form of holds emblazoned on a sheer headland awaits a climber, a positive relief, sticking out from the cliff – either the rock around it must have been painstakingly chiselled away to reveal the relief or the message had always been there, erosion resistant, waiting to emerge. Somers thereby rejoices in the familiar climber's love of great moves *'The what the heck made that move so good?'* somehow conjured up into the rock. Casting rock as the star, he brings up the curious notion of consciousness dwelling inside or both sides of the rock (or everywhere?) This expressed itself when trying *The Quarryman*'s crux, I reprimanded the rock: "If you think you're a foothold, why don't you function as a foothold?"

Right up the centre of The Rainbow Slab was an ex-Nick Harms line that had also sprouted enhanced holds. Proving too tricky for Nick at the time, super sustained, it'd help me work up to a natural project on Twll Mawr, *The Meltdown* (more of which later). Nick's line had 40ft of hard climbing. It demanded strong feet and fingers, excellent flexibility and a high pain tolerance. At one point I had to squeeze fluid back into the tips of one hand with the other to continue. Summer 1990, some days the dark rock was so hot it burnt my skin. Size 6 feet squeezed into size 4 Kevlar Sprints, soles manicured per attempt, it called for concentration on tiny specifics while holding full body awareness. Friction level and shapes lodged five days in, intuition finally turned up unfettered on the crux to give the hardest route on slate, *The Very Big and The Very Small* E9 7b or 8c.

Slate is known as the rock-over capital of British climbing, yet the project *The Meltdown* barely has one. Instead it has 10 moves I'd never come across. The technicality of these highly positional unique cruxes is such that any limb's contact can fail. Tiny slivers as sidepulls in spookily appropriate positions: round mounds for feet naturally expertly inclined to limit the sweep of the hand, a cluster of three holds do exist where three are necessary to swap hands. There is a rest before the top crux traverse which takes six moves to establish, culminating in a heel-stand in a starred out position facing outwards for a hands off. Just mega…

Earlier in late '86, I did the hardest link I'd done up to that point on the project. Eight dynamic 6c moves up a rib sandwiched between an ankle height drop down to a layaway involving precise rotation of the whole body, 7a, and a highly compressed mantelshelf and traverse 7a. Repeating this marooned link in 1990 I found it harder than *The Very Big*… if that link was 8c in '86, perhaps it was the hardest sequence in the world at that time.

Horses for courses, *Meltdown* presented Jerry Moffatt playing away on slate with problems. When they met, Zippy said Jerry was that rare thing after he'd been unable to do the eight moves: silent. *Meltdown* would've been world class but unfortunately I broke a hold. I almost grabbed it, but watched horrified as the crux elegantly rotated into smithereens. I toyed with moulding a gold filling for the toothy hip-hop overlap but that might rob us all of a 'Stone Boat'; a vehicle to touch the extended mind of gravity authentically. James McHaffie has since done the move. We'll have to see who prevails.

There are other things to concern us for sure, like genocide, environmental catastrophes and the new world order, but I think they are all part and parcel of our lack of respect.

Can you hear a route Geiger? As if at a certain frequency in the alaya[37], how close human and slate have got to *Meltdown* is recorded, left as a residue in the *schwang* of the route. For me, *Meltdown* is this experiencing of the fusion of man and maker; what it is that makes the *climb* not just the rock. Climb the route well and you may notice how the rock is. How *it* as you.

[37] The ground of all experience.

The Fall

Cloggy's East Buttress resembles an Indian chief, especially so after snowfall when the chief's headdress feathers out from The Pinnacle. This is what my friend Gabwt called 'The Indian Face'. Midwinter, I'd look up at the cliff, ponder whether the aid placements masquerading as gear on the unclimbed scoop might hold, imagine what I'd do if I did actually fall.

The hardest sequence ends 60ft above the RP2 at 65ft. Coming when you're tired, sticky boots dirty, a nearly handless foot-change, long pivoting slaps – feet on blind smears – tenuous crossover, all precise, demands that you stay relaxed.

Perhaps the gear wouldn't strip. Even with a shocktape[38] on it, the manufacturers warned me the lentil-sized brass RP2 would melt in such a fall. To give the RP's thin wire the best chance of not snapping, I'd use a large diameter screwgate. Backing this up was a Chouinard 1 in an expanding flake and on the other rope an RP0 in a solid placement and 3mm sling on a tiny spike.

On the day, Bob and Sean rehearsed walking some steps down, taking in as much rope as they could, then reeling out the rope as softly as possible, as if stopping a Barracuda from snapping the line. I actually thought that, with this precaution, the protection might've been enough. The next best hope was that these would at least slow me down once flung at the ground.

It was crucial to avoid cart-wheeling, but perhaps this might not happen. Once, failing to clip a bolt on Pritchard's *Cure for a Sick Mind*[39], I fell 100ft, Pritch on belay ending up above me[40]. Crucially, in relation to the line on Clog, what had been interesting was that instead of grinding along the lower angled slate, I'd flown parallel just above it, able to control the angle of my body to some extent. In retrospect this parallel flight might've happened off the unclimbed Cloggy scoop, giving the scenario envisaged below a genuine chance of success.

---

[38] A sewn folded sling designed to unravel to reduce the peak force a runner will take.

[39] Placed high to avoid ruining the boltless *Rainbow of Recalcitrance.*

[40] Fortunately I was wearing two woolly hats but even so suffered concussion although that didn't kick in until after I did the route. Head injuries are nasty. I was depressed for quite awhile afterwards. Not a cure for a sick mind.

Tensile bone is surprisingly strong for something so light, but only in exactly the right direction – misaligned, a bone is little tougher than a brandy snap. Whatever happened in those few seconds of falling, it was essential to hit one of the intermittent grass ledges just beyond the rocky foot of the face – the greenest softest part, then lurch again to the steepest, most heavily gravelled scree beyond. Gear on *Master's* would hopefully hold the fall by then.

So if a hold did snap, pump become irreparable, or boot skid on lichen, I planned to immediately accept it and launch into this fall. Practising this in my mind, I would first turn and run down the face then, when the runners started to reel me in, I would wait for the end of the rips, right myself and aim for the turf and scree beyond. This flimsy paper chain of deep uncertainty was what let me finally really go for it.

Indian Face

Much has been said about adventure, the call of the wild, and other trite phenomena, but in the final analysis climbing is a personal affair; like the dark brooding immovable love one can form with a stranger, it has a definite but subliminal character. For me the *Indian Face* came as the final realisation of a dream held solid and perfect some years ago. A purity of expression that was able to be so personal that it could transcend the obvious cosmic futility of life; friendship and activity are some compensation for a deep seated hopelessness, but only climbing appeared to have a germ of profound depth in all its excited little plays of life and death. Cloggy's east buttress was the idol. So the beauty of the *Indian Face* lies not in enjoyment or in achievement, but in the rejoicing of the exorcism of a self-made destructive cage; and perhaps in the faint possibility that it may even be a scant record of such.

For seven years, I have gone through many of the recurring experiences of history. The initial joy on the crags has, with age, led through to a desire to improve my ability in the belief that it would deepen my enjoyment. But as in the realisation of any worthwhile dream, what man loves he inevitably kills. His efforts eventually fill a polished cupboard full of weird and wonderful trinkets; of ink, of brass.

Climbing for me provided a means of self-expression through this. In addition, ability has often meant a wider social acceptance, even if only in a 'one of the gang' way. To a young, socially immature person, that grew as a cancer, to a stage where my climbing was taken out of my hands to an extent. The end of this lies in photographs, sponsorship and in ugly tights, and in a dead end with a bolted door. Eventually there comes a time when you have nothing else to prove. You have made friends through compassion and that new side to your climbing disappears. With its departure there is left a strange beast; more able mentally and physically than before but without the naivety and wonder of youth. Its direction becomes an anguished cry to complete fate in the cycle of time; and after, to move on to new, more dilute and comprehensive ambitions. For me this involved many dangerous, yet necessary climbs, the culmination of all this being the *Indian Face*. The mechanics and story of this climb trace my liberation from something.

…It has been nice for three days!

A nice day sneaks over Crib Goch while I sleep, and Cloggy creeps slyly with its keen climbers towards dusk. In Pete's, I find the team has gone to Gogarth. I sit and tear out my hair, with tea that dries my upper palate. Keith tells me to get my feet off the chair, and so I order a salad. The WALL envelops me for a moment sometimes. The cage is not continuous around me then. In places it is very thick, and permanent, other borders open and close like a heart, and my nausea belches steam up through my skin, to my head.

Trevor, 'Carlos the bandit', who threatens to join the PLO, walks in wearing a wide brimmed hat and dark glasses: another late night. They would not put up with it, I tell him. I charmingly offer him a small coffee and a sustaining breakfast and ponder the next move. He's fed up with slate, and a little with climbing in general just now, but he is a sucker for a good long walk.

I smile – matter of fact – and suggest Cloggy, no strings attached. Trevor after much convincing that he is keen, agrees. We walked up to the crag, and started up. I got to the move left next to Johnny's bolt and Bobby watched me from Llanberis – 'ghoul below the Eigerwand'. Down climbed and lowered off again. Trevor felt ill so we walked down and had some food and beer.

The next day I was much better prepared, mentally and physically, but deep down knew something primitive was being expended on each effort. I was getting more psyched out rather than familiar. The wall's mechanics were becoming exterior and disconcerting. There is never a place to get into the rock, no groove to shadow your fear, just blankness and no gear. Abbed the climb a third time, getting the holds clean after the long rains and to practise the entry to the upper flakes where I'd gone wrong twice previously and had had to climb down 30ft on side pulls and smears to escape.

Tested the Rurp[41] in the top overlap. It is in only an eighth of an inch, but is tied off with 2mm rope. The Rurp is at about a 100ft – above that there is no gear that would hold bodyweight until the belay at 150ft. Thirty foot below is an RP2, and this on shocktape provides the crucial protection. This is backed up by a Chouinard 1, half-biting in a loose flake, and below this a 2mm Perlon sling and an RP0. For the other rope at that height, RP's 3 and

[41] 'Realized Ultimate Reality Piton': a teeny aid peg.

4 in poor placements on nobbles and a situ nut 10ft above which came out. Low down at 45ft there is a stopper 6 (filed down on short kevlar rope) held between two fins that represents the best runner on *The Master's Wall*.

The climbing itself is hard and, with eight bolts, would rate about E6 6b/c, but there is only half a bolt and that stares at you while you laugh at your runners, a tribute to a man's vision and short sightedness.

John Redhead's voyages on this wall deserve special praise. He had already done *The Bells*... at North Stack and was working on the sweeping scoop right of *Midsummer's*... He had one near fatal fall high up when placing a small wire. His foot slipped on a smear, the resin worn off his Canyon boots – the Stopper 6 took the fall and back up he went. This time he lowered off a Stopper 1 which skated visibly in its placement as he was lowered off. Another effort had him jumping for a 9mm abseil rope.

Redhead, frustrated, placed a bolt like a dog pissing to mark his territory and retreated to recover. An 80ft cameo *The Tormented Ejaculation*, graded E8 7a, still unfinished in his portfolio, but **the** line remained.

Jerry Moffatt arrived, chopped the bolt and *The Master's Wall* remained. Previous to these two, there had been other efforts. Ray Evans and Hank Pasquill had tried the line from the ground, inciting no rumour of practice. Failed, their efforts could be seen as more impressive than later ones. Mick Fowler had climbed an impressive climb in *Spreadeagle*, which starts in the groove left of *Master's* start and finishes in part left of the top section of Moffatt's route. It was my turn to struggle with my obsession.

There comes a time when the romance of the climb is crowded out by the raw danger of the route. This happened on the third day. On the fourth day I walked up and for the first time I wondered if I would walk down; somebody's son and friend.

Imagine the wall...it is a random woven wire mesh, tilted so that it steepens towards its top. At the base of the wall, two thick cables disappear into the turf. The lights in the town flicker as you touch the rock. Each move forms an electric circuit between your hands, you see. As you move, you worry about the outcome of that move. The tension at present resides in a dull Dinorwig power generator hum: "Woo-woo...woo...woo." Then I make a false move and the rock barks out a spark, a whip sizzles down my arm and fades to a sickly warmth in my shoulder; I try another hold but which one to use? Use the wrong one and retreat may become impossible. The gear is poor and a bad mistake could mean a death jolt full across the heart. So you move taking note of your position and the holds, but as you move higher the voltage grows and amongst the myriad connections there lie false trails that can kill.

A body makes
a sound like a
a fly hitting purple café killer lights.
Dizzscht, dizgg,
and your world is no more.

I went up with sticky rubber soles, which do not conduct electricity, and two friends that knew the score.

At 70ft I felt OK; automaton in a plastic bag, my brain floated out in space behind me. It had slim threads that blew in the wind but did not seem to be catching on anything, so I continued.

As I climbed I felt as if I was not there, but I wasn't somewhere else either. Just nowhere, alone on the surface, I arrived on the flake, the moves a blur. The body smudged over the rock. I was playing chess with the 'Gort'; the animal form left of *Woubits*, two olive eyes and daggers for ears.

In went light pieces of metal, fiddling with pieces of unfloured pastry on my mother's birthday cake when I was 12. The assymetric stopwatch was complete. All the time my mouth would give out these little tunes which disappeared. Then heavy breathing, and then short jerky gulps; shallow panting. In went the RP2 just above. I climb up on undercuts and dimples just below the point of commitment. I'm 10ft from gear and decide to down climb as if on the last training traverse on the wall. Coming level with the gear. I look at them saying: "Sloow and smooth."

I lower off for a rest, to let them take the stress from me. 'Splendid isolation' over for a little while. The release of tension was enough to make me want to stay on the ground, but I knew I would be up here next year. I had no choice. Twenty-five minutes rest and a cigarette and the two sides of my feelings still do not converge. I need to do it, but I desperately want to walk home happy, but I knew that would be a lie; so I go up to die a little more; homeopathy.

A hundred feet up, out above the last gear, I am faced with the first of the hardest moves but it is all in the wrong place. My body feels heavy, and lumpy…I slapped out right, a move that should be static, and was committed to the crux; a precarious mantel onto a rounded boss. If I fell off this move the gear would rip as it is off to the left and in downward-only placements. A blind foot feels for a twitchy notch. Once on this you can step up, rest and clip the Rurp.

You stand on both heels so you look out to the left, your hands by your side. At this, I noticed a friend I'd met in Verdon Gorge on the belay of *Great Wall*. His face spoke volumes. I tried smiling to relieve his tension but that made me relax and so I collapsed back to rest. I was there for half an hour; totally alone, the overall crux ahead, yet my position, physically comfortable. Rescue 20 minutes away, I would have to say 'Yes' and 'No' to the finish five or six times by the time they had reached the top and lowered me a lifeline.

I contracted to think of a comfy sofa, and watching the telly with a carry out. I went for the crux, the motion startling me like a car unexpectedly in gear in a crowded parking lot.

I swarm through the roundness of the bulge to a crank on a brittle spike for a cluster of three crystals on the right; each crystal crucial and separate, like the keys for a piano chord. I change my feet three times to rest my lower legs, each time having to jump one foot out to put the other in. The finger holds are too poor to hang on should the toes catch on each other. All those foot changing mistakes on easy moves come into mind. There is no resting, must go for the top. I swarm up towards the sunlight, gasping for air. A brittle hold stays under mistreatment, and then I really blow it. Fearful of a smear, on now non-sticky boots, I use an edge and move up. A fall now fatal, the automaton stabs back through, wobbling, but giving its all. Crossed way over my body, my left hand low below my knee, my right can extend over my body and mid-swing grab a jug. I grasp a large sidepull and tube upward, the ropes dangle uselessly from my waist. Arthur Birtwhistle on *Diagonal* I grasp incuts and the vectors recede.

Gabwt's *Indian Face* is climbed. I can rest and feel proud. *Longland's*, *The Drainpipe Crack*, *Troach*, *Great Wall*, and *Midsummer's*… smile in me, again, but like fine antiques; the gallery.

*

The essay above was written in the week after the ascent.

….it was good to finally make it down the Eastern Terrace. I pause, collecting gear from the base and look up. In the closing darkness the chalk trail hangs in space. The Indian summer will pass over and erase all trace but for now movement still twists above. In an hour the cwm will be left behind to hollow and reflect. In my mind the jade lake will come down with me to join my friends in Llanberis. This is the time. What I sensed it could be like.

It is the culmination of my dreams from school. The goals written and pasted in my book have been accomplished, at 22 my dreams have been fulfilled. Few have that happen. By that you see how true the vitality is in them and notice the warped drive in them too.

What was to do now?

But back to the present, in the past, Bobby, Sean and I walk down alive, lighter, tired, all in one piece. It is great the Dolly disco (at the Dolbadarn Hotel) is tonight. Friends, climbing partners, lovers, ex-lovers, enemies and people unknown to me are swept along by the achievement.

No longer invisible, some of the fractured energy burnt off, a softness in me can accept people's praise. The last few days I'd been drinking whisky from a quarter bottle, now with the unexpected break in the weather, success and survival glow. The sense of quiet reaching a certain level of mastery has given me nourishes a sense of inner satisfaction. I dance, clink glasses, shake hands in a new way and feel a historical dimension around me.

A week after the ascent *The Guardian* ran a double page spread: *Indian Face*. (Facing page). For a day, climbing had the oomph to squeeze Nigel Mansell and Gary Kasparov to single columns. The public could not be expected to understand fully, probably thinking the climb merely scary, tricky, not the equivalent of racing a crystal decanter car around Monaco.

Still aloof, "You always have to be different" I hear echo from the kitchen. I still didn't fit in but now I was distinguished.

A quarter of a century later *Indian Face* has only had three further ascents. Mine, pre-prepared on abseil, Nick Dixon's and Neil Gresham's after top rope, Dave Macleod's too. The climb has still not been climbed 'au naturel'. It is amazing but obvious – things change. Finger power, science and jet tourism have relegated the high mountain crags with their feral weather, 'snappy' rock and lethal delicacy to one choice among many. While sports routes of the day have become oft climbed, the 1986 canon remains threatening. The ground remains hard.

Extreme Severity, and more

Rock athlete Johnny Dawes has pushed climbing into a new era with his ascent of the hardest climb in Britain. David Rose and Roger Alton report

ONE hundred and twenty feet above the rocky screes at the foot of Clogwyn d'ur Arddu, a towering cliff on the north flank of Snowdon in Wales, rock climber Johnny Dawes moved up and on to a ledge just four inches long and two inches wide.

This minute resting place was smaller than a bar of chocolate. But it was the key to Dawes' historic ascent, earlier this month, of a new climb on the cliff's featureless Great Wall. The climb was so difficult and dangerous that it marked a turning point in climbing, as significant for this high-risk sport as the first four-minute mile was for athletics.

Reaching the ledge, Dawes was at the outer limits of his physical and mental capabilities, and was able at last to est the screaming muscles in his arms and legs. Any mistake as he inched his way up the verticality below the ledge would have meant death or serious injury. The rock was virtually bereft of cracks or niches in which he could have slotted metal wedges, attached to his ropes, to limit any fall. Above lay more of the same.

"I stayed on the ledge for half an hour," recalls Dawes, 22, the former public schoolboy who is now indisputably the bravest and most gifted rock climber in Britain. "I was literally too 'gripped' to move. I thought, I don't have to be doing this. Then I saw a friend away over on the left. We looked at each other, but we didn't smile. Any break in my concentrtion would have been too dangerous, and I could have fallen off."

Dawes had been psyching himself up for months, waiting for the fine autumn to dry out the high and sunless crag. But even then, he says: "as I walked up to the cliff, I knew I might not be coming back." Yet he felt it might be his last chance. "By next year I might have been too old. I don't think

HIGH FLYER . . . Dawes at the outer limits on Indian Face in Wales.
Picture by Paul Williams

I'd be prepared to accept that level of risk again."

Even experienced climbers find it difficult to comprehend the technical demands and the risks involved in Dawes' 150ft-high new route, which he has called Indian Face. None of the holds had positive edges on which to pull up. Dawes had to use tiny ripples in the rock to lever and balance his body in a symnastic sequence of moves, using subtle shifts of weight from limb to limb. Tiny flakes on the rock face, on which side pulls could be made, also allowed upward progress.

"it was as if the rock was wired up." says Dawes. "If you touched holds in the wrong sequence, it was like a short-circuit through my body, and I quickly had to think again — otherwise I'd have been electrocuted and fallen."

He gave the climb the ninth grade of Extreme Severity, E9, the first ever of that standard. Dawes was also responsible for the country's first E8, a blank groove he climbed earlier this year on a gritstone outcrop in Derbyshire. Few climbers, even those of the highest skill and ability, can manage E3 or E4. A small elite in British climbing goes on to E5 and E6, and occasionally E7. Only Dawes has gone beyond that.

Dawes is obsessed by climbing, which has dominated his life for the past few years. He is a small, wiry, affable man whose climbing makes up for lack of inches with supreme technique. Supported by wealthy and indulgent parents, since leaving Uppingham school he has led a peripatetic existence, moving from crag to crag.

Of the many new climbs he has established in Britain, the central line up the Great Wall of Clogwyn d'ur Arddu (or Cloggy, as it is known), has haunted him — just as it has every other top climber over the years. For

Cloggy has been, since its first routes in the 1920s, the spiritual heartland and forcing ground for aspiring hard men of the hills. Great climbers of the past such as Jack Longland, Joe Brown and Don Whillans have all made their mark on its awesome, rearing bastions.

But it was not until 1962 that Pete Crew, a college lecturer, made the first impression on the Great Wall. His line — still a magnificent route, but now graded a mere E3, only skirted the edge of the huge triangular buttress that is the focus of the cliff.

In recent years other top climbers, such as Jerry Moffatt and John Redhead, have made attempts on the blank central line, knowing that once climbed it would be the hardest route in Britain. Each had either to retreat or move away at half height. The difficulties were too much.

Only a man with a unique combination of boldness and skill could hope to succeed. Says Steve Haston, a Llanberis climber and himself responsible for several ferocious E7s up the overhanging sea cliffs of Anglesey: "Johnny's like a fighter pilot in the war — it's all or nothing."

How good is Dawes? Where does he stand in the great tradition of British rock climbing? One who is in no doubt is Trevor Jones, author of the definitive history, Welsh Rock (Pic, £16.95), and a leading activist of the Fifties and Sixties. "I rate him the best in the country," he says. "Dawes is a diminutive King Kong; small, powerful and very brave. And, of course, he's a purist. He won't use any artificial aids. With Johnny's ascent, the great challenge of Wales has now been met. A 30-year dream has been realised."

Dawes himself feels that, in spite of the danger, climbing such a route was a creative act. He compares it to music and poetry, and he talks of climbing as a means to achieve a unique and harmonious relationship with Nature.

"When you look at the great climbs of the past, they seem to have the personalities of the men who climbed them," he says. With Indian Face, Dawes has not only pushed British climbing into a new era, he has stamped his name indelibly on the sport.

Above: In common with *Gaia,
Braille Trail, Sad Amongst Friends* &
Salmon, Indian Face has a hands off
rest, the perfect place for your body to
relax and mind unravel. RP2 on shock
tape and a 3mm line sling are the
genuine runners. Laybacking around
the overlap, handhold and foothold
need to get on well. Stumble or doubt
and suddenly you have no holds at all.
Left: 1st ascent. Sean Myles looks down
concerned. Photos: Paul Williams
Right: A late start. No time to drop
the rope on the effort the day before.
Photo: Jon Retty

Above: The unhygienic *Janitor Finish*. See note l. Photo: Craig Smith.
Below: *Taboo Zizi* 8b, 1988. Video grab from 80s Extreme by Alun Hughes.

Above: *Conan The Librarian* E6, 6b, 6b, 5c. See note m. Photo: Heinz Zak.
Below: *Hardback Thesaurus* E8 6b (7c) on dreadful rock. This video grab is of a 50
footer taken before completing my hardest ground up climb. Video by Alun Hughes.

Left: Big G sporting the Moss Cap that lives on a certain rock in Glen Ulladale. Right: Waddy 'long arms' in homage to Joe in The Hard Years. Photos: George Smith

Above left: ★ 2nd pitch, a hand crack appears around the corner. Pritch relaxed on bold ground.
Right: ★ The last hard pitch has slopers, nasty fall potential & massive exposure.
Below: ★ *The Flying Groove* 7b+. Crimps, heelhooks to fingerstack, to hands. Photos: Paul Pritchard.
Opp: On the left of the face is Ben on *Mosskill Grooves* E6 6b, 6a. See note n. Photo: Gordon Stainforth.

Top: The suitcase was an ill-advised last minute decision, and the sweater!? Photo: Paul Pritchard. Below: Pritch, Ben and I wait out Hurricane Hugo in a corrugated hut in Glen Ulladale. The bucket is loaded with salad. Photo: Gordon Stainforth

Strone Ranger

It is September, 1987. It has been a quiet lazy year messing about in familiar haunts. The weather has been poor. Now and again though, a long treasured fantastic quest presents itself. I fish in the Padarn Hotel Bar for a Batman or a Robin. Discussing the adventure with the regulars, though they're keen, they've got a lot of beer to drink. It is the Aardvark who finally bites. Great, he is going to try it with me. Nutter! We are going to try and free *The Scoop* (A4) on Strone Ulladale. *The Scoop* was on a part of the huge, overhanging Hebridean cliff without any free climbs. It would be the first aid route either of us had tried.

pic: See note r.

We had plenty of experience of each other's moods and habits. I knew "slack on brown" could mean either more red or green rope was needed for my colour blind friend. He knew "This will be my last go…" was a barefaced lie. He had a long reach, was sometimes dangerously brave. Take climbs like his Scimitar Ridge E7 *Surgical Lust* if you must. Look up, squint and spot the first gear, a peg sticking way out, 60ft up, archetypal of the scary, foot dangling, cross-roped style of the wild Lancashire black dog Paul Pritchard.

Two agreeable weeks pass umm'ing and ahhing the likely realities of the coming siege. We visit Paul Simkiss – DMM International – to whom we smile a lot…two ice screws, crabs, rollers at cost! From Paul Trower, an old hand on big walls, we receive all manner of weird contraptions including étriers, hexagonals on rope, pegs for rock *and* mud, as well as unusual tobacco with which we hope to out 'Doug Scott', Doug Scott. All there is now is to grovel around in the oily Clog bin for any 'seconds', a task for which Aardvark enthusiastically volunteers. On Monday Paul will cash his giro and we will be off.

A stroke of luck – on our way, we decide to make a quick detour to Gogarth. Paul has a yoghurt bar, a set of Butthole Surfer tapes and three bandit scarves but has neglected to bring his bloody climbing gear! Fortunately we find a spare harness in the van and go down into the base of Wen Zawn.

Opposite our E7's of last year, my *Conan, the Librarian* and Paul's harder, more serious *The Unrideable Donkey*, there is a heinous overhanging wall. Between *Games Climbers Play* and *T-Rex*, it has features that look as if they offer protection so I set off, traditional climbing – ground up.

A jagged ramp rearing progressively to the left of the line meant that, even from quite high up, should you fall, protection would not ensure you would miss smashing into the spikes at its base (where Paul would nearly drown 10 years later…).

The face immediately proves more quixotic than hoped; both powdery and damp to the hand. The sea had got to work on the 600-million-year-old quartzite as soon as it could. Like a mad archivist searching through one folio after another for a missing word, one solid looking plate levers easily off, only for another that looks the same to hold, then ping unexpectedly at the last moment. Both leave pistachio-coloured scars behind, clearly telling me this rotting tramp's Mac is no tableau on which to search for technical 6c.

What holds are left lead me to an overlap at a 100ft. Above, the rock sweating in the sun, though more vertical looks more tender still, impregnable and blank. Possibility above time had eroded down to a coughing, diagonal crimp. Faint. A skyhook perched on forgotten Parmesan would be the best to hope for in need of retreat.

Elbows up and ground to a halt by a rock hard pump in my arms, and with no hooks, I pucker in relief to spy another slot. From below, quite invisible, it is now crucial as the sole alternative to the useless feature I had planned on using. We retreat. Back at sea level, I knew the line would be on my mind during the quieter moments driving up to the Hebrides.

Llanberis again, for a brew – and Paul's rack – and, as fortune would have it, it is the end of summer party. In blustery weather the hosts used to tie two ropes to the telephone mast and, with a blanket, fly out from it one on each end.

Today all manner of electrical devices are on, music blaring, drills drilling thin air, strobe and bubble machine on, electric heaters. The Lecky man was coming to read the meter!

Morning...I find Paul snoring, crashed out zig-zagged on the stairs. It's easy to leave as the kitchen door is off its hinges. A great party.

Finally we are off. We stop at Nobby's for further pegs and a brew, then go on past the turn off to Malham... Kendal.........Carlisle. For a long while the squeal of tyres seems to play a knowing duet with the music on the radio, and so to sleep, 50 miles shy of Glasgow. Down a side road, trucks' rumbles traverse the ridge half a mile to the west. I can vividly recall the hoots of Scottish owls, flashes of torchlight outside obscuring a clear moon, merging into the sleep we had been waiting for since Leeds.

Morning, Glasgow, we breakfast in a weird Italian café for a full English. Next door, we buy red and green cabbage, grapefruit...on past the Rannoch Oak, the Buachaille, finally to Nevisport to test the water. To blend in with the other shoppers Paul toys with some red socks while I purchase more midge juice. It was quiet, too quiet. When, from behind the cashiers' desk the man, deadpan, says: "That will be two pounds and thirty seven pence please", there was no way of knowing, for sure, if the grapevine had twitched this far north.

Past Fort William things really start to get fun. Paul poised on the dashboard, foaming at the mouth, crams his fingers into an "evil" jam on a "mental" runout. We have no idea what is going to happen but know for sure it's going to be exciting. We do not know how big hitchhikers can be either! Let me tell you, they can be very generously built indeed. We pick one up, well I don't. The thumb we first caught sight of is no clue to the prodigious bottom beneath. I watch, biting my lip, as Paul attempts to push her physically up into the van, then hands her her double bass. On lefthanders our new cargo is a boon, while rights become a death or glory mission. As often when faced with the ludicrous or embarrassing, the Aardvark starts to judder visibly and looks as if he is about to let himself down.

We arrive at the coast just in time to miss the ferry to Skye. We settle down to sort out the gear in a lay-by. We had just started the task when this moaning Scotsman arrives; all bagpipes and 2nd World War.

"Wharrrr dya thaynk yooore doin laddee? Woodie yaa do this on a road in England?"

"Of course", I say, when Paul unhelpfully hurls something clattering down on to the man's driveway, then whirls around like a dervish, screaming. When he starts to splash water from a dirty puddle on his face, the Scotsman turns and strides back to his house in disgust. Whatever Paul dropped on the drive flashes a warning as it rolls by: "DO NOT PUT ON METAL OR VINYL SURFACES". Paul has got 'Jungle Juice' in his eyes.

We half expect the highlander to return with his regimental sword and cut us down but instead he brings back a camera and shoots a couple of cheeky portraits of Paul. They would have been quite blurred, but he seemed pleased and told us:

"I've got evidence now, I'll be taking it off to Angus"??

Paul having recovered somewhat, we dine at the pub on fresh local salmon, salad and beer.

We wake to a fine day, in time to see our intended ferry cruise out of the harbour. It gives us time to finally sort our gear. Here is what we considered necessary for ten days' vacation for two on the Isle of Harris:

Gear	Food
20 pegs	Two cabbages, one red, one green
4 bong	Onions and garlic
2 ice screws	Raisins
2 mud screws	Three grapefruits
8 Friends	Carrots
4 Sliders	Two cheeses
12 Rocks	Olive oil
10 RPs	Vinegar
6 Hexes	Six eggs
2 skyhooks	Three loaves
90 crabs	Three cans of beans
1 nut key	Two cans of corn
4 jumars	Two cans of tomatoes
2 hammers and 1 bolt	Muscavado sugar
kit (censored)	Coffee (Nescafé), very mellow taste
5 ropes	Marvel
2 harnesses	White Horse whisky
3 pairs of boots	Tea bags
2 chalk bags	Muesli
Box of chalk	Two blocks of chocolate
2 sleeping bags and 1 pillow	Peanuts
2 karrimats	Cigarettes
1 TENT?	

4 books – White Hotel, Wilt,
The 4th Dimension (And How To Get There) and one other Clothes
Stoves, pans and cutlery
The midge armoury: Moskil, Jungle Juice, (spray and liquid) and Combat.

220lbs in all.

Out on the water, looking back, our blue Rascal van looks lonely. We'll arrive too late to get to The Strone tonight, but it's always wonderful to get to somewhere unusual and new. On arrival at Tairbeart, South Harris, our first sight is Abdul's mobile shop parked outside Abdul's grocery store. The store, half boarded up, had recently suffered a broken window and had Gaelic graffiti daubed all over it.

We take a taxi as far as the castle at Amhuinnsuidhe (pronounced A-vin-suey). Mr MacKinnon is not a ball of fire behind the wheel.

The big march begins. Without the keys to the gate to the road that leads up to the dam, we have a longer than necessary four mile walk ahead of us.

Each of us carries a 110lb load. Paul has an Alpinist rucksack, me a red Petzl caving sack Ben Lyon had given me without a waist belt – and a small suitcase for the rest. It is good to be in the purple green hills, but difficult to enjoy the beauty when you are so miserable. Why are my rambler's sized thighs failing me so cruelly? The rucksack on my back is *a complete bastard*.

We make the dam – over a mile down – by dark and immediately fall asleep from exhaustion.

"…YEEEE…YEEEEEE…YEE…"

The midges, invigorated by dawn rain, are especially chirpy. Paul is already on his feet but does not talk to me. Teeth gas or melting legs, walk too slow the midges feast freely, too fast the hill gets us.

Tears indistinguishable from the rain and sweat, unaware of progress for a while, I look up hopeful to see the distance covered but it is a sour disappointment. A midge bites me on the scalp, another on my eye, cheers for that. A cabbage leaf makes a fine improvised skullcap. Paul is way ahead but unable to move. He has fallen over backwards, and with shoulder straps tight and with his waist belt buckle inaccessible, he's kicking around unable to right himself. Carapace down, he resembles a beetle, one with kicking skinny yellow Lycra legs. Bloody funny.

Sack off, suitcase down, I roll him over. We have actually done the first lake and cheer a little. The sun even makes an appearance for a moment. In any case the rain slows, eased by a lovely little breeze. The m–i–d–g–e–s are gone for now so we can safely stop and tuck into my Brassica hat.

We can almost smell the 'big stone' over the hill. I've never seen rock so warped and rough as in this Glen. Orchids, giant moss, the rumble tinkle of the stream make this valley a great reward. Ulladale, open floored, steep sided, holds a loch at its foot with an islet home to two lonesome pines, and rearing above all of it, The Strone.

At last we come below the cliff. It is not as impressive as you'd expect, weaned on crags brute as Burbage South, and of course Pritchard had toyed with Wilton's Main Wall.

We set up camp, put up tent, stock our bijou open plan cave (with combined kitchen/living space) and unpack the rack.

Paul is really keen, but also anxious. After all this is to be his first try at a route from *Hard Rock – The Scoop* A4, 400ft, continuously overhanging at 30° and the sole aid route featured to ensure no-one could tick all the climbs in the book.

Personally, I was more concerned about our provisions than the climb. A ravenous Aardvark was beginning to graze freely on our supplies. Unrestrained he would've happily stuffed himself silly, prepared to eat nothing for the rest of the trip. Perhaps my sustenance might have been safer carried on my waist 'à la Whillans'.

We had a brew (more of those later), then set off to take a look. It would be nice if we could make some headway to chew on over supper.

We uncoil our ropes, tie in – an excellent moment.

The initial rock is dubious and frighteningly unpredictable. Hoping it was not to be the norm, I move up on to a jug on the lip of a slanting roof feeling a bit jet-lagged. Above there is a small niche. Tentative, like an elderly woman easing herself into a chilly pool, I find I can swing into it to face out and place a pin. Above there is a bit of old tat. Knot that and clip it and it might protect a traverse left on the lip of the roof.

After a long, strenuous struggle I commit to a move up, hoping a clearly sloping shelf isn't too sloping. The old tat reveals itself to be tethered to nothing more than a rusting Rurp. Appalled, a mantel on to an outward slanting ramp reveals itself as the meeting place for many rolling stones. How many years debris clatters away? Four RPs go in good rock. I start to relax and contemplate a vicious looking compact rib above.

Slightly tilted, leaning, flaring pinches and twisty footwork set up for a dyno to a sloping edge. It puts a rusted blade peg in reach for a longer, easier dyno to a loose looking jug and Rock 5 in a flare. A traverse right looks on, but it is a tottering bulge. Lower off, happy to see Paul have a bash. He succeeds on extending a further steep pitch into the base of a schist groove.

We trot down, happy at our first day's progress and prepare a slap up meal.

I finish washing the pasta pans in the loch, quartz gravel at the water's edge a handy scrubber and return to the cave. Arriving back, without saying a word, Paul squeezes my shoulders and turns me around.

Each footprint left on my return from the loch has lit up, as if my feet had been painted in light. Snaking up from trees silhouetted against the glistening water is a trail of successively brighter lights, the activity of glow worms whose light shines upward to meet the giant luminosity coming in from the universe. The crystal night sky frames the silent clatter of the aurora borealis.

We wake to a cloudless day – finally our things would have a chance to dry from the walk in. Yet for climbing the weather hardly matters. What Pritchard calls "…the Big Umbrella" of *The Scoop* will shelter us from any rain.

A later trip freeing *Knucklehead* A5, at E7 6b, 6b, 6c, 5b illustrates this well…

Paul was recovering a cam that had fallen behind the belay ledge on *The Nose* A4, also a Doug Scott climb. The contortion required to reach it necessitates me guiding the unsighted Paul in, like on the '70s game show 'Bernie the Bolt', "left a bit, right a bit". Beyond the cam I spy a white object, balanced precariously diagonally across the crack. Paul's swollen knuckles snag something slim and conical already poised between index and middle fingers. It can only be the long lost property of hippy Doug Scott, as dry as the day it was rolled. We spark it up, in delayed camaraderie.

Back on *The Scoop,* we jug up swinging ropes to the ledge. Paul sets off in a state of amber alert in big country. The cliff has gifts waiting for him, big jugs, where they are needed. It looks so intimidating but conceals a handjam crack. He follows it easily around a jagged bulge up into a small eyrie-like cavelet, 6a. The crack leads out again then fades, turning thin into the back of a *Venom*-ous groove, 6b. A determined effort thin laybacking, slick open book pasted bridging succeeds. At its top I lie down comfortable and content. Each time we arrive at a different stance, it is intriguing to come across an old peg or jammed cog, like sharing curios at a stall on *Antiques Roadshow.*

Back on the deck we get stuck into our brews. They taste really good – peaty water (full of minerals and protein), Nescafé, Muscavado, Marvel and a wee dram of whisky prove an awesome combination when you're really shattered. A roll up, a good book and sleep.

We never knew what time it was when we went to bed or rose in the morning. We didn't have a watch or a radio. It was good not to live by time but simply by how tired or keen we felt, which inevitably meant late starts.

The next day, getting up there seems much more exhausting. Our deliberations on which pitches would suit us meant Paul got the pitch *Hard Rock* had gripped us up about. A ghostly echo, "Our blades only bit for quarter of an inch for twenty feet", float into mind. Paul flashes past this section.

He finds good nuts and an in situ peg, taking the piss out of us hauling mud screws and ice screws to overcome the mica schist. He continues to a peg-hungry hanging belay in the base of the large central corner, where the pendulum was made on the first aid ascent.

The big corner was a soaking wet drainage line and pretty blank. There is only one feasible, if ludicrous looking alternative – a super steep flying groove to its left. I aid out and inspect the first part of the pitch. It is a shallow right-angled cut into a square arête formed from a vertical and 45° overhanging wall. It has a saggy crack in the back and a thin heel hook on the lip. It will be hard and scary. We didn't have what it would take just then.

Down on the loch some fishermen are at work. As we touch down at the base of the big cliff, they shout up their encouragement so we go down to meet them. Moved by Paul's skinny frame, they offer us fresh sea trout. Paul shows me how to gut them, his dad a poacher. I sauté them in some garlic (Paul would have fried them of course), serving them on a bed of rice with a side salad.

In the morning we wake to horrendous rain. It has been raining all night. My 'Asda high altitude' sleeping bag, as Paul puts it, is completely soaked. There is a puddle at the end of the tent, which flows towards me if I try to move. I eventually mop it up with my pillow. Damp Moskil won't light. Holes in the canvas had let the night shift in. Paul also stank. So did I, I guess, but Paul hadn't washed for a week before he came to Scotland!

We settle down and read; Paul *Wilt* and I *The Fourth Dimension (And How To Get There)*, and I was going to need to know how if I was going to pull off that next pitch. We could see all the way up to the crest of the scooped face through the tent door. Off the lip, torrential plumes snake down to the valley floor – a dreadful Medusa, frustrated, writhing towards us, defending the scoop's secret.

The next day at our high point, 250ft up, we are tired. Re-climbing the ropes with jumar clamps is taking its toll. After an effort, I drum up a tenuous sequence of jams that actually fit the features well. From sharing on a little finger edge a 'bosting' hand jam allows a heel onto the edge and a swap from jam to pumpy underclings. It's *Bananas*, but crackers and nuts too. A paddle around blind for a hold uncovers a crisp sidepull. It allows a splayed out semi-rest where you can look down through your legs at the lake.

At E6 6b (7b+) the pitch beaches on a perfect flat piece of real estate, the most premium of deckchairs. We are now only one rope length from vertical ground but the aid route we want to follow is steep as …. flushing with lichen and moss. Eventually, after dodgy forays direct, we opt for a long detour out left to the very edge of the scoop face.

Paul's traverse into virgin territory is a particularly gripping lead. The rope snakes around sharp fins, the gear appalling – a fall would leave him 40ft out in space unable to extricate himself unless he could catch a thrown rope.

Paul faces a quandary. To get in any gear at all, he has to hammer a peg under an American refrigerator-sized block, off which he is already hanging (!) – seemingly glued on by barely a tenth of its base. The only spot where the peg can go is the juncture of block and cliff so each tap runs the risk of catapulting Paul and block into space. (I remember grins, but no hesitation).

The peg holds of course, Aardvark's judgement of scounson[42] sound. The hard won peg protects a technical traverse on slopers to a thin blade belay right out on the edge of the whole valley. We swing leads. From here, a classic exposed pitch follows a teetery arête, up and over a roof, on up a slabby groove system, finishing back right on a sofa-sized ledge beneath the capping ceiling at the Strone's centre.

For a moment just sat there in shirt and corduroys, blade, RP, there's a sense of satisfaction, for below on the edge of the air, pegs on metal loop, hammer swinging free, it'd felt how I imagined '50s climbers must've enjoyed their pioneering. Something had come right down there. Paul comes on up. I'd have liked to have shared my reverie but sometimes talking can trample experience. In any case, we have the challenge of where to go next to share. Ahead looks horrendous.

A circling golden eagle passes by. It looks straight at us. Perhaps it thinks we are stranded sheep; some sheep. It catches an updraught and wheels round the buttress out of sight.

We decide to rest a day before the final roof so abseil to the ground. Above the roof it looks to ease considerably, but the roof itself looks hard and bold. We go down to the Post Office at Amhuinsuidhe to get provisions and to ring our next of kin.

---

[42] The ability of a sculptor to know how the rock will cleave.

It is raining again, but that doesn't stop the Postmaster, who clearly enjoys a drop, saying, "It's clearing up boys… it's clearing up". When we visited The Strone the following year, it was reassuring to discover again that according to him the weather was still clearing up.

Some Cadbury's chocolate éclairs we bought tasted strange. The packet reads "Best before Dec 1982". There was no bread but the Postmaster insists, "Hamish will be along presently." Over an hour passes without the present coming, so we decide to make a visit to the castle's kitchens. The cook lets us in, says we can help ourselves. The place is deserted, no hunting stags or salmon fishing this time of year. Suddenly Paul is nowhere to be seen. I spend a perplexing couple of minutes looking for him, encountering stuffed animals, suits of armour and freshly laid grates. Giving up I decide I'll get the bread myself.

The kitchen smells as you would imagine, evocative of cold hills and the sea battered exterior. Huge steel tabletops, a vast walk-in fridge, and racks of knives make one imagine the castle cooks in full spate. The heavy fridge door swings open easily, there's the bread, oh… and there's Paul, his hood done up tight, hands in pockets, looking at his Converse grinning. He'd locked himself in.

Dusk, back at the cave making supper, we see dark shapes moving far off in the heather. Are they Scottish climbers? At first it's difficult to even pick them out. Later on we see them close up. On top of an outlying hummock they prove not so sinister and they even stop to look at us. Meeting wild animals is always special. Transfixed, I can't say how long we stare at the stag and it stares back. The meeting swept my heart clear, made the valley grand.

Back on the wall, it now took a full hour to reach the top belay. Tumbling around in a swinging sky you might think we would be above the midge line. The golden eagle had fixed us with a glare, but had not made me taste my mortality. Now ravens circling and bobbing in the wind make me shrink. The exposure is unrelenting. Five hundred feet of overhanging rock sucked in beneath us, a thousand more of space to the boulder field.

We try to break through the ceiling by following a diagonal overhanging ramp. However it is filthy with slimy lichen, hidden holds prove disappointing and yields little gear. There are some nuts away to the left in a big flake.

They aren't brilliant. Above me and to the right where I want to go, there seems only dampness and sloping nothings. The only option visible is to try and place a no.1 Roller[43] in a flare. It might take enough weight to place a peg up and left of it in a hairline crack.

It was bloody dangerous. Any fall would be diagonal, unavoidably swinging loaded rope along the razor lip. Pumping out on a pinch trying to place the Roller, facing a 30 footer or more, I am really scared. Roller finally seats itself, the tiny wheels of the device slightly out of line with the slim wedge designed to work up against it. It holds my weight. The physical relief is immediate, the mental relief monumental. But while looking for a spot for a peg, I can't help but notice the outer wheel skating slowly but definitely outward. Settled down on the runner, out of reach of any holds with which to try and climb down, I'm locked into a subtle duel with the schist.

You can think of the schist of Strone as granite if you want, but I wouldn't advise it. Heat, pressure, and mineral altering chemistry have been at work on this clanky giant. Just because it has not fallen down does not mean it is solid.

Desperately tapping blade into seam off to the side, it sounds all dull wrong; rising and falling in pitch. Somehow, whatever is done to brace my body, each extra blow seems to unseat the Roller further, "Oh ..no........"

Horrororrorroorrorrooooor… the fall spools out, a smell of burnt nylon, my body yanks about chaotically in the air like a whacked conker, drawing the ropes again across the sharp edge. Paul struggles to ram his foot between edge and rope. I cringe as I swing to a momentary halt one way, aware of gravity's insistence to throw me into the valley. A chopped rainbow of coloured threads dart wildly in the air. Paul lowers me a loop. I immediately wrap it around my arm. One rope is almost severed, the other's sheath is badly torn.

Ravens circle.

Safe for the moment back on the belay, we share a tab. Paul is spooked, shaken up. Haven't seen him like this. I hardly experienced it, so quick had it happened, but Paul saw it all unravel, full screen 3D.

Rewind, in slow motion – What had happened?

---

[43] A metal nut with a wheel device next to it which sometimes works in shallow flares.

…hammering…a rising scale of tones. Peg steadily enters the rock. A slight jolt at my waist had come into my mind without me thinking anything of it, so subtle had it been. Mid-swing the same feeling rings through me again; a silenced hunch realises something *is* amiss. The last blow *had* sounded hollow. So what, it's not too bad a peg; but then late, mid-swing I see it; the crack the peg is going in snakes down off to the right, around a dome in the rock back to my waist. Too late to stop the blow – the driven peg splays the same crack as the roller is in – I hammer myself free of the cliff.

Paul is not keen to try the pitch. In any case I know better what is up there. There is a hold up and right. If I can get the peg in off that, it may protect me to a prominent jug spotted further up. Frayed ends chopped off, I tie in again for another look.

(*It would be good to say we did the rest of the climb without inspection, but having to catch the ferry back, we opted to inspect the pitch from above. Just iron that out of your mind. Don't let the truth get in the way of a good story is what Al Rouse used to say.*)

Now the make or break moves of the route. A fall from here will launch a 60 footer. A fall had already cut my ropes to the core from half that distance. Retreat was now unthinkable. The top was so near. We had released the fixed lines. With 1,500ft of exposure, terrifying gear and uncleaned terrain above, I had to be determined.

Moves flow together well and before knowing it a final rub of the rock with my frayed 'Wendy Lawrence' jumper reveals the last smears for my feet. I contort in a crouch to rest and compose myself for the final hand traverse. The end of difficulties is a class act; a jug positioned right on the very rim of the scooped face of Strone Ulladale. It seems almost a shame to take it and there it is. Slow, careful…fingers curl around the trophy jug. "We got it Paul".

"Nice one" in Lancashire floats up.

We cruise a long delightful pitch on perfect black rock to the summit tufts and unimpressed sheep. We have a team photo and celebrate with a sesame snack Pritch has squirrelled away in his jacket.

Next morning it is overcast. In a cloak of mist the Sron regains its aura of impregnability. Thoughts swing to *Knucklehead* (A5), *The Nose* (A4) and

Sidewinder (A4). If *The Scoop* goes, maybe they will. This was to become a long obsession, this big cliff with its stupendous unclimbed lines and aid routes waiting to be freed. We'd be back one day to rob more Hebridean treasure from the ravens.

A Swiss banker called Gerald Panchaud owned Glen Ulladale and Amhuinnsuidhe Castle. Thanks for letting us on the big stone. Walking out, salmon in the burn are dying from the effluent from the fish farm, the deer we met are to be stalked at £400/bullet, on some highland estates eagles are killed by leaving poisoned carrion for them to eat. Perhaps that's reasonable to save the wee sheep, but sheep, intruders in their present numbers, stop trees and a whole host of compromised species growing in Snowdonia and the Lake District.

Waiting for Mr MacKinnon's beige Sierra 1.6L at the castle we watch the fish leap out of the sea. A mother and her kids watch too. Helpfully pointing out to an ungrateful mum that her daughter's fly was undone was when I knew we should be on our way home and that our solitude was over.

We dossed in a woodshed that evening, like 'up t' dale' in Stoney, while outside it poured down yet again. In the morning at a café in Tiree, we're served Earl Grey tea from fine porcelain by a woman with appley breasts the same circumference as her spectacles. It is with our little fingers nicely stretched I can still picture Paul and I heave our hideous loads on to the boat.

Buoux

Ben Moon and I follow a Formula Three single-seater close. Even show our nose in front at the hairpin. The car is hot, the brakes are starting to smell, so we come in. The pit lane at Paul Ricard is quite long. This time it's Jerry's turn to hide down in the footwell, away from the marshal's eyes, till we are out on track.

I had already completed three laps and was familiar with the circuit from TV. The trouser filler is a 60° kink right, at the end of a long straight at the back of the circuit. In my Peugeot 1.9 205 GTI, it is possible flat out at 120mph. However, immediately after comes a short straight where you must shed 50mph before a tightening right that banks towards its end.

When I was on my own, the teeniest of lifts would dip the car's weight enough to guide it through but now I have human ballast.

Belt only just clipped in, Jerry visibly squirms in his seat as he sees the kink approaching – unsettling the car – and lets out a girly squeal as we enter at over 120mph. The instant we enter the car is unstable. To make the corner at all, I leave the steering on till after the kink, well into the braking zone of the tightening right that follows. Slightly askew, 5mph too fast and 10 stone of extra legend on board, the Pug slides violently at the rear, throttle buried to brake the car, broadside on.

Slowed to 70mph, over the curb, it hops, twirling on to the dust and old Renault F1 rubber at the edge of the track. In just eight laps, with the coarse surface and hot ambient temperature the 1.9 already needs new tyres.

It is a rest day. Usually we all spend it in the caravan, but this once we find ourselves overtaking 2CVs and being overtaken by sports prototypes.

My experience of racing up till now was a day's karting in Senior Britain. Numpty, I'd bought a wet weather chassis. Too soft in the dry, the kart would break into lurid slides, just when they were least expected. Each lap as I came round, the crowd, seeing this possibility, retreated from the retaining tyre wall and my kart having passed, the crowd, relieved, moved back in again. They gave me 'Driver of the Day'.

Hanging out with Ben and Jerry and old friend Sean Myles was enjoyable. I knew Sean from Oxford where Mike was the president of the University

Mountaineering Club. Mike out-climbed Sean and I with a sustained footless traverse on the university's cobble dotted climbing wall. Though Ben and Jerry were world class, they would likely have struggled on those greasy, big butch moves.

Mike had taken me on my first trip away to France, to the Gorges du Verdon in 1981. I'd had a go on *Papi On Sight* 7c+, by the star of the time Jerry Moffatt and managed to do most of the moves though I was little more than a slender armed, rock-over machine then, while staminoid Moffatt would soon flash *Phoenix* 5.13a in Yosemite.

Now, 1988, Jerry, Ben and I are on our hols. Jezza was recovering from tendon surgery, training again and on the rampage. Ben Moon with his deep elbow insertions and dread lock off, and me, green on bolts, as big as a house.

Their fresh approach then was to alternate between the power and precision of Fontainebleau and the long steep cliffs of southern France – the philosophy: power made you quick, able to do moves easily, so stamina was less important. Over the following months, each of them aimed to reassert their grip on world sport climbing – England v The World but also Jerry v Ben.

Provence was fashionable, Swedes, Italians, Japanese and us Brits, the unfortunates, all gravitated to the squalor of Estelle's campsite in Apt, while the French elite waited for good weather to leave gay Paris for Buoux. (They knew places to slip off the auto-route and avoid the péage.) Always immaculate, the 'toe pointers' disappeared to a swish gîte after climbing, to fine wines and fresh outfits.

Sean and I start off the trip in a dodgy tent but one long night rain ambushes us. By morning Sean, bless him, bone dry, finally asleep, is floating oblivi-

Apt campsite.
Photo: Mark Pretty

ous on his lilo. Soon after we are four up in the caravan – the *Monte Carlo Deluxe*: sandpaper grinds away splits in skin, topos, half-used oval vitamin E pills perch on the aluminium rim of double-glazing cloaked in condensation. Crappy French papers necessitate yet another go.

Lager research had swelled me to a portly 11 stone. At five foot five inches, white all over, I made quite a sight for the locals when Sean and Jerry hid my clothes somewhere at the *TCF* warm up area – cherub in the sun! At first my lock was non existent. Tendons weak, skin too thin for the angle of the dangle and rough pockets, French 7a was hard. I found it difficult to relax – it was boring waiting for muscles to grow and stomach line to shrink. *Les grandes bierres formidable, chocolat et frites* put aside, Zipster's gam à l'oregane would have to do.

Meanwhile across the field the Austrians of 'Team No Motivation', complete with deadhang board on their bestickered Toyota Hiace, weighed out their 'power muesli' on electronic scales. They could all do pull-ups with just one arm, yet each evening had tales of where they had fallen off routes that I, by that time, could do OK.

The euros were an amusing bunch. I remember Didier 'Rambo' Raboutou, Jerry's diminutive nemesis on the competition circuit, would warm up in white gloves. When he had done enough he would do a final stretch of his hands and announce "Didier is ready!" and have his sexy girlfriend peel them off. But the King Ego must have been Mr Ed – Patrick Edlinger. From the south, he was the thorn in the side of the poshies from Paris. His style was bendier and trickier.

One day below Cimai, eight climbers are attempting to recover their tent which is underneath a boulder a freak storm has loosened from a slope above. The storm was so fierce, that fortunately, the owners of the tent had slept in the car. Mr Ed arrives with his entourage of lady friends. He sees the tent under the boulder and gestures for the group to stand back, taking up position single-handedly.

Jerry knew them all and had their respect. Recovering from injury, it would be two months before he would repeat Jibé's *Spectre*… 8b+. Ben had his eye on a steeper project to the left – perhaps the English reply to Antoine Le Menestrel's solo of *Revelation* 8a (the first E9?). Moon's *Agincourt* would become the world's first 8c. While they did laps on the *La Rose et le Vampire* 8b, I quietly improved. Or not that quietly!

One freezing night, Sean, also a legless wonder, Ben and Jerry were talking about routes I could not do, wittering on about power and this and that 8b. Bloody boring! I attack, they try to restrain me but because they hardly weigh anything I spin the three of them around on my back roaring "That's power you b…..ds!"

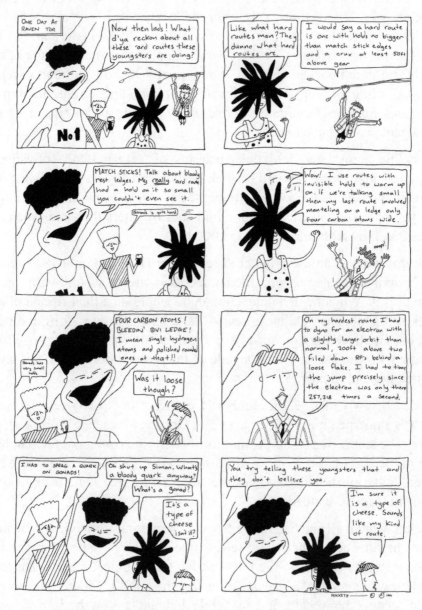

Check out **rockfax.com** for the other episodes of Pokketz.

My goal was 8a by the end of the two month trip. I worked five 8as and an 8a+, but I was still frustrated. A few weeks later I had done two 7b+s and lost four pounds or so, but the moves I thought basic and in essence the sport to be largely about power to weight ratio. With persistence and planning, of course you would improve. Zippy taught me a lot about how to work routes move by move and shared his short man sequences. Ben was an inspiration, pushing the envelope, Jerry too, with his clear distinction between working and doing. *Not* doing was important; *not* climbing to recover, *not* trying moves other than those necessary to unlock the sequence. But where was the drama?

The main adventure was at night. One evening a 2CV parked next to us with two attractive German sisters aboard. I helped them pitch their tent but in the end it proved *impossible*. The three of us bedded down in the 2CV! Ben and Jerry were shy then and pathetically single. A small victory; I awoke warm, smug, refreshed for another day of cranking, while Ben and Jerry looked really grumpy emerging from a freezing caravan.

Oil free salads and runs along the train track eventually leached off the lard. Eking out effort on the steepness became enjoyable. We also went to Volx, France's answer to Stoney Middleton, polished and grotty, but great roof climbing. It stayed dry and offered a different challenge, as well as a project across a huge roof. In any case it was worth making the trip there, if only for the road.

In the UK, in shorts, I'd once 'borrowed' Jerry's GSXR 1100 to learn on. It was an unmanageable lump. Coming to the first corner steering in and realising the bike was going off the road I eventually cottoned on – to steer the wrong way. On a rest day in France, I see another motorbike on its side stand ticking over… its rider is talking on the phone about 100 metres away. The others are at Volx and I could do with some transport. I stare at the bike, estimating his running pace from his physique and try to gauge how the bike works. But when he turns his back, bold white letters on his leather jacket spell "Gendarme". Best keep to four wheels.

On the way back from Volx in the 205, celebrating after Ben sent *Maginot Line* 8c, with the cream of British climbing Chris 'Plant Pot' and Jerry on board, Sean and Zippy in the Escort behind get to watch the action.

…entering a corner fast but fine I get back on the power early…but instead of the corner opening like it *should*, it treacherously starts to close up.

Realising immediately and lifting off the gas puts the car on a teetering knife edge – hands all crossed up, back end swung around, rear tyres bite…tall, a slow truck is rolling up the incline, Film Noire, we're hurtling sideways down the gravel, the verge's edge lined by square stone bollards that feel sickly close to the back bumper. Breath held waiting for car either to clip them or grip to return so the car can straighten. Thank heavens, grip comes back. Paying off the steering at the right moment to catch the slide, without flip-flopping back at the truck, catastrophe is averted.

Two corners later my mistake becomes obvious. Rolling gently through a corner that opens rather than closes up, the corner's look-alike, shows it had been a case of mistaken identity.

The clinical style of climbing was getting to me. It was the last day of the trip. I'm attempting to do *Fissure Serge* 7c+/8a, *Bout du Monde's* entrance exam – a wall climb below a long sluice crack. Painstakingly acquired technical adjustments logged, with just enough 'resistance' harvested into my arms, just as I enter the crux it becomes a race – the sudden shower gradually wetting the fissure, rivulets gathering together above me are running as one towards the crux's finishing crimp. All my redpoint eggs are in one basket. The route overhangs so I remain out of reach of the deluge…for now.

 "Allez…Allez…"

Water already drips on to my hair and the back of my shirt. Chalk is wet, yet the holds are still dry. I rattle through the seven move short man's sequence quicker than ever. Slapping the last hold the first drop of rain falls on the back of my hand. It's in the bag.

Two weeks later, clag and crag have drawn me back from England. Within a week or two, six days on, I do *Rêve d'un Papillon* 8a. In the next two weeks I do four more 8as; *Diagonal de Fou, Elixir de Violence, Les Mains Sales* and *La Nuit des Lizards*, 8a+ in fact.   All that had changed was my fitness.

The big goal was *Chouca,* soft 8b. At the time, 1988, it was the entrance exam to hard sport climbing. It involved a footless start, a huge dyno and a thin crux on to a teetery slab. Marc Le Menestrel would fiercely chuck away the boulder cairn that would develop at the base, ensuring the first three hard pulls were done.

There was a lot of banter and camaraderie. Gaelic wit 'Spider' quipped

"There's a nip in the air!" as a Japanese climber tumbled off *Chouca*'s dyno. Darius Ozin, an American, commentated on efforts, shouting "Allez allez" before the dyno – and if the climber succeeded: "It's in the hole…it's in the hole!" But Darius, the self-confessed 'king of the dyno' could not do it. He came up with the famous 'figure of four' move instead, where you put your leg right over your arm until sat on it, you can reach the pocket, *Chouca* dyno static – "Sacre bleu!"

La Falaise Au Boute De Monde – the cliff at the end of the world – is a shock to see for the first time. The raw effort needed to climb up there, that was new to me, and by dispatching *Chouca* I proved to myself what I could do playing away and it is a brilliant climb. The technique was different, tolerating methodically a blend of pain and concentration but steep rock was ok. Another 8b to the left, *Taboo Zizi* falls next. In essence though there seems little difference between them all. Work more than play; even the names of the training arenas of the time let the cat out of the bag; The School, The Foundry, The Office. It all seemed a trifle conservative.

A week later, belaying the talented Baron Arnould t'Kint on *La Mission* 8b, the will to succeed is proving too much for the lovable but mentally fragile Belgian. He is able to read a book while balanced on the back two legs of a chair for God's sake, what does he care about this long, steep sheet of weight training? Yet Arnould had a hefty bag of pills and would ring his sports psychologist in the evening if he failed on a redpoint.

This day he had just fallen on lead yet again. I eat a pear, not a particularly loud one, but it sends him over the edge. He holds his head in his hands yelling: "I hate the sound of that fruit!" Swinging feet free, placing and locking as logged from Arnould's goes, I tickle the top hold first go on lead, having only made a slight mistake choosing a too low foothold.

For a little while I was even at the blunt end of sport climbing's cutting edge. Marc Le Menestrel's *Mauvais Sang* was a bouldery 8b. Unrepeated, Ben and Jerry had had a look at it. Its thin deadpoint move suited me. Five days later I'd done it, could even reverse the crux.

It was interesting, improved fitness didn't have an entirely beneficial effect. For some reason I was unable to repeat familiar stock in trade dynos back at PYB wall. It *really* was a case of chalk and cheese. For me, the most compelling climb on the whole Buoux trip had been at the campsite playground – a standing jump onto a revolving roundabout. But I had found this sport climber's body in France. It was ready to try lines waiting in the UK.

The bold headwall left of *Strawberries* fell first, *Llanberries* E7 6c – unrepeated – then a steep line in Wen Zawn came to mind. I'd tried it ground up before. Crispin and I were engaged in trying a still unclimbed line under Wen Zawn arch we referred to as *The Tesseract,* because of its 4d tortuous geometry. Across the Zawn from the abseil point was a scary unclimbed wall. You could see it had some gear at half height, but would involve a weaving rope length up overhanging Parmesan cheese-rated rock, and looked to meat out a possible ground fall when you'd be finishing pumped.

Crispin Waddy and later Bob Drury in tow, it took six visits to solve it climbing ground up, taking a 60 footer on to a duff salad of shoddy pro. No 'jiggery-pokery', no rumours of three ropes, no local youths messing about, no doubters, bolts or pegs. *Hardback Thesaurus* felt every bit E8 (7c French). I think it was a new level for truly traditional climbing but I gave it E7.

Around then I did an E7 direct finish to Noel Craine's *Kaya* and repeated his *It's a Broad Church* E7, both on sight.

On sight was what Jerry was known for too. He'd soloed gnarly trad but it was for 'on sight' sport he was best known. Remember the fierce excitement when Jerry did the final route at the world championships at Leeds in 1988? Dixon and I, unusually fit for us, dipped our toe briefly in the water. I'm not sure if I found it too hot or lukewarm. My folks came to watch me compete. When I came out from 'isolation' the compère gushed: "Johnny Dawes…first ascent of *Gaia*, the unrepeated *Quarryman* and *Indian Face*, the world's first E9…Johnny Dawes…"

An expectant hush.

…without effort to the second bolt, I settle into a relaxed hang on an edge to ponder a bulge, resting, feet smeared like on grit. The resin was unforgiving of that schoolboy error. Left boot scuds off, my body rotates, until humiliatingly I hang facing the crowd, unable to turn back around, and fall.

"…Johnny Dawes…"

"I thought you were supposed to be good…?!" my father soothes me, in that classic manner only the well-to-do can truly nail.

III

22

Sleep-overs are fun. They can last for over a year! Zoë Brown's house, 13 Snowdon St in Llanberis, was one of my favourites. There was the odd object to suggest she was Joe Brown's daughter. A tarantula, a wooden box he'd made with an intricate lock made of slats to be slid about in a definite sequence. It was a hub for visitors: debating hall, gym, with a couch to kneed on or receive analysis. Sometimes she got heartily bored of my histrionics and irresponsibility. Ben Pritchard and her even made up a song about me to the tune of Robin Hood. I recall the last verse as:

Johnny Dawes, Johnny Dawes, going round the bend,
Johnny Dawes, Johnny Dawes, but he is our friend,
Takes from the poor, gives to the rich,
Johnny Dawes he's in our fridge…!
Yes he is…!

The silver spoon was well and truly tarnished by now. Along with the occasional TV job, lecture and sponsorship from HB, Lyon Equipment, 5.10, *Halo* the hairdresser and *Flava* an organic vegetable shop, I'd managed to survive, stretching a £60k trust to last eight years or so, travelling to India, all over Europe and the US.

It'd all boomerang back when I bought 22 Wath Road S7. I managed to get a mortgage for a terraced house in S7, built in 1896 with an outdoor loo and set to work. More Castro than Gastro, *The Broadfield* was the spot to get things done. Kirstie, Claire and Airlie joined me tearing the house down. When the dust settled I wondered how to build it. Lounge lizard raconteur Martin Hoyland advised helpfully, moved flags sourced from a disused quarry in the Peak and kept score. Pool shark Little Chris did the woodwork, Big Chris the plastering. The hose was always attached for the next round of gobo so when ripening plums were spotted by the local kids I was ready, waiting until they were right up the tree…hee…hee…hee!

It became a smashing little house where we hatched a lot of ill-considered ideas: with Liam to turn the cooling towers near Meadowhall into a lead-climbing wall, to travel the jet stream using kites towing articulated balloons, one of mine that. In order to be able to rent out a room, I hit upon an open plan bathroom lay out (saving on walls and cash) which meant the loo and bath were open to the elements at the top of the stairs. Silvia, Argentinian ex-model, weapons grade mountaineer, liked to sing in the Victorian slipper bath. That made me happy.

Doctor Evil had mini-me, I had Pat, maxi-me, but Pat King and I weren't lovers as many assumed. He'd attract the lasses, I'd chat and dance with them. At *The Forum*, seven Yorkshire'd boyfriends in Fred Perrys look on

Pat and Moose in the Hoose. Photo: Dawes Collection.

paralyzed with cool as their girlfriends sashay around us. Pat and I liked the same things: pottery, grit and pool. Floppy, unreliable, but lovely and very inventive on the rock, Pat had a childhood to catch up on, I one to extend. Son of an East Ender, he was generous to a fault, inviting a drunk in out of the night to stay at 22 for a while when I was abroad.

Malcolm Camp was a favourite housemate too and an enthusiastic decorator of the house with stuff from skips. A 'creative in waiting' who loves to play honky tonk on a kid's keyboard, he was committed to repairing the pin and string portrait of Sheffield city centre. I joined him on his trips to the reservoirs where he was developing a new swimming stroke that involved a 360° rotation of the body.

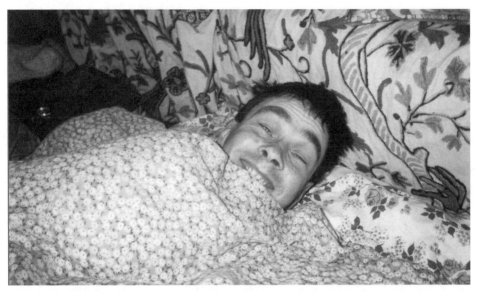

Jim Tuohig was a treasured resident, intelligent, reliable, handsome, GSOH (single), blues guitarist and runner, committed armchair mountaineer, fond of tins of lentil soup.

When the contradiction of living in a house being built got too much, we would wander around to Andy Peat's. He liked skips as well. One day Andy, (downhill mountainbike world champion Steve's brother), who can climb up a lamppost by swinging around it, jumps into a skip. He pulls out a green ash stump resembling a dragon's head, serendipitously sawn at the rakish angle for a wall mounted hunting trophy. A cracking BBC natural history camerawoman Justine Evans and I carve it further, smooth it some horns, wax them to an ivory sheen, burn charcoal into a snout we've chiselled and leave bark for its hide. It was fascinating how 'The Moose' became a loved member of the household. Back from Hampi, I find him hung precariously above the woodburner by a single hook, reminding me of Jerry Moffatt's tale of Frankenjura boulderer Flipper Fietz's sleeping arrangements. He slept in a bed with knives lightly pinned to the ceiling above.

Writing this I realise it may have been a dysfunctional time for some of us. It was a childish but enjoyable phase. Hindsight suggests I'd have been better off capitalizing on my name rather than balancing 19 *Jenga* blocks end to end and getting Donkey Kong to work on *Supermariokart* or getting caught making love on the centre spot at Bramall Lane with Claire and running naked with a visiting Canadian girl across the river plain below Chatsworth House chasing the Duke's deer. I was trying to find someone to settle down with.

Fine days still involved trying the last lines of the Peak, then on the way home came a regular challenge in 'Bowzer', the Subaru estate; to roll all the way back without power from the cattle grid on the Burbage North road to 22 Wath Road. Three cruxs stood in our way: getting up Psalter Lane, carrying speed enough to make it around the roundabout at the top of Cemetery Road and making it over a main road in Nether Edge itself. Psalter Lane reached, lights permitting, its shallow angle meant crawling along for 500yds at 10mph, hazards on, nothing amiss, under the guise of mechanical failure, Tuohig cringing. Roundabout successfully passed, 90° left rights led to a T-junction on a big road, well before Andy Peat had to be let out while we're still moving. Sprinting to get to the junction before we get there his job is to usher us across fast enough so we have enough speed to get over the speed bumps.

We also made expeditions to Boot's Folly opposite Strines Inn over the back of Derwent Moor. Building magnate Henry Boot had built the square 60ft gritstone tower to win back the love of his wayward wife, to no avail. The lower part of the spiral stairs was removed after a cow had become stuck in the keep's main room. A crag with a fireplace, we went and climbed there inside and out, in fair or foul. One stormy night, when the world was prophesied to end by Nostradamus, Pat and I roasted chestnuts for some girls hoping the grand surroundings and wartime-like moral laxity would romance them. That was our folly.

Pat was with me too when I bought a silver 205 Mi16 from the manager of Morrisons in Huddersfield to replace 'Bowzer'. The manager had fitted hideously stiff Koni springs and warned me it was a handful, as it was bound to be: "You take it easy, it is very fast" which bent Pat over double. Gas-filled Bilsteins, race brakes, fresh Michelins and a limited slip differential soon made it sticky and wonderfully predictable. Once we took *Suicide Roundabout* at race pace. In spite of the name the police have for it, it's a rare corner where you *can* scan well for pedestrians and cars and prime evasive manoeuvres reliably.

…There's a car coming but we're already well clear of it, 205 *countersteering* – a little left to weight both tyres to turn right. A front wheel drive's front tyres will still be loaded too much so *left foot braking* – applying brake and throttle together carefully – retards the un-driven rear tyres, slowing and turning the car. Mega-hatch is on the limit: obvious to a car approaching the roundabout, the one with the flashing blue lights…

"Bugger"

The officer walks to the window, asks me: "What is it you think you're doing?" I know precisely but omit the discourse above, but before I've time to frame a sensible answer my big mouth has said: "I'm really sorry, we've just been to see a James Bond film, I got over-excited", which amazingly seems to explain everything to his satisfaction. Biting our lips we watch him in the mirror walk away.

Another friend of mine in Sheff is Alistair, six foot two, 14 stone, skilful with it, likes a wrestle. I can keep him at bay for about 30 seconds. A model inmate, he developed Doncaster Prison gardens which received "Britain in Bloom 2003 runner up". At his house he cut the tops off two fir trees so they were the same height. I liked to stand on their tops. There was a great view of Ecclesall Park from there. One foot per tree, it feels like surfing. If it's breezy you must go with the trunks as they go where they will. He kept piranha as well. I liked to play his Hammond organ to them.

I knew all this larking about would have to stop. I did some great climbs during this period but not as good as the ones I didn't get up. *Warmlove* named after a cat is a despy mantel, *Smoked Salmon* is a super thin steep slab and *Avoiding the Traitors* is a beautiful roof and runnel problem. It wasn't as if my interest in movement was fading but increasingly I found myself sad, confused. I spent hours setting up a Lister Storm for the Nurburgring on Toca 3 carefully and then watch the result on replay with a doobie. Pot had a lot to do with keying in a depression that was there already, but also I was not trusting of myself, or others. I cared about others but was distracted, consumed with myself. I needed to find a new direction. I decided to go back to University. UEA this time to read Development Studies.

I may not have got in. At a particularly emotive question during the interview I ejected some spit from my mouth, which landed on the professor of sociology's glasses. I looked away and back. It had gone. I was accepted as a mature student!

In Norwich I lived under the stairs at my girlfriend Nat's. If she was happy and excited she would actually spontaneously jump up and down.

It was a great opportunity to learn more about the world and meet other types of people. There was a fine library where I came upon interesting things.

For example, at Gaviotas, a late 60s project in the Savanna of Colombia, to provide materials for fuel and buildings they had planted pine. These grew but had proved infertile. The canopy they provided had made conditions

Graduation day at UEA.

184

conducive for a wide range of dormant local species. Today it is a 75% biodiverse rainforest and The United Nations describe the village as a model of sustainable development. Gabriel Garcia Marquez has called founder Paolo Lugari "the inventor of the world."

Another revelatory book was ex agri-scientist Fukuoka's 'One Straw Revolution', about the most calorie productive farm in the world. Run with a *do nothing* principle, it uses no artificial inputs or ploughing giving him time to write 'bad poetry'!

I also had time to look for explanations for the sublimer experiences of life. I found some science/spiritual books struck a chord and some theories, particularly former Research Fellow of the Royal Society Rupert Sheldrake's theory of Morphic Resonance compelling. The theory suggests activities themselves have a universal memory associated with them. Statistically, someone ignorant of an activity would learn to do the activity more easily once others had done it. Sheldrake did experiments timing water rats negotiating mazes to test his theory. He found successive fresh populations of water rats in distant locations using the same configurations went

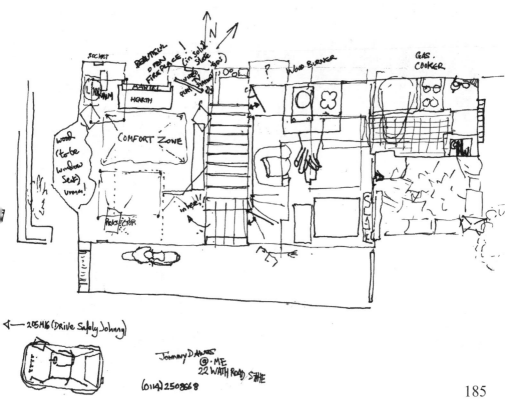

185

through quicker and quicker, until eventually they went straight through. Ha... I knew it. It reminded me of the famous Einstein-Podolsky-Rosen experiment that demonstrates *Non-locality*. I'm paraphrasing: *electrons in love* – entangled, spinning in different directions are split apart and taken to opposite ends of the earth. I know, I know. But when one has its direction of spin changed, the other reverses its spin as if somehow they are always together. Spacetime is clearly not what it seems. Quiet crags seem to exude this quality sometimes when one relaxes. Carrots, hunches about pebbles, I'm a bonafide hippy nutter.

But where *was* my social responsibility that might arise from all this discovery of interconnection I'd unearthed in the bookshop, library and from friends? Was I still more interested in my own thoughts, still notorious in some circles for drifting off or interjecting to guide the subject back to me? Full of myself.

Pain was still there. I was still heartily bored, self-destructive but admittedly without the proto-suicidal edge I'd had. Development Studies was great socially and a great education. My friends from this period I remember fondly, all the others actually. We're all in this together I begin to realize.

Norfolk winter Zimmer sports.

The still unclimbed Meru shark's fin. Mum pointed out I wasn't strong enough to be a mountaineer, although before falling a kilometre I did do an E5 pitch on sight. (So there). Photo: Paul Pritchard

Above left: After coming down off the Ak Su, this fabulous character, who reclaimed a part of the river after the fall of the Soviet State for a garden, brought us all a meal I consider the finest I've ever had. A long procession of raw vegetables straight from the ground, washed in the glacial river. He is seen here picking almonds.

Above right: Friction only, it took 45 minutes to get all limbs to work together, V10.

Below: The BBC took two years to find one of these chaps. We had one put in our laps on our trip to Ak Su in Kurgyzystan. The Snow Leopard cub's price was 5000US$. It was to be sold as a guard cat for Russian Mafia in Tashkent.

Very smooth dynamic mantel problem involving box splits. Bhagrathi III in the background.

Above: John Rosholt on Jardine's *Owl Roof* 5.12c. See note o. Below: Font by name, font by nature.

Above left: See note q. Photo: Rich Heap.
Below left & right: Jumping for joy. See note p. Photos: Simon Nadin.

Above: Phoning Virgin radio with a big mobile. Photo: Simon Nadin. Left: The paparazzi heard the Crane was in town... Photo: Sean Smith. Below: Getting an invite to stay in an igloo. Photo: Simon Nadin. Opposite: The first time I climbed Nelson, with Noel. The banner was like a sail, I'm sure Nelson would have approved. Photo: Sean Smith.

Police hand Jerry a caution. Naughty! Photo: Simon Nadin

Troll Wall

There was a hot woman at UEA who refused to sleep with me. So when she invited me to accompany her to Norway to visit a fellow student, I leapt at the chance. On our arrival, the siren waft of foreign perfume on the doorstep in Oslo made me think I'd landed on my feet again. My friend is welcomed in with open arms, but pulled to one side she is also informed "that it will not possible for *him* to stay". That was me, I realised.

Oslo is expensive, too much so for me to stay there with ten days to get through until our flight home. I'd once seen a BBC film of 70s Derbyshire legend Steve Bancroft climbing in Trolltind with Hans Christian Dosieth and a strong team of windblown Norwegians in stripy sweaters. They attempted an ascent of the Trollveggen without artificial aids. It had left a deep impression of colossal cliffs rising out of a tight valley.

It seemed a good idea to go up north on the train, but without a partner to climb with and no rock shoes or guidebook, in Åndalsnes I ask around in the hope of meeting local climbers. I'm successful. Nevertheless, two days later the decision to leave the local climbers to it isn't difficult. Waking up on the sofa, my first perpendicular glance is of a long line of empty whisky bottles, arranged in perfect order, worryingly. It was time to escape and explore the valley of the trolls alone.

Myth has it that Trolls are turned to stone in the full sun, so it was good the weather had been uncharacteristically dry. Bouldering on the sunlit gneiss erratics, high above the northerly spurs of the Trolltind boom and whistle.

Any designs on the Trollveggen (Troll Wall) were quickly dropped after learning it had suffered from recent rockfall. In the end serendipity intervenes. In Romsdal village, enquiring about possibilities, a German couple with pointy hats hand me a topo[44] of the Trollryggen – *the* longest upward route at 1,800m – in the whole of Europe. The topo has unfamiliar UIAA grades, a key a parochial Brit could only hazard a guess at, with one section obscured by a worn crease. Fortunately the giant saddle is clearly visible out of the window, the closest climb to the hut.

---

[44] Diagramatic illustration of a route, showing pitch length and belay positions, overlaid onto the crag or mountain.

Though I was without proper rock boots, fortunately, I had come to Norway wearing approach shoes with sticky soles. A full chalk bag from a boulderer joins peanuts, dried fruit, two litres of water, plastic sheet and duvet jacket in the pack. The only thing to do now is to get some sleep.

…Seeming to wake as soon as my head hits the pillow with dark and light in cahoots, dreams etch-a-sketched away by wilderness, night has passed. All around nylon pupae swell and contract, betraying there are creatures still asleep inside them.

In the tight silence of first light, slipping the heavy bolt softly aside, by swinging the hut door open and looking up, the gnarl of where I am going can grip me cleanly.

Out in it, at the shallow ford across the river, trouser legs rolled right up past the knee, a boot in each hand, feet immediately lose all sensation in the icy meltwater. Now feel the speed of the walking move still crisp air clean across my face. Pining sweetens the higher I go. Until all of a sudden, eyes down, the rhythm of swinging arms and singing muscle on the path leave the trees behind with the first steps on to solid granite.

Here weather can change mountain fast but for now it is still asleep. Cosy and moving silently makes it seem like my sleeping bag in the hut must still be warm inside or as if something of me has not left it quite yet.

Almost 800m up the slabs, already it's time to stop for a drink. No need to break open the pack, the cliff serves up an airborne drip trail from a roofline far above. Only because the air is so still can the ticker tape of drops gattle accurately into my mouth without even touching the sides, if you concentrated (but not exclusively or you could fall off the ledge.)

Before I continue, let me tell you about my previous experience of going solo.

Climbing without any safety bollocks has always appealed: the clear intent, the physical freedom of when and where it unfolds. Danger can be a balm that forces intuitive parts that are usually too bored to turn up to make an appearance.

Partnerless from time to time, in North Wales I find myself entertaining crazy ideas like soloing *Left Wall* to get fit. On form Tremadog E4 *Cream* feels exciting on solid edges and good jams while *Fingerlicker* calls for a cool flow. Even classic E5s like *Cockblock* and *Right Wall* feel OK. *Cockblock* seems, unfeasibly, jump-offable and apart from greasy undercutting out of the hole, cutting edge ten years before, *Right Wall* feels safe and fun. Familiar, these climbs felt mellow but on occasion things went nicely out of hand.

…Pretending I'm still on *Gogarth* E1 – still courting the idea it's not too far above the sea to dive off – deep down I suspect I've strayed onto one of the big lines. Jamming like a king, 200ft up the overhanging flared crack feels like grit HVS until stopping too long on a greasy break. Rhythm lost, stalled, forearms swell hard as a drum… peering at me from the crack is a wooden bong. Before paranoia about viruses in bird guano grips me, I bite into the salty block and rest. Soon I've enough grunt for the strenuous exit off-width of *Citadel* E5 to be a tricky joy.

Trollryggen was easier, but forty times bigger than the Welsh aperitifs above – gulp – twice as big as Yosemite's El Capitan!

At 800m up comes the first full-blooded climbing – where you must use your hands. At first it felt strangely easier than walking, arms seemingly positioned deliberately at the correct angle to use the slab, by push or pull. I remember thinking: "This is the optimum angle for mankind to move easily on in its evolutionary passage from jungle to savanna".

Climbing aerobically, weighing less and less, I grind to a halt at a short steep slab. Sack on it feels tricky, at least 6a. To reverse feels possible but these approach shoes feel more reassuring on the scamper. Right foot brought left of my left foot and high, allows shared hands on a slanting crimp to work quickly. Soon sat on a gravel ramp, munching raisins even though I do not feel hungry, I see there was no need to have climbed the slab, an obvious easy rake skirting it. Frayed damp topo makes it clear no part of the existing route is 6a.

A half hour of pleasant climbing brings me to a band of overhangs. Do not recall these from the ground, conversations, or recognize them from the topo either. There is a measure of reassurance. The cliff is low angled and needs must, could be carefully down climbed – if it doesn't rain, and I think to try to solo this roof is not so barking since it has a shelf 10ft below it to catch me.

There seems to be three possible lines through the overhangs. One is a flared pod on iffy rock, destination unknown. Another is a lottery of flat loose holds. The last though more solid is harder, a discontinuous crack, without footholds, no change out of E4 and not the HVS anticipated…

For now, to reconnoitre each line the sack sits safely on the shelf. The groove feels wrong. The loose one has me palpitate feeling the space. The crack has interesting climbing. That and the updraft on the big cliff, somehow silences the exposure. One look up the crack system on the steep headwall, sirens begin to pull me up; exciting moves uncurling in my mind start to happen in my body. Gaga, the exposure makes me feel safe, but from the feel of rock under my fingers a mental klaxon shouts me down. What the hell are you doing up there?! Down… get down.

On the shelf I take stock. The options aren't good. That is how it is sometimes:

> … Bhagirathi III, exhausted and lazy, Paul and I had stayed in our pits for far too long, joining the face when it had long become a funnel for melt-loosened rockfall. A whistling stone had narrowly missed me, something making my body flinch out of the way, but so doing consigns Pritch unsighted to yet another quality accident. Paul is in shock and needs water. It's up to me to find it. There was an audible trickle, fascinatingly a smell to it too, rising up from deep within the Himalayan mega gravel below.

> Entering the morraine would be a calculated risk, the mathematics of which no one could possibly know. Water bottle in hand, I crawl headfirst into a chaotic jangle of blocks, random shards, crazed dust. There is a way down. There appears to be a space big enough to accept me: under a large boulder, and around another. It seems safer to go on my back past the first – the prospect of the boulder moving is too horrific to dwell on. After, a twisting very slow dive to pierce a tighter gap still, I chock the boulder with a rock hoping to stop it settling. Wriggling through, the boulder moves, pinching my body, narrowing my only exit.

> …Drops start to join up in the bottom of the bottle, boulders all around groan but I can't leave yet. It takes forever to fill… one could get trapped here, water freely available.

> … Can I get out? Has Paul passed out already?

190

…Go back through slow or fast? How was I to know? First push the bottle through to where it can't fall. Avoiding contact with the unstable boulder I go for it, bench-pressing on the only block properly jammed by others. Smaller chunks rattle down. Chest clear of the constriction, quickly, before its mass can notice, jabbing on the very centre of a block that seemed to have stuff behind it I push for the gap… feel my legs meet chill air.

Paul's torch malingers in the gloom.
"Get your laughing tackle around that"

Now, back in Norway – Vikings, long boats, fabulous blondes, that sort of thing, I've broken out the water from my sack and wonder which way to climb?

Clouds emerging from behind the cliff give fresh urgency. Left is vast, glassy schistose/wet flaky death. Horizontally right is the vastness of the Troll Wall, with giant bands of overhangs and just one free route, notorious for difficult route finding and perched flakes. Above, you know already. Retreating down seemed unappealing, the slab now greasy with the sun tracking across it. There was one last possibility. I thanked myself for briefly considering it from the ground before.

Trollryggen is effectively a long lens of rock bordering the Troll Wall, below which is scree. My plan was to down climb a crack system I'd spotted from the road and jump horizontally across the 100ft drop to fall a lesser 40ft to slanting scree. Loose, it could potentially absorb a long fall quite well.

Leaving my sack for the reconnaissance I traverse around, climb down to explore what I cannot see from where I am.

I move down the line precisely. That classic over-carefulness advertised to me that things were more serious, although in reality the actual dangers were exactly the same as before.

Around the corner the crack steepens, plastered with ungainly jugs that looked like they had been glued on badly and slippery wet. Stamping on them first tests they aren't loose. The scree is not as far off as suspected – the plan *was* in with a chance of success. The leap runs over in my mind. Something else too, even below the jugs, was a mossy knoll that might further trim the length of the fall I'd have to take. Back up to the sack.

The one worry was how far away was the scree exactly? No trees or people there to confirm the true scale of the yawning drop I throw the sack on the trajectory my body will take to see. It took longer than I thought to hit the scree but it still looked like the best option – particularly now since I'd just thrown my gear, food, water and sleeping bag away![45]

Climbing down, hands on a wet jug, careful to pull out precisely, giving it no chance to spit me to one side or the other, a gentle swing and lurch to the grassy lump. That moment, finding it solid, body twists from facing in to facing out to leap – spread out like a cat – I launch out over the violence of the void.

Oh my lord..... oh my looor....ccuuuurrrrunCH.....

Scree loosened from above goes for my legs, but by sprinting diagonally back upslope, it's easy to scamper clear of the spinning blocks.

Time for breakfast. Vodka is already out in the hut but a nice cup of tea seems far better for a sobering look. Matching what remains of the topo against the hard copy through the window reveals I'd made the right decision. My 1800ft highpoint had been 400ft off route. I wonder how my sexy friend is getting on in Oslo.

---

[45] I bet Harold Lloyd could have judged how to do this jump well first time off. It was a jump like any other if a bit bigger. It was not as precise as the potentially lethal dive down Zoë Brown's stairs. First time you had to miss your cranium on the stair lip while making sure you reached the softness of the sofa, clearing its wooden arm, releasing the main horizontal push/leap after your body had already fallen below the top stair! At least the Norwegian scree would be softer than the flagstone floor of Sheffield nurses' hall of residence, where, brogue-clad, the steep grind down mahogany banister involved a gradient change midway at a dogleg.

On The Box

Foula is an island west of the Shetland Isles. Two and a half miles wide, three and a half miles long, it has one road with a family at either end, who reputedly didn't get on.

I found myself on the island in remarkable company. We had been gathered to attempt an assault on the second highest cliff in Britain at 1,220ft, Da Kame. The project had been hatched entirely by a forthright Jewish 15-year-old called Abigail Mann. Five foot two inches tall with blondish hair, and, Dave Thomas remembers, a generous application of foundation. When Miss Mann had been 'relieved' of her place at school, she'd hit upon the idea of making a film of her climbing this huge cliff on Foula. We heard little about how either her leaving or commission had happened. If I'd had a hat, I'd have taken it off to her.

Her 'butter wouldn't melt in my mouth' approach had convinced venerable historian, Himalayan veteran Paul Nunn, super-bold Lakes hardman Pete Whillance, soft-spoken Scot Murray Hamilton and rufty-tufty Lancastrian mountaineer Ian McMullen to come. Dave Thomas a.k.a. *Joe 90* and I were to represent the new generation. *The Climbers*, for the Beeb, was to be the handiwork of a mellow chap called Sid Perou, revered for his cave-diving films.

A flight from Manchester to sunny Shetland left us squeezing into a small boat to chug out into the Atlantic; loaded with crisps and chocolate bars (teenager Abigail had done all the catering). It was a rough crossing. Only late in the voyage did Foula rear up out of the waves through the fog. It had the fantastical appearance of a gigantic golf course that had been compressed until its smooth greens were angled at 1 in 1.

We were all billeted in one compact white hut. Steel bunks brimmed with kit and, with late night head torches bobbing across tense novels, the ambience loosely resembled the Second World War submarine epic *Das Boot*. In silence we waited, not in dread of depth charges but in the vain hope that the rattling gallop of rain on the tin roof would stop.............. for a whole week.

Involved in TV projects a number of times, they seem to me to be strange, disembodied affairs, if often played out in remarkable places. It's the queer

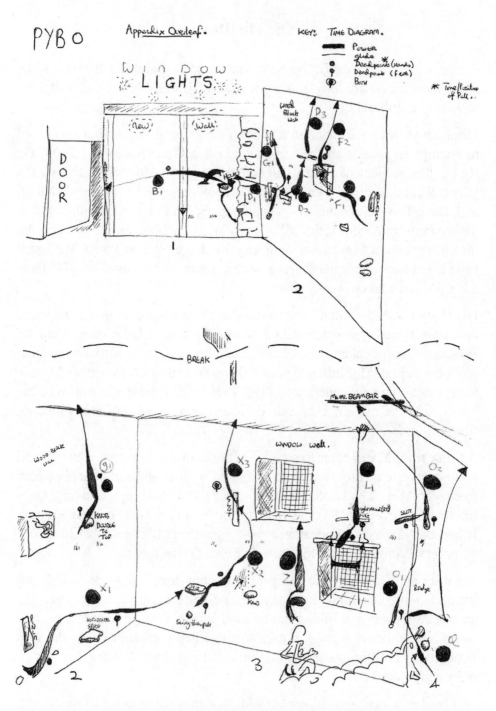

My storyboard and directions for Stone Monkey. One dangerous problem was running full pelt at the bottom alcove, tucking yourself into a ball, sliding to land sat down.

motive and peculiar coalition of people that would ordinarily not be doing such things together that make for the unravelling of dramas.

In the mid 90s, I was involved in another film commission from the BBC described to me as being about: "*A man and woman attempting to climb a big cliff*". The big cliff would be St John's Head on Hoy opposite the Old Man I decided. The woman: Airlie Anderson.

Airlie Jane is a heartfelt two stroke kind of girl – explosively honest, with a great turn of phrase and a glorious bottom. We have a tradition between us that whenever we meet, *wherever it is,* she knows to turn around and offer me her bottom, at which point I give it a loud smack. This has happened in some ludicrous public places. With *Master's Edge* E7 6b and 8a *Rêve d'un Papillon* in her back pockets, to attempt to free climb Drummond's *Long Hope Route* with her was an exciting proposition.

You can have a proper laugh with Airlie. One time on our way to Curbar, Andy Peat wanged a pebble that hit my head, making a hollow sound. She thought this was unbelievably hilarious. Cackling, she shut her eyes. About 30 feet away I pick up a sheep pat. Inspired by her mocking open mouth, I spin it, and very out of character, deliver it right on target. But she had a temper on her too.

Which one would turn up on St John's Head?

We make an un-filmed trip up to Hoy for a reconnaissance. I didn't really notice because my mind was on our pace but once on the cliff Airlie Jane was already spooked. We had to get to a particular ledge before dark to bed down, so I ran keenly up the steep grass slopes below the great buttress to a small overlap of feral red rock that had a faded rope in situ to pass it. Grabbing this I shin up it. The rope snaps…I freeze in the air, *Tom and Jerry* style, launch back, landing on all fours like a cat on the steep lawn below. She squirms, squeals and tells me off, unsoothable. I'm unrepentant – you couldn't hurt yourself there if you tried – and press on until finally we're at the rock proper. But Jane is "not amused". She thinks someone is going to die at any moment. I've clearly made a miscalculation…but once she punches me in the face she starts to calm down.

With all the calamity and histrionic delay we've failed to reach the bivouac. My partner, emotionally exhausted, hogs the teeny ledge we end up on, but cuddles up. Really it is rather beautiful how we have ended up like this. It would have made a great film in itself. I smoke, watching galleon clouds patrol the ocean as night descends.

Early heavy morning rain comes in off the sea. We rappel off. Dragged down by sodden gear and mood, we grumble like only the two of us can. We scale the big gully roped up. Eventually we get to the crest of the uphill, and pleased to be over it all, resume our reverie by hurling our sacks down the huge steep slope over the other side, then rolling down try to catch them up. Dizzy useless at the bottom, stumbling, unable to lock in on my sack, I give up, tackle Airlie instead who's giggly wobbly trying to stand up.

The slopes on Foula were every bit as good as those on Hoy but no one wanted to roll down them with me. The atmosphere was dour, the inclines merely a daily obstacle to the chore of hoofing vast mats of moss off the Kame. Performing a cartwheel on the 'first pitch' to make plain not all of the Kame was a cliff didn't go down well with the crew. Pete and Murray were always hauling Dave and I up in front of 'The Mann' for not doing our fair share.

My daily distraction was a sideways dyno along the side of the hut: a 6-step sequence on a foot wide ledge ending at an arête. It was hard to slow down enough to layback the smooth arête you were flying past, yet hard to accelerate enough to even reach it. My earnest precious insistence that this should form the centrepiece of the film rather than the vegetated mediocrity of our goal the Kame, earned me the nickname '7a Dawes'. Whillance also insisted there could be no way *Indian Face* could be E9. Outrageous!

The real shame was that every day we walked past incomparable lines on the most perfect pocketed ultra solid sandstone. Eventually we got on one. It yielded a three pitch mega-route that meandered around a 70ft roof via a 50ft traverse on its very lip, then took a square 100ft arête. Unfilmed: *The Big Movies* E4 5c, 6a, 6a.

I insisted TV commissioners don't have a clue, but the venerable Paul Nunn took all the film hassle in his stride, regaling us in his rolling dither with great stories about Rouse teaching University Mathematics with no qualifications and of epics in the big mountains. It was an amazing lesson in humility to see the troll-like Nunn being happily ordered about by Madam Abigail.

We found a use for a Hex 10 – to defend against huge birds called bonxies[46]. One knocked over our friendly unsuspecting sound engineer, Gavin. They're capable of taking a small sheep, or … young girl for that matter. In the end, the film was smashing. Despite the fact our heroine couldn't climb it quite as planned, the Kame looked dramatic. Footage was shot of other escapades as well. Pete, Ian and Murray explored a sea stack. Pete swam heroically across swollen water to fix a rope. Ian and Murray found a telegraph pole which they had caber-ed up to receive the rope on Foula itself, rigging a Tyrolean so we could all get across. On the stack's unusually glossy solid rock, we did a magic E5 arête. On the main island, Dave Thomas and I climbed an incredible arête with a sole peg for protection, with a cool cha-cha-cha sequence:

*** *The Colonial* E6 6a, 5c, 5b.

Long nights in the hut were dull. Still with a mountain of chocolate, we held a Mars Bar eating competition. I ate 14 and won. But we're still bored – 'the devil makes work for idle hands' – we fashion a noose, blindfold Abigail's teddy and light a candle for her arrival. On the boat home a love bite had mysteriously appeared on Abigail's neck. I shudder to think.

My biggest appearance was on *Stone Monkey*. Noon Boxing Day it was watched by 2.5 million people. Channel 4 did well from it. *Stone Monkey* had cost them £10k. (Repeating it four times, they filled the airwaves with a six times award winning film for 4 x 26min/£10k = less than £100/minute.)

Cameraman Alun Hughes and I first met in the Pass. I'd soloed up to place gear in *Cockblock* then down climbed to complete my warm up with some stretching. I then rodeo-clipped the crab from the ground, antics that impressed him.

We filmed a trailer.

Alun showed the head commissioner all manner of dynamic footage: white water canoeing, soloing etc. Incredibly he fell fast asleep. Alun Hughes having to actually nudge him awake. Instead Alun tried second generation dynos on him (one dyno flowing into the next). His eyes widened…"It's the leaping boy…let's have the leaping boy!" Commissioner Metcalf exclaimed.

With Alun armed with a commission for a 10-minute film, I set to writing a non-climber/climber friendly storyboard, featuring climbs that show tights

[46] Great Skuas.

197

at their best, music beyond our budget, spliced with a hammy narrative to make the show flow. (No, that wasn't Mum and Dad). The idea was to allow the rock to be director, choose the camera angle so body shape fits into the TV screen. That way hopefully the climber's mind at work would be apparent.

Metcalf was keen to fund another four shows, after it won so many awards, but he moved to Sky just a week before the go ahead.

Eventually Channel 4 wanted a piece of the stone monkey again – *Design Awards* was a competition for design. I was employed to judge a thermos flask against a school amongst other things. I climbed the grand hotel boulder at Stanage no hands, carrying coffee to supposed newlyweds on the top. I was then presented as married to rock. *Downhill Racer* E4 solo right-handed was captured using a Polecam on TV for the first time. I criticised the flask as it only held three cupfuls, not enough for the couple to both have a refill.

Motormouth, a kid's show, was quite funny. I was there to jump about. Presenter Gabi Roslyn had dressed in tights, which somehow looked inappropriate on her. I told her so live on air, a bit rich bearing in mind how I looked in mine. On the show was a young lad. Later he'd out-manoeuvre Jeremy Clarkson bodily and verbally and become the mascot of Kendal Mountain Film Festival but when I first met him his voice hadn't broken. He'd just been on Hoy too, on the *Old Man* with his old man – no one as young as 11 had ever done it. Leo Houlding was unfazed, appreciated the impact of a well-judged reply even then. His Dad and I shared a love of Zappa.

At our swanky hotel after the show trouble lies in wait for Leo in the foliage of a large tree in the lobby. Pouncing out, I shoot a handful of ice down his back. He gives chase on the marble floor, the two of us sliding by the guests on the foyer settee like Indians circling an upturned stagecoach.

A month later, on his own, wide-eyed, duffel coat, school bag rammed with sandwiches and climbing boots, I go to meet him on the platform at Sheffield train station. He greets me in a high-pitched Lakes accent: "Would you like a Solaaaro… Johnn…y?"

S7. Leo hung out with the homeless in my half renovated terrace playing *Supermariokart*, skiing in socks behind the sanding machine. On the crags my friends and I did as we always had, while Leo spent much of the time swinging around just trying to hang on this or that ludicrous, still unclimbed line. At an early age he encountered what hard might become and developed a natural talent for speedy slaps.

It wasn't very long before he was repeating the hardest climbs, so when I canvassed Berghaus for sponsorship and met with a curious lack of enthusiasm it was no surprise they'd signed the young blond comp-winning Houlding. When I courted Helly-Hansen, Airlie had also pipped me to the post. New clothing brand Stone Monkey had taken on Ben and Jerry and because of tardiness my nom de plume! Deals done. Buggeration.

India

India is a beautiful name for a middle class child, an even better name for a country. I'd always had a hankering to go there. A passing interest in enlightenment and all that had inspired me to imagine encountering gurus levitating, melting the snow around them.

The late Mo Anthoine, irrepressible wit and mountaineer, was the first to sow the seeds in us to set our sights higher. A photo on a civic sign opposite Joe Brown's shop of he and Joe smiling at Everest base camp in 1986 captures the jovial spirit of their times perfectly. Mo suggested us craggers in Llanberis go to Gangotri in Northern India's Garwhali Himalaya. Mo described it as "A parking lot for El Capitans". As I once pointed out to Reinhold Messner I had probably climbed more 8,000 millimetre peaks than him, but that was for me to miss the point. It wasn't how many or how high, the challenge of huge gloss walls in thin air promised its own rewards. For me those proved shy.

Pritch, Bobby Drury, Joe Simpson and I on our first trip to Gangotri camped on one side of the valley, a bigger team from Llanberis at Tapovan on the other. They came to attempt Shivling, we the unclimbed west face of Bhagirathi III.

Overhanging shale would greet us at the top of a 3,000 foot face of fluted granite. New to the game, it seemed clear to me Joe thought we might be a danger to ourselves, and so to him. Before we could get stuck in, worryingly Paul nearly fell unconscious from cerebral oedema. In the meantime, Bob and Joe go on the *Scottish Route*. I help Paul down to the highest huts where he recovers almost immediately.

Our Nandaban camp was not relaxing. Our cook wasn't one really. Our sleepyhead liason officer just ate our food and complained. One day at camp, pulling on my boot, just about to kick down past the restricting pinch of the plastic shell, I feel a jab under my heel. I pull my foot out to discover the source of the sharpness, a razorblade pointing up! It could scarcely have been an accident as the blade sits in a cut slot, keen edge up. It wasn't auspicious. Paul and I eventually went to try and free *The Spanish Pillar*, but rock fall badly smashed his arm.

Passing time on a still sunny day at Tapovan I try a slim perfect groove on a boulder. I hear a soft padding behind me. I turn to see a baba walking barefoot in the snow. Om Giri is a Hindu holyman who lives at Tapovan above the glacier. There were a lot of babas bodding around, many keen smokers of charas; wickedly powerful hashish resin. To the untrained eye, some babas looked like 'chancers' who lived off the tourist fat, but Om Giri spent winter on his tod in a cave in the rocks. His stove had a 20ft flue so it'd work even under the snows that accumulate there at 3,500m in midwinter. One day he invited me to visit him. I felt touched that of all the mountaineers at Tapovan, he'd asked me. The reason he gave was hilarious – he could not service his wives for religious reasons, and I was being offered the job!

Though my first mountaineering had been a flat experience, India itself was anything but. The place and people were extraordinary, at one turn sickening, the next fantastic, all the clichés you've heard smack on target. In India the feeling you are in a spiritual place is tangible. The idea the world is an illusion is considered normal here, not held by everyone, but somehow obvious nevertheless.

In Delhi I see a tiger ride a motorbike, in Bombay, a girl for sale in a cage. I remember one content legless rickshaw driver grin ear to ear as he peddled us around with – wait for it – the only thing he had to do it with, his arms! At a crag in Maharashtra having a pee, I find myself snake to snake with a king cobra: no contest! At Ramanagram, while I am cleaning off a gently overhanging unclimbed rib, my friend Adam Wainwright scrambles up a gully. I am shocked as a big round boulder rolls down, "Bloody hell Adam, what the …". Then I notice the boulder is hairy. Thinking this unusual, the penny finally drops when the boulder starts to walk! Adam had roused a hibernating brown bear. As it runs along below the crag, our Indian hosts squeal with laughter, one announcing later, with a chuckle: "Afterwards we will all go for a swim – in Crocodile Lake".

I tried mountaineering again some years later. We would try an even tougher challenge, the unclimbed legendary Meru Shark's fin, **6,66**0m high! This time in the company of a good friend of Paul Pritchard's, the late Phillip Lloyd, a very strong South African mountaineer and Noel Craine who'd later team up with Paul on Baffin Island and on the Towers of Paine.

When Noel acclimatized badly, his load carrying duties fell to us. The Shark's Fin juts into space above a mile-long snow slope. My job was to clear the diagonal fixed lines from the slope, coil and carry it up to use to fix the fin itself. The snow was un-compacted two steps up, three back tiring. Climbing diagonally in the full sun meant braking trail without steps with a growing weight of rope. A full day's effort doing this was way too much for me. By nightfall, in an ice cave cut into a mushroom on a ridge at 4,500m, I'm totally exhausted.

Next day, it is as if I had never slept. Pulling my outer boot over my inner is too tiring. Instead I loosely lodge outer on inner, swing it back, to kick it on by kicking it into the rock. But on the back swing, the outer boot flies off. Remote control, it almost carves to a downhill racer's stop in the snow but instead flicks its heel at me before diving off into another valley. Why did I not think to clip a sling into it before I kicked it in? Can't think…

My feet had been freezing all the time but once I had a boot fashioned from Karrimat and duct tape, at least one foot was warm. We all had to go down. That was the cost of my idiocy. I insisted on glissading; sliding down. It went well for a bit. I thought I had a measure of the snow until I rode up on top of ice. The ice axe, on the back of my sack, was not useful as I accelerated down the mile long slope! I cleared my sunglasses of snow when I could, to try and spot any approaching bergschrunds (I think that's what they're called). The thin air and glossy snow did little to slow me. Far from being scared, I was finally actually enjoying myself. I know falling is supposed to be bad but this was more fun than anything we'd done so far. I went floppy in case I hit something but all that happened was I eventually flew out of the shade flipping around coming to a halt in soft snow, in the sun. Comfy, I gazed leisurely up at the long arc my body had made, and at my fucked off partners trudging slowly down. I feel something in an inside pocket, retrieve it for a classic *Hamlet* moment.

Some of us baled from the mountains after that. You have to abide by group decisions. In the lowlands and by the sea, we visited new crags and ate royally. At Savandurga, a summer storm filled a sluice in the granite dome so it squirted like a giant tap. At Varkalla, swimming in the ocean we treaded water amazed as raindrops leapt straight back out of the water as if it was too cold. A few minutes later we were fighting for our lives, slowly being pulled into the fast offshore current of the Indian Ocean. The monsoon had schizoed the tiny stream leading down to the beach into a torrent.

My third trip to India was with Jerry Moffatt and Kurt Albert to Hampi. Hampi is an ancient granite cityscape in Karnataka. For miles all around the uninhabited city, as far as the eye can see are boulders, ravines, abandoned quarries and ridges making you want to explore.

I can scarcely think of three more enthusiastic climbers than us but for raw glee Kurt could not be matched and his big joy came in a ridiculous superhero's body. When we first got to the little modern village that has grown up to tap the tourist trade, one local, feeling Kurt's impressive German muscles, exclaimed, "Big guts!" and stroking Kurt's face added "Nice mooooustache". Kurt was so eminently approachable and lovable, this happened a lot. Mischievious, once eating in a posh coffee house in the Frankenjura he held a loaded butter knife, one hand on the end, exclaiming: "There is no way this will come off" referring to the large dollop of butter on the knife! Then he flicked it. It flew across the room, coming to rest on the diamond-encrusted glasses of a stately frau. "Oh no…I'm so embarrassed..!": he said in a big stupid bear voice.

I loved that Hampi trip, especially pulling scams on Jerry. Jerry is more business minded than me, in the markets he'd haggle then beam when he made a good deal. One day I went to the market early to bribe all the stallholders to not budge on price on the things Jerry liked to buy for lunch. While Kurt and I haggled easily getting "Best price…?" Jerry was greeted with waggling heads and wavy hands. Once on the train Jerry, dopy, was asleep as we entered a station. While the train was still moving, Kurt invited me to get out and run down the platform with him. "Jerry…Jerry, quick, get out, the train is leaving…", Kurt hollers through the open cabin window. I have never seen Jerry move so fast.

It was fab watching the countryside change as we trundled through at a human pace, a 20s pace. Sat on the roof of the train, I had a big surprise when I saw a horizontal black stripe approaching separate the smoke from the engine into two. Just in time I realise what it is and vault the bar landing with a bang on all fours bringing enquiring heads peering up from the carriage below. I learnt later it was for collecting the mail without the train having to stop.

We find some great climbs in Hampi although it is boiled blanket hot. I get hideously ill for some reason.

The thing I remember fondest are the monkeys. We three made our living from climbing like them. They're quite like us – one white bearded fellow lived above the gate into the main temple. He had a collection of items he'd curated lodged in the nooks of the carved Hindu reliefs. When we saw him he'd just nicked something new from a tourist and was working out what it was. He tried to eat it, prod his neighbour with it, finally holding one end of it, he moves the other up and down his teeth. He had discovered a toothbrush.

He was a silver Hanuman, the ones who frequented the cliffs on the dome above the temple were little brown ones. There was a chimney there which was too wide to bridge, but they could still climb up it. I even saw a mum with a baby on her back zig zag up it, bouncing off the walls.

I once set a climbing competition using Blu-tack in the bath, for a spider, even adding a bonus hold, but it made no difference. The spider did not improve with experience, all it could do was throw legs at it but monkeys seem to know immediately what to do. The monkeys in Hampi didn't climb up everything though. Once Kurt chucked ripe banana high onto an unclimbed face with a short leaning crack at its base. It was incredible to see one youngster try and layback the crack, then, jump off, linger then go back up and try and jam it. At the top of the crack, it shared both hands on an edge. Then to our collective amusement, it wiped its hands on its fur. It looked up, then down as if pondering: "Am I too high up..?" Then dropping back into the crack shuffled its hand along the edge, came under, crossing through reached up to the banana, locked off and ate. Watching our little cousin climb, you could see it working out moves like we do.

I will miss Kurtle. He died in 2010. Jerry was lovely when I asked him about the funeral. I got a clear impression of a joyful occasion; of many people remembering a happy wiseman.

Action Directe

A rainy day in Llanberis, two bars too few, three too hot, the red phone rings:

"Survival International here, we have a mission for you…"

At once I imagine myself as Virgil, head doddering, poised on Tracy Island, arms suspended on string, neck wobbly. 'The Crane Fly' Noel is to be the 'Brains' of the outfit. Data-driven, polite, he considers my 'Oh John, petulance…petulance' to be a problem.

Our mission to:

'Save the World, Stop the World Bank'.[47]

Survival International is sadly not a charity for traditional climbers, it defends the rights of tribal peoples, but it'd do for our purpose – to scale an illegal 185ft tall alpinist's delight of granite, sandstone and bronze.

Its first ascent was by an anti-apartheid team in the 70s that included the curious visionary Edwin Ward-Drummond. My climbing career has been strangely spent in his orbit:

- Wen Zawn, *Conan the Librarian – Dream of White Horses.* 1986.
- Great Wall. *Indian Face – Midsummer Night's Dream.* 1986
- Troll Wall. 1993
- St John's Head. 1995
- Curbar. The lampoon of *Drummond Base.* 2003. An unchipped E8 6c direct on his sculpted *Linden.*
- and here with Noel Crane on the rocks of Trafalgar Square. 1991

[47] Our objective: to raise awareness of policies arguably designed to put poor nations in debt, a cheaper means of control than military power.

An Oxford Doctor of Epidemiology, expert in Lyme disease and 'Oh so correct', one gets the feeling Noel enjoys a stiff quiz more than a stiff drink. Here are a couple of events so you can get a measure of the man. The first is in the heyday of the Plas Y Brenin Wall. Noel, a gangling, button-challenged gent had a beloved party piece where he would squeeze a key between thumb and index finger, slip it into a slim slot adjacent to a tiny gloss-painted dink which he would pretend to crimp, and, casually as you like, long armed, reach up to a ludicrously far off hold. Dave Towse, a head honcho then, baffled, would fail to do the move, hilariously, every time. On another occasion in Kyrgyzstan, Noel cautions me when I'm offered a go on a wild-eyed border guard's Rambo-stickered AK 47 with a screwing of his forehead and a disappointed deep "NO… John".

So to the 'Monumenteering'…

We had particular problems to surmount. Noel and I had not bargained on the rank rich guano on the sloping mantel on to the square pedestal at the base of the column itself. We were going to have to deal with this swiftly to be out of reach of the long arm of the law. We weren't on a trip to the beach and had not brought our towels. One way or another, guano or no, banner must get to the top. The obvious solution was to strip off! While Noel educates me about viral disease, testicles grinding into the back of his neck, I take off my fleece to scrape off the pigeon's donation.

Where I judge the perfect mantel would leave an impression, I try to clean off small patches in the thick mats of acrid shit; one for the heel of my foot, one for one hand, and where the heal of the crucial turning hand must go I struggle to get a tiny patch squeaky clean using my pristine t-shirt. Gear capricious, mantel dangerous, any imprecision and we really would be in it. Reeking, I pull off Crane's screaming shoulders to do what I was built for, a slimy mantel. Standing up carefully on the slick lip, teetering on to one foot, a horizontal step over a wide treacherous sluice of guano to flat stone is possible.

Second pitch, 1a is a circumnavigation of the column to arrange a belay. Now Noel can climb the ropes and saunter easily around the pedestal to the base of the Corinthian column. The boys in blue have arrived too late. Noel thinks they look friendly enough.

The long third pitch, up the column itself, faces the National Portrait Gallery – a long uniform pitch on exquisitely hand cut, metre wide granite scoops bounded by square pinches. Questionable protection comes from a lightning conductor, an inch wide zinc strap running up the full length of the column, coupled crudely to the granite by brass dowels. Where strap meets dowels, a sling can be slung. This is not as safe as it sounds. Were just one part of the ductile strap to snap, all slings below would certainly also fail.

A full metre and a half between the slings, it was clearly a job for the taller man. Noel stands precariously off the apparatus then, by reaching up, fixes the next. Eventually he arrives at the bronze Acanthus leaves at Horatio's feet – the filigreed enthusiasms of the victorious English's remodelling of French weaponry into something useful – an overhanging free section; a thrilling doddle to climb.

On the summit we juggle tasks. As I pull over on to the slanting plinth, Noel offers me a hand, as is customary at heroic times, shortly to be replaced by something to smoke. Into the other hand he places a blocky 80s mobile phone, already ringing. On the other end, mock cool, a Virgin Radio DJ spins me, "What do you know?" Parliament in view, drawing deeply for inspiration for a second time, I point out: "It's just **not** on…"

Survival International had chosen the day well to maximise exposure. Lady Di was signing Andrew Morton's book 'Diana: Her True Story' on The Mall. Once done there, the Paps were likely to spill over to milk the bonus photo opportunity nearby in Trafalgar Square.

Hanging with Horatio was a hoot but it was a surprise that a cursory glance at the handsome sculpture reveals not only has battle rid Nelson of eye and arm, but it seems 'column' too.

Time to plant the flag. Strung between us, the banner reveals itself to be a huge sail. We're hurled about as we struggle to tie it around the shaft. In high wind, it's quite impossible to tame without weighting it down. The Friend 4 clipped through a make-shift hole in the banner eventually tears loose, free falling for a 100ft, narrowly missing a pigeon-feeding tourist and policeman.

Back down, the Old Bill greets us. Wincing at the aroma of our '*eau d'oiseau*', standing as far away as possible, the Peelers take our particulars

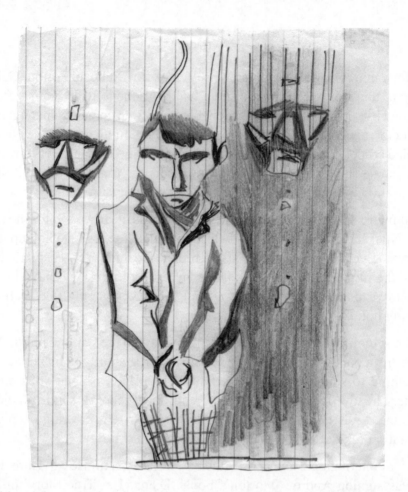

quickly and overlook the cam incident. It is only a civil offence to climb Nelson's Column, so we know we aren't going to jail. The press gathers. Noel is sheepish in front of cameras. Already tipsy with Champers, I feel bullish, a warm fuzzy feeling of success. Mission accomplished.

We had succeeded in climbing the Monument, sure, but like the three ascents before us, we had aided it. Nelson's was still to be freed.

Luckily the red phone would ring again just two years later. The task this time was to:

'Save the Innu'

Canadian fighter planes were destroying the Innus' livelihood as surely as if they had bombed them – the noise of the jets had made hunting in Labrador impossible. Survival International chose Nelson's Column again since it was directly opposite the Canadian Embassy.

210

Nelson free is a job for 'The Champions' – two world climbing champs – modest Simon Nadin, the perhaps less so Jerry Moffatt and little ol' me. We aim to start at first light to avoid the rush hour and the Busies. We plan to solo the same bronze frieze of the Battle of Trafalgar but then this time to climb around the lip totally free.

Trouble is Muppet has left the banner in an East End grocers. We must wait till it opens in the morning, landing us at the column's base slap bang in the middle of rush hour, anything for attention.

…Rope ready, uncoiled in sack, harness loops ready to poke through undone flies, we scurry across and storm up brass mouldings to the cleaners' bolts. Car horns toot. It feels like a carnival. Most were on their way to work while we were off to the best seat in the house.

Below us the Innu elders have arrived. The Chief, in thick national health specs, looks up. His daughters peer from behind their hands, hardly daring to look. So far we've avoided the cops. The aroma of coffee wafts across the square.

The crux would be safe, a 3.5 Camelot between two castellations under the bulge of the pedestal. I place a rattling heel/toe in the castellations beyond, crimp a digit wide flat edge at their base, wide pinch another and set up for the hewn horizon. Cautiously rapid, I slap out for the anticipated sliminess of the smooth granite lip. Surprisingly, this time it is perfectly clean, the swing out ok to hold. Tacky even, the following mantelshelf proves enjoyable this time around. Hook a heel, roll around, over onto it and lying down, surprisingly comfy, pop my head back over the lip like a meerkat: "Hi…*guys*". (6b/c)

The scene is electric. Sunlight bathes the damp stone silver, multicoloured merry makers in their finery each on their own trajectory, nubiles sprawl over a bronze lion.

Simon aids up the column to get a good vantage point for a photo – another special talent of his – and brings us up. I try and follow free.

On the ascent with Noel, belligerent wide slings had slowed progress and I'd taken two rests. It is bizarre climbing, the exact same move over and over: straining the pint-holding muscle to the limit, a fast breeder of a pump threatens to overhaul me, but this time sailing up in a helpful breeze my forearms last until I crawl on to the plinth. *"Explosé"* as the French say. We're treated to a wave of great Innu cheers, audible even over the Trafalgar swell.

Out on the jutting promontory I perform a 'Victory Roll', jumping feet through clasped hands.

Remember the man hanging off the clock in *The 39 Steps*? It's like that up there. We forgo a clamber up the fragile sandstone uniform of the admiral to the cocked hat. The column free inspires a not strictly British group hug. Simon shares out sarnies and pours a hot brew out of his Mum's thermos for us to savour the unrivalled panorama. You can see down The Mall to cheesy Buckingham Palace from here, down Whitehall to the Houses of Parliament.

Survival International had devised a swanky new banner made of net with each individual letter sewn on. Easy to hang, it sat perfectly still in the light breeze blaring out: "Save the Innu" for the cameras.

Back on the deck, the Rozzers congratulate us too: "You were two hours quicker than the last lot" (Joe Simpson et al). However they assure me: "If you do it again you *will* be going to jail". Jerry breaks out that unmistakeable smile and passes the champers. Arms to jelly, I almost drop the bottle.

Members of the tribe embrace us warmly and take photographs of all of us together. Their chief even invites the three of us to come and live with them in their igloos!

Nelson's had been a capital success – £80,000 worth of publicity raised a sufficient enough stink that the Canadian Air Force stopped their flights over Labrador for two months a year. The Innu could hunt again…and of course a free ascent (Yorkshire style) done of the incomparable:

*** *Absolutely Fabulous* E6 6b/c, 1a, 5a. 185ft (Dawes/Moffatt/Nadin 1993)

Afterword

To savour the politically and legally independent City State of London's atmosphere like that was interesting. Once the dust settles, in an office doorway, still holding a victory bottle, I cut a dash as a tramp… how passersby on their way to work look at me or don't – never wanted to wear a monkey suit anyway.

On my first night out on the town in the Big Smoke, when the nightclub shut, my 'sure thing' for the night was nowhere to be seen – where to sleep now? My idea was to walk all night to keep the frost out – that makes you think what it must be like if this was your lot every night. However in Drury Lane, the theatre district, just starting to feel properly chilled, spying a large cardboard box, somehow I instantly sense I'm in luck. How does one know a box is empty from the outside? The box wasn't snoring I suppose. I tap politely. Sure enough it's empty, apart from several clean blankets. I'm soon asleep. In the morning, waking late, I'm extra lucky to have a fine 'breakfast in box' of coffee and pain au chocolat.

Nelson's had gone well but I'd been on other actions that hadn't gone to plan.

The British government had failed to honour pledges to label wood origin, so once again something had to be done. Oli, a mate from UEA and I, discussed the issue during a takeover of the Bursar's Office to denounce the first illegal Iraq War. We happen upon 'Earth First', quite a different deal from Survival International, much less regulated and anarchistic. The forthcoming action was in London where we were to make an attempt to scale the Houses of Parliament.

…We walk back and forth in front of the West Tower, waiting for the time to vault the fence. There was scaffolding on the tower, a stroke of luck since we intended to place a banner there and take photos pronto. However, in black 'Socialist Worker' raincoats on a sunny day, both with matching hunchbacks concealing our equipment, the guys on the CCTV must've been splitting their sides. Once the coast is clear we vault the fence and make for the scaffold. But our timing could not have been more comic. Our assault coincided with a sushi of Japanese tourists catching sight of us. Pointing, giggling loudly, cameras flashing, our goose was cooked. MI5 up to the task this time, we're marched off down Blackrod's Passage to the dungeons.

It is sobering to note that in this the mother of democracy, we had no right to a phone call. The Houses of Parliament being a Royal Palace our actions were punishable by death. Whoops.

I don't regret much. However, along with not accepting the offer of holding the late Wolfgang Gullich's ropes while he was solving what became *Action Directe* and turning down three girls' offer to 'bathe' me, when I had the opportunity to pinch a Houses of Parliament's blanket perhaps I should have.

A Sense of Direction

I got a B in Geography A Level so you might think when planning a week's climbing trip to Colorado, I'd have thought to book a flight to Denver. My fellow traveller, whom Neil Foster to my amusement called 'Dawes' erstwhile sidekick' in *High*, also failed to realise New York is over 1,500 miles from Boulder.

Paul Pritchard and I encourage a juvenile sense of humour in each other. Take a situation on a crowded ferry to Harris. Each of us ordered two fried eggs and chips. No comic potential – until a woman sat down opposite us. This too would not have raised a titter were it not she possessed breasts of dreadnought proportions around which she had to manoeuvre her food in a long, straight-armed arc. All it took was a look down towards the two eggs on my plate, the mildest of grins and the 'Aardvark' had let himself down badly, again.

Like the Pilgrims before us, we set off bravely west. Paul, with no relevant driving experience as such, must share the driving if we've any hope of doing any climbing in Colorado. It's good we've hired an automatic brand new Corolla.

Driving for hours is tiring; soft rock then Bible readings take turns to drone on the radio. We stop regularly for Taco Bell burritos and sodas. At one gas station, we pick up a hitcher.

Like *Withnail,* Paul is hunched over the wheel, "making time…" Cooking engine inadvertently gases us with soporific new car chemicals. An hour later, it shocks me to hear a monotone American drawl rise up from the backseat, even more so when I clock what he says: "You guys…like…the dead?" As casual looking a glance as possible in the rear view mirror fails to reassure, so it seems a good idea to discuss how I do feel about those in the afterlife.

"I don't really know how I feel about them, it is difficult to know surely", I say.

Paul laughs. I look at him reproachfully.

"*Dude*…no duuude...*The Grateful Dead*." The hitcher shakes his head in disbelief.

Overnight, Paul takes the wheel again while I get some shuteye. Comfy dreaming away, suddenly snapped awake by the ***"BBbwwwrrrrrrrghhhh"*** of a huge truck, I flip up, like a sprung 70s executive address book. Through the windshield I catch sight of Paul running down the road chased by a truck. Confused, faced with a junction, he'd stopped, leaving the Corolla in the centre of the turnpike and simply run off. Relaxed enough to sleep again, I'm roused by a strange lurching, this time greeted by the sight of Armco racing at the car and grab the wheel. With both of us asleep the car had decided to bale.

The Rockies slowly rear up out of the plain from a sea of California grass. Two days on and spent, in the middle of the night we arrive in snowy Boulder. Our sense of direction somehow disturbed it was fortunate we've instructions written down for how to get to our doss.

Off Main… pass Dunkin Doughnuts… go second left…then first right, No 24.

Hmm…but the road we arrive at only has 20 houses. We wonder where the other four houses have gone. We try again. End up in the same place. We experiment with the same route for almost an hour with the same results. It's bitterly cold.

"Let's just stop Paul, we can put all our clothes on, if we keep the engine running we'll be ok."

We pull into a parking lot. Paul winds the window down to ask a man something – writing this, I can see Paul's smiley face again now, imagine how it must've changed… when the man pulls a knife and pokes it through the window. Paul ducks into the footwell, darting for the window button, door lock clicks shut, open, shut, open. I gas it hard but the automatic just burbles, "Sshh… ssh… sh…" Our new acquaintance calling us: "Honkies, honkies" attempts to climb through the narrowing aperture of the window. We get away.

Later, Paul has a brainwave. It's clear, there are two – yes of course – *two* Dunkin' Doughnuts on Main Street. A possibility we scarcely could have foreseen. We continue further along Main and there it is; our directions transformed by our new orientation.

'Crusher', a loose desert sandstone specialist, shows us to our big clean beds. We're lucky not to be still out there frozen in celluloid, lost like in the movie '*Slackers*'.

Once settled in, we track down Derek Hersey. Early 1983, new to the Peak, keen to share my enthusiasms, 'desperate' Derek had been one of the few to bother to see past my public school brashness. I've still a soft spot for 'Chesters', 'Plant Pot' and all the other hardmen who lived in the woodshed, for introducing me to the richer tones of British climbing. Passing years make folk more precious. Derek was wonderful and unchanged, attentive and genial as ever. Derek would soon be dead though. While soloing the *Steck/Salathé* he'd fallen. I noticed this morning that I'd lost my favourite drawings. All life fades like pencil drawings in the end anyway, but the love for them remains.

Prior to our trip, lager research in the UEA student union bar debating Development Studies had me weigh in at an impressive 11 stone 2 pounds. I perfectly work and by the skin of my teeth 'send' the tasty Eldo testpiece *Rainbow Wall* 5.13a. I can't remember what Paul did but at least I got a climb in on the trip.

Coincidentally we'd bumped into our feral scientist compadre Crispin Waddy[48] out there. Our surprise at how this possibly could of happened, was greeted with a signature Brando-esque: "Ummm…" Crispin once spilt

[48] A great exponent of the deep-water solo, discoverer, pioneer of Chile's Cochimo Valley and developer of Strone Ulladale who used his knowledge of rock's curious twist and turns to design fantastic climbing walls – Livingstone.

a tin of sardines into my new van's air conditioning, thinking nothing of it. Another time, me courting a boil on my bum, sitting on my foot to avoid exploding it, he kicked my foot out from under me. What a bastard! Once, walking in to a cliff in Pembroke, an officer in an army truck full of soldiers, asked us for directions. Crispin told him to take a right and left, after that there was a right apparently and then another left I noticed. By now I had an idea where this was going but the squaddies hadn't quite. Crispin repeated the directions again, a little more jauntily: "You go left…right…left… right…left …right…You'll soon be there!"

We all had a grand time together for a couple of days. I did grinds in our dear Corolla skateboard along the lip of the packed earth banking of the new Morrison by-pass. We escaped just in time up the twists to Red Rocks, blue lights flashing in the valley below.

Back in New York, our Corolla, now not so new, having already had a more than full life, smelt rich and although subtly dented and louder than standard, miraculously attracted no costly attention when we handed it back. Celebrating, Paul and I go to CBGB's drag night but leaving too late to find a place to stay, we sleep on the subway. In the morning predictably, we end up rushing for the plane. Lost down a steamy deserted Manhattan side street, incongruous Alpiniste rucksacks on our backs, it slowly dawns on us we're not alone. From behind brushed metal doors, some locals slip in behind us. Thankfully just then a cop car wallows into the alley and we jog alongside our escort until we're back where they overdo the cinnamon in the latte. Totally knackered from our holiday, dirty but happy, we slump in the 747 draining our miniatures.

Face Mecca

On the couch a fit of keen inspires a climb on Cloggy. On reaching the base of the crag, eyes tilt to see *Face Mecca* arc out from *Great Wall* belay into the steepest part of the shield. This phenomenal Nick Dixon route, companion to *The Indian Face* on the Great Wall of the East Buttress, had remained untried and unrepeated since 1989; one of a handful of British climbs graded E9 6c.

Slightly steeper, rearing up more abruptly than its neighbour, it's only because gear above the *Great Wall* belay is said to stop you hitting the floor that I even entertain it. There is said to be no gear of note on the climb itself apart from a tiny pin, 60ft out, in half an inch. Even with pro 10ft up *Great Wall* 2nd pitch you'll face an 180ft fall. Unfit, it was wise to practise the 7c+ climbing on abseil. An hour or so on the face had it feel ok.

Knots tied small, rubber squeaking nicely, two quickies and a small screwgate are on board for the 100ft pitch. Scooty on the stance, mulling – *first not too steep, beautiful moves on beautiful holds* – chalking up I blow smoothly into my palms…

…A sub-marginal Rock 1 I've managed to find on abseil, 20ft out in the initial section, is nothing an aid climber could rely on, though it does encourage me to head on to the pin at the overlap, a potential bail out. Rusty, once I've run 50ft out it becomes clear that this rehearse and ramble up approach is weak and that this route is complex, tricky and terrifyingly strenuous.

Composure wobbling like a water drop in deep space, the decision to climb down is a good one, but Rock 1 half-biting is now 30ft down the face, the safety of the stance 20ft below that. Down climbing, approaching the piece from the left, finally almost level, pulling two tiny flakes together, the right hand crimp snaps impressively. The '*Have I fallen off?*' shock-rush gives me the sensation I've fallen through my feet. Shard tinkles down the face as the action of still crimping the remaining flake pulls me off. As if the hold is red hot, body flinches, letting go completely I tip unavoidably backwards. Feet somehow still on, I crumple still edging on a slanting crease, allowing a slower fall to arc onto the terrible nut. See it start to pivot in the rhyolite, aware that if it snaps or strips, a massive tumble is let loose.

Drop hanging, afraid to speak, mouth mouths: "*Down…*"

Treading smoothly so my weight is taken by the rock, I ready myself to sprint headfirst to escape the first bite of the meat grinder by jumping the *Midsummer's* ramp and also scan the surface so I might grab a hold to avert such a fall. At the belay I slip my leg into the thick tangle of ropes to mash myself immediately to the belay.

Half an hour later the climb regains my attention. I go again. Flash pump gone, way ahead more swift to track, by the first 6c undercuts cleanly the overlap arrives without incident. Pin clipped, poor wire placed, you can gaze out left to the crux and at a sucker rest just before it. It's this that feels like the next place to go. Body not recovering enough, it moves left too soon, my mind is tripping itself up.

Pulled into the crux by mixed enthusiasm, the span to the top is somehow too far. Suddenly the section seems to have stretched, or have I shrunk? In the barrel of a human cannon, I need to work out what the hell *is* going on. Pulling harder, persisting, tiring further, to my horror, it finally twigs. Left foot is too low. Just above it is the rim of the crucial dish. Now, the only way up is to reboot the move: to peddle smears in an untried sequence off poor underclings. Starting this, noticing doubt encroach on hope, I detect I'm preparing to fall; and ludicrous, hear the word "*Take...*" judder cheep in my skull.

Feeling for it, finally foot seems to have found the correct dish. Shaking the free right hand mid-move, to drain some lactic acid away, I thumb a bump to reduce the demand on my left hand, if just for an instant. My body shapes up to best hit the top knowing the move is right on my present limit. I sense my grasp of the final hold grow in my mind while at the very same time feel the strength to hit it with my body diminish. Unseen these two graphs align triggering a snatch but fingers catch at an awkward angle. I'm forced to shuffle again to recognise where the best spot on the hold is. Tentative, feet fast, I suck out my waist to hit a shape to hang not pull …and as body goes back in, jab at full stretch – any possibility to try harder, or again, gone.

Got it.

One hundred feet out, heel pressed to the back of a flat ledge, the *easy* mantel, arms bombed, is suddenly treacherously sketchy.

Up, all in, left by the climbing facing out, it feels incredible on that diving board ledge, that the concavity below is slowly being eaten away by lichen.

IV

A Real Buzz

Luckily the Cambridge Audio CD player from Richer Sounds had come with a promotional lollipop.

The van sets off down the hill, but on the windscreen, motionless, is a bee. Before wind-speed builds up to spill the bee to the mercy of road and tyre, I slow the van and stop. A car impatient behind, my bank card is already out of its holster. I rush out and lift the creature off into my hand.

By licking the lollipop – red like the van – and by dripping the syrup into the hollow of my left hands anatomical snuff box, the bee placed alongside it can start to feed. Her mouth is extraordinarily thin and long, like a straw.

We go around town and shop a little, I even take her to The Forum for a coffee. By now she is showing signs of a lively character. To attempt to put her at her ease, I stroke her thick fur as she feeds, but instead clumsily get syrup on her wing at which point a short sharp head movement points back up at me.

I watch as she works on the task of renewing her wing. Half an hour of meticulous cleaning with no discernible waste of effort, makes her look like a knowing miniature helicopter able to repair itself.

What had seemed like an abrupt reproach after my clumsiness with the syrup is now forgotten. Bee turns its head, this time a full 270° – show off – then tilts her head, and then again, as if to say: *"Do you understand what I mean…?"*

My companion's gesticulations so precise, seemingly deliberate, make her appear not just sane, purposeful and certainly skilled, but generous of spirit. I have come to love this beady-eyed bee. She seems to say thank you and, slipping out of my cavernous hand, is gone.

Little Wing

Raud O'Brien was recounting his circumnavigation of the five southern capes in winter single-handed. He went on: "Snapped awake, floating in air…looking down at my bunk…in that instant I knew *Little Wing* had come off the top of a huge wave. What I didn't know was the angle of the boat, how it'd hit the water. Off a crest she could be at any angle, could even *pitch pall*…go in mast first".

Little Wing is a 36 foot steel ketch Raud designed and built himself. He'd secured a spare mast to the deck, but refused to fit life raft or GPS. We met at the Blue Mountains Film Festival when he was promoting his book 'Little Wing' and I was giving a talk. We warmed to each other straight off. He invited me to stay with him in Palm Beach.

Before visiting Raud in Sydney, I take a trip to 'Earthcore', a rave up north on the Murray River.

Japanese hotties in towering platforms and huge silver flares crouch in the back of *Mad Max* pickups, scraggy sounds, big Eucalyptus. It's hot. I swim across the river. Hand on mouth, "Woo, woo …woo" I tear naked along the far bank, Red Indian brave. A tussle with the stiff current on the way back raises an aussie chuckle from the shore and a wry, "Look out for the *Salties*!"[49].

In the morning, fully awake but disassociated, looking up, lying in the dust of a burnt out gumtree it feels like I'm a giant in a miniature cathedral. Fire has left four elegant arches in the hollowed tree. No more than curious of it, I watch a large orange and yellow beetle go up and down munching skin from wrist like a diligent cricket groundsman mowing.

A rum new acquaintance seeing me in the tree laughs heartily. I relate some unlikely experiences, he belly laughs again but I'm plugged into *the field* baby. Kookaburra laugh precisely on time to back me up. Acquaintance still doubtful I clasp my ear to the sky, as if to say: "Listen and learn fucko". Birds' mock laughter breaks out on cue again.

Back on Palm Beach, in need of somewhere to pull myself together, fortunately Raud's house stands out. A large square woodshed cuts a feral dash amongst the exclamation marks of surrounding condos. The O'Briens

---

[49] Big seawater crocs.

225

were one of the first families to settle there in the 50s. Raud opens a door in a wall and I'm safe again.

His cabin is awash with books. Just to get to the loo requires a car dealer's forecourt shuffle, backing up into an alley of novels, engineering books and maps. There is hardly room for a single person so it's best I stay on the hilltop with his friend Jackie. Jackie had been an estate agent but decided to quit that lucrative job and care for the elderly instead. She had an open bungalow high above the bay where she took care of all kinds of creatures, pets, local animals and now a drowsy little man from Sheffield.

Raud is a little at sea when he is not at sea. He loves to run about, he says it stops him from wobbling on land. In the afternoon we get into a routine of sprinting downhill to the store, near where *Home and Away* is shot. We'd buy a couple of cold ones, spark a doobie and watch a giant sun sink into the sea.

Down to the bay wound a wild path through the bush to a comfy perch on which to look out to sea and recover. On Barranjoey headland at the edge of the ocean was a smashing little crag that eventually gave a fantastic long no-hands expedition. On Palm Beach a sandstone boulder gave some sweet, high solos.

One evening as dusk fell, lettuce spinner out of the cupboard, Raud's cheerful head juts around the kitchen door. He announces a sail would do the boat good.

It would be my first experience of sailing, except for a tame family outing on the Solent with family friends and a wild effort on a closed Rutland Water when my school pal Tim Stratton and I capsized a Hobbie 18.

There was just enough time to get out to the ocean before dark, sufficient diesel to reach the wind but not enough to run the engine once out on the ocean. To be honest Raud and I were a bit worse for wear, giggling way too much to put to sea.

Raud deep in thought, Johnny oblivious…finally the engine starts… propeller in gear, steel ketch immediately accelerates away from the jetty. From below Raud asks: "Do you have the tiller?" then "If not…could you take it?" Sprinting the length of the boat, almost running straight over the stern, etched in my mind's eye as I find the tiller tied down cobbled together from motley climbing ropes, is the sight of Raud's Swiss banker

226

neighbour's pristine 19th century mahogany steamer, growing bigger, directly in the way of *Little Wing's* steel hull. As Raud will soon explain: "a long rope *is* essential to manual steer engaged elsewhere up the boat" – but it is tied around the tiller to avoid flaying the freshly painted deck in a long series of wind/salt tightened knots. Clove hitch - clove hitch, reef... clove...hitch...da...da...da. Finally tiller turns, bow bite rightwards and I can look up. In fading evening light, the japanned mahogany steamer's panels look almost maroon...and how smooth to the touch!

Out in the Sydney shipping lanes the water proves choppier than expected, unfortunately the wind weaker. What wind there is, is diagonal and on shore. Raud isn't feeling well. By the time he was 12 he'd already done four Sydney to Hobart races, during which family life would continue as usual aboard but today he is seasick, worse, relegated to a muffled sailing coach below deck.

I see some lights brightening ahead of us in the gloom: "Raud, what does a red light turning to green mean mate?"

He tells me they're the lights of a container vessel. I'm informed it cannot avoid us. It is up to me to miss it.

"Go to port", he answers.
"Which way is that?"
"My left."
"Which way are you facing Raud..?"
" Urggghhhhhh"', Raud clarifies into his bucket.

The hand on the tiller has to be expert to keep momentum, though with current, wind and pitch ajangle, just whether the cliffs are getting closer or not is difficult to fathom. The ships in the lanes are not always visible either. This, the fading light and the churning brine give me the fear. Not a short go for it climbing crux fear, balmed with brief precision, but a long traffic queue "Did I turn the chip pan off or not?"

Once night fell, fear's complexion changed again. Couldn't see the coast any more, just did the best I could, using eyes, ears and *ummm...* to best get us through.

Two hours later all is well, sea calm and rhythmic, the wind keen and steady. It's a great privilege; she's been around the five southern capes cheating icebergs off Antarctica, accompanied storm petrels days from land skimming the sea for ground effect, fallen down waves the size of hotels.

I scan the waves, surfing the boat. Most waves go easily under but occasionally a big one wells up so dramatically that even if I do bend my knees fully feet still come completely off the top of the cabin deck as the boat draws away.

Snoring below, Raud's competence helps me out as *Little Wing* reassures me with the care dreamt into her, catching wind clean, cutting waves sweetly. Raud's ingenious self-steer runs no more than 15° off true; predictable enough to help me anticipate where she will land. I haven't even told you about the swift water lapping musically as I lay contentedly on deck, or that it was a full moon.

LA LA Land

I have no idea who you are or where you were when Twentieth Century Fox famously ran out of copyright. Fed up dodging emotional mines that litter my life inexplicably, I was in the desert, in the City of Angels looking for psychological solace.

I'd done well for myself in many ways, yet often still felt terrible.

After the kids from next door had left with Johnny Dawes the kitten, I reopened *New Primal Scream* by Arthur Janov and choked back the woodburner. I learnt how Primal therapy had helped John Lennon with his demons, I hoped it could help me. In Janov's theory of neurosis and anecdote lay a hope that my unexplained unhappiness had roots I could unearth; by honest discussion, feeling one's emotional back catalogue neurosis could heal.

…5am, December 29th 1999, I rollerblade snaking carelessly towards the ocean down a silent Wilshire Boulevard. *The Braille Trail* has led me here. Not only the past assaults me but the present too. Bought prematurely, I'm stranded living in the faded velour of a Mk 1 Honda Civic in the suburban back streets of Venice.

I came to Los Angeles with the promise of a coaching job at the climbing wall but it didn't exist so neither would the money to finish therapy. Just $22 dollars left, I'm getting about on a skinny emergency tyre. It is liable to get me pulled over, which is serious as I've no insurance. Even when it's parked there is a problem – living in a car in California is illegal. Last night in Santa Monica, before settling down under my disguise of boxes on the back seat, I'd been asked for my documents by a cop. I had no option but to say I had none and that, "If you want to ruin my chances of getting on my feet in the USA then now's your opportunity…" Somehow, like Obi-Wan hypnotizing a droid saying, "There's nothing to see here, move along", the trooper glazes over, loses interest and rides off.

It's another sunny day. Off alcohol, pot, anything that keeps me emotionally defended, tears skew my vision. Overcome, worried about money, finally I find a public phone that does work and call an English acquaintance. It was the eve of a new millennium and I had nowhere to go to celebrate. So quickly is Matt on the line I hope my voice doesn't crack. Matt works at

James Cameron's *Digital Domain*, he modelled the passengers on the deck of the Titanic seen in the long shots from the lifeboats. He tells me he and his artistic director girlfriend are off to a party in Malibu, says he'll SMS me later when he knows what is going on.

Matt picks me up in his Plymouth muscle car. Soon I'm quaffing vintage bubbly from a flute. To suddenly be at the party of the man who wrote *The Simpsons'* theme tune was quite a turn around. Before the other guests arrive, we watch Mike Leigh's *Topsy Turvy*. Danny Elfman, our host, had written the score, so had a first print of the final cut.

Sleek women, polite conversation, the last thing I wanted to do was *act out*. I'm just too fragile. The difference is I notice when I'm fearful now. Come "Auld lang syne…" Clinton grins wide on screen, they laugh as if Mickey Mouse had turned up.

Dawn is spectacular. Danny takes us sea kayaking, for me it's the first time. Scooting through small channels in the erratic salty surf sees me enter the new millennium, for the time being with no bugs on me.

Every morning now I take to swimming early in the ocean and in the evening go to yoga, fortunately contributions only.

I have managed to get a job out of the LA Times delivering packages around the metropolis. From 8 a.m. to 7p.m., from San Fernando Valley to Huntingdon Beach, finding the way with the Thomas Guide, I drop at Sony Studios in Culver City, HBO in Santa Monica for *Curb Your Enthusiasm*, Warner Brothers in the valley and to private individuals including Faye Dunaway (her house was exquisite and subtle), Steven Spielberg (big and scary gates) and to a certain *Buffy the Vampire Slayer* office.

One day I have a puncture in Compton where the riots kicked off. A homie scarily pulls out a wrench but kindly uses it to undo a wheel for me. I enjoy chasing blondes in Boxsters down the hairpins of Coldwater Canyon and after a hot smoggy shift sipping strawberry smoothies down by the beach even more. Refreshed, I relax playing chess on the boardwalk, getting my arse kicked by serious Russians.

More often than one would expect, one catches sight of well-known faces out on the road. A way of changing direction on Sunset is to use the fore-court of a plush hotel. Generic 'Radio…radio on', me puffing on an organic

American Spirit, I see Sly burst from a limo. No dry cleaning or ironing in evidence on my side, I toot the horn and wave from my steaming heap. *Rocky* in a silver suit disappears into another part of his lifestyle cocoon. He always tipped well I was told, always time for the little guy. It was a shame there was no opportunity for us to remember Wolfgang Güllich together, his *Cliffhanger* double.

One day in the valley, someone I realize immediately is familiar says he recognizes me. He can't work out where from but it dawns on me he's off *Starsky and Hutch*. It's Huggy Bear! I detest menthol cigarettes but share his just to hang out. He is easy to get on with. We chat about jazz, which he plays now, climbing and the UK. Fresh with the *'word on the street'*, a Friday, I put in my worksheet and retire to prepare organic salad from Trader Joe's out of the kitchen/trunk of my car on a pine chopping board I'd found and dress it with lemons scrumped off a tree in Venice. It is good to be short sometimes; Jack Kornfield's *A Path with Heart* keeps me company on the backseat.

Though I lack the cash to do much primal therapy I scrape enough together for a visit to a *Treager* expert. My shoulder's rotator cuff is still damaged; the legacy of doing *Master's Edge* right hand only, to avoid hurting my left wrist, the main reason I didn't climb much in the 90s. Dressed in a baby blue tracksuit, a plump woman inadvertently releases two terriers from her door that sprint down the garden path and bite my legs. I'm not sure if that is a part of the treatment. I'd recently read acupuncture was discovered when some people struck by arrows actually got better. I hand her $25, the lowest fee of anyone I'd been to. She's got to go shopping, she tells me, and without delay lays me face down on her kitchen table, lifts the offending arm up and drops it. It doesn't fall straight away. She says, "You don't know how to relax…Imagine it's a dead fish."

Step by step she reintroduces me to my body as she bends me unconventionally on the table. She locates 27 pressure points for shoulder muscles, shutting down each in turn. I lift the arm, let it fall easily and walk happily away, a two-and-a-half year injury fixed for peanuts.

At a climbing wall I bump into one of the 'Stone Masters'. John Long, beefcake 70s climbing legend, is a fabulous storyteller and practises healing using a therapy called 'Somatic Experiencing'. It works by placing your attention close to bodily tension, letting the resulting vibration release stored trauma.

I continue to go to the Primal Institute when I can afford it. The full primal process is confidential, definitely useful, but I'll run the risk of sharing a few things. We practise saying what we really feel, use 'I' not 'You'. I listen to how others experience me; fearful, unsure, judgemental, defensive, funny, caring, whatever it actually is. Clearly the habit of guessing what others think, a mainstay of my adolescent survival efforts and beyond, no longer worked, if it ever did. What to someone else might be obvious – that we don't know what others are thinking – is made clear simply by asking them. Imagined and actual never matched.

One prescription involved me carrying a teddy bear around everywhere. One sneering woman on the bus openly laughed as I got on. One Friday, last chance to get out money for the weekend, I was still letting tears flow after a session. At the till, when the bank clerk staring straight at me greets me with a stock: "How are you today?" I can finally break into a full belly laugh. It *was* good to feel more, not care what others thought *about* me.

I slowly grew to be less defensive, less judging, more caring. Thanks everyone for helping me. Amongst the fragility of being open, I found myself getting more confident and some of that unmistakable *you can do anything in America* started to shine through.

As Matt buys plane tickets online, I mooch about the car park. An enthusiastic woman had set up a telescope amongst the jeeps and muscle cars pixel workers like. She first trains the interplanetary lens, the size of a papoose, on Saturn, the '50s pin-up. I look at my favourite heavenly body, Jupiter's moon Io, send out thousand mile flames. Then we gaze at our sombre moon, craters picked out distinct by oblique rays, imagination could place you right there, feet lightly in the dust – and just one shadow, no conspiracy.

We hook up with Matt's brilliant Brit friend Colin, at his pre-visualisation company, PLF, *Pixel Liberation Front*. To save money PLF maps out in advance where super expensive rented cameras will track, to get shots as quickly as possible. Time to kill, I construct a cone on cutting edge CGI package *Houdini*, make the sun move around it, a shadow track behind it. Early evening, in Matt's hot gruff Plymouth, we drive to Colin's birthday party at a zany restaurant at LA city airport. To my horror, multitudes are on the menu; ants and locusts. Wish I'd known then what I learnt later about karma. Afterwards, up into the hills to hang out in a dark bar where they still sell Watney's Red Barrel. The crisp banter is great fun; a special effects Oscar winner's thoughts, a cute musician's and so on's reflections, I don't bother to second guess any more and just enjoy.

Mandatory in LA as well as being in therapy is writing a film script! Mine was about 'The Vegetable Car'. A child's design rescues not only the family home from repossession but the world from ecological disaster! Movie plot clarified, I come down to earth again for a coffee, Wilshire and 3^{rd,} Santa Monica, but instead meet one of LA's wild cards. (The madman on the bus again picks me out.)

"𝔒ne of my reincarnations was '𝔖parhawk of 𝔅elgorad', you see 𝔍'm a vampire living out my search for my spirit wife." The man tells me by way of an introduction… learning he lives in a lean-to amongst bushes on the unstable cliff top… 30 minutes before he'd been told by his *brown haired witch wife*… who now lies with her throat cut underneath his hovel… he was to meet her tonight, to suffer to join with her; to meld as 𝔖atan and 𝔖atanessa.

I decide to start writing on Abbott Kinney instead. I roller-blade there with sad beautiful 'Chemical Brothers' on, but another shade of the greasy computer hard-drive that is LA shows itself; a strange experience reminding me how 'the other' could still upset me. How could I be and be separate? Here are the notes I wrote then to remember the encounter.

… A much helloed elderly man in a wheelchair talks for an hour.
He told me about mahogany steamers on the Thames, riding his tricycle around Blenheim Palace, the servant he'd ordered then to oil his chain: "almost certainly dead now", he observes.

"I knew the Whitneys and Astors", he says.
In Sergeant's portrait of Nancy Astor he sees his own mother.

"No family hand me downs for me. The power of my Wharton College doctorate was what got me my positions, any one of 31 choices open for two years."

He is a man of structured knowledge, expansive, inflexible, his power he projects through his eyes, and by jerks and pointing.

"…my children were no problem, they were fun, but my wife was killed in a plane crash in Greece in '68. I threw a plate at the window at 'the meeting', a bullet-proof window, big finance; Lockheed pulled out of the $900m monorail deal, a bad year for them."

"As 23rd Prince of Rome I stood by Martin Luther King; lost my teeth because of it."

Then, he explained how:

"The Hursts relayed the position of 'The Lusitania' to the Germans every quarter of an hour, the wealthy on board a sacrifice to fuel The LA Times reader's anger, effectively declaring war in 1914 before the president.
All planned from within the walled community, motivated by the $700m war bond."

He was like a huge compacted snake, his time in the sun fading. It was as if he was a larger creature pumped into a tiny human body, a worldly God. His simple acceptance of his place, what he is, rocks my beliefs. Momentarily it's as if my beliefs have become irrelevant to my experience.

Only by saying: "I cannot say I like you" do I reclaim composure.

Already rolling in his perambulator he leaves me with a physically sinister shake of the hand: the same hand that was there: "when he met Hitler", the hand that "doesn't like Africa".

Giving me an instant knot in my stomach, he says: "I enjoyed our conversation".

When I was little I'd insist: "Keep it separate" when Mum served a meal with one food touching another. Where was me? Where was the other?

I've business with Barking Pumpkins next day. I'd sent Frank Zappa's record company a VHS seeking permission to use 'Yo Mama' off live album 'Sheik Yerbouti' for the DVD of Stone Monkey. 'Yo Mama' accompanied the cut of *The Quarryman* groove. With the music from claymation 'Nightschool', 'G Spot Tornado' and 'Peaches in Regalia' it's one of my very favourites. It was interesting to learn Frank thought it was one of his best solos.

…waiting in a diner in Hollywood for late Frank's wife Gail to arrive, I don't know what she looks like but I needn't have worried. Big silvery hair, massive frizzy white dog in tow, we're soon winding our way up to Mount Olympus in a blanche Mercedes V12.

She has an extensive tea cupboard. Over Jasmine tea she tells me a story about a hobo that slept in the garage one night. Frank, too soft to kick him out, allowed him to stay for months. She calmly gives me permission to use the solo – the first time Frank's music had been released for inclusion in another's work. The Zappas all liked *Stone Monkey*, Mrs Zappa paying me a compliment: "There are not many people in the world like you and Frank".

Downstairs, Dweezil Zappa is working on music for *The Grinch* in a small cabin he's built in a corner of Frank's studio. Guitars on their haunches face the door, expectantly? I pinch myself, sat at Frank's mixing desk, imagining 'Watermelons in Easter Hay' being mixed. Bakelite on the knobs is almost all gone; Zappa's voracious attention to detail and prolific output has revealed the metal bones of the mixing desk.

In the early hours Gail takes me back to the coast. On impulse, I ask Gail if she ever thinks Frank is still around. I swear at that very moment the rear windows wound down. We look at each other, neither of us having touched a switch.

Quiet once more, walking in past the Gardenias I ponder Gail's offer to do the choreography for Frank's final project – 'Civilization Phase Three'. But a line in time approaches fast, a date on an air ticket, before I know it I'm back in cold damp England.

Harrison Ford

I got a call this morning. On the line was a London based Rochdale born sculptor John Frankland, whose works, *"You can't touch this!"* and *"What are you looking at..?"* had been displayed at the Saatchi Gallery.

"We want you to climb on a boulder" he said.
"Where is it?" I ask.
"It's down in Portland…at the moment", he replies.
"At the moment..?"

We struck a deal. I was to be the 'animator of the rock's choreography'. Over a week the 70-tonne rock made its way at 15mph from Dorset to Warwickshire, to the front lawns of Compton Verney, a striking country house set in an 18th century landscape by Capability Brown.

Compton Verney's grounds make an immediate impression as you round the gates when one is greeted by a parade of Giant Redwood. Silver Mi16 hot hatch crunches up the gravel, slowly rolls over a glorious bridge of Cotswold stone. There it is – like a big box that has been sat on, one side overhung, one a slab. Was it just a pose, this juxtapose of big pebble with

Compton Verney is a remarkably grand spot to start one's climbing. Alex and I celebrate his first climb. Photo: John Frankland.

Georgian house and garden? No. One had to admit it, on first sight, it had a certain tearaway beauty to the eye and while it is my least favourite rock type, the *lager* of the kinaesthetic world, this rhombic chunk of limestone clearly had potential to throw shapes.

John, tall, softly spoken but a little punchy too, remembers me as aggressive the first time we talked on the phone. Apparently I'd honoured him with a long rant on the evils of chipping, complete with a cautionary tale about the deepening melancholy of the instigator of a quarry near Matlock who saw his ambition slowly consume a whole hill, eventually driving him to take his own life.

Rock is a universal template with which we can rejig ourselves back into true like a flick of a creased, damp sheet. Cliffs are a unique library of kinaesthetic phrases, having the same creative authorship as we do. To destroy the fine detail of the rock's surface is like finding a lost Mozart piece and putting a match to it.

I'd suffered at the hands of chisellers, you appreciate. *Perplexity* at Millstone lost an unlikely V7 Greek dancing sequence up a groove. *Warmlove* was kindly repaired by Andy Barker before I'd heard about it. Incomprehensibly, six climbs were chipped after my first ascent. But here was I taking the money and running, right up this quarried block with my sticky trainers.

The molested slab proves interesting no hands – that means no knees or elbows either. After that, a big smooth foothold at the slab's foot inspires a move, a rough hub for a horizontal 360° spin. The start and finish is identical apart from a new glee at the end.

Blue sky, I sit contented on pristine lawn and imagine hopping up the boulder.

…Look for the angle to best buoy the boot as it lands. Wait for the sense of how knee and body will *Tetris* up above to do this. Wait patiently, listening for that shape to grow and a sense of where to prime a leap to hit this imagined apparition slowly gels…then motion will emerge naturally. A relaxed mind can watch and wonder at the giddy flavour of a …h…O..p.

Far apart, each hop must load up enough residual wobble for the next. Slowly this 'rattling chain' wobbles less, more closely mimicking the 'snaking rope' of easier movement that will eventually characterise the actual hops. Sideways motion imagination had so far failed to discover in my leg was thereby coaxed to emerge, seemingly miraculously, from a to and fro of wheeling arms and a time soothing counterbalance of the fallow leg.

I hop up John's boulder, landing on top as if magnetized to a stop like a commissioned figurine. Hopping for a climber may appear an evolutionary dead end but it feels very good and the boulder suddenly feels like an old friend.

"You're like ...Harrison Ford...you're like Harrison Ford, youuu are!"

A huge fleshy head stares up at me, somehow fixed with an even bigger grin. The animator of this smile is my height with an awkward gait and an intonation that tells me this profound enthusiasm comes from a young man with Down's.

"I...I...want to climb the mOWWNTin toooooo Johnny", he insists. Somehow he knows my name already.

I remember how thrilling my first climb had been; now Alex was going to have a go at his. To this day I can remember the whole encounter perfectly, which is rare for me.

Communication with him was very direct. I literally impress upon him how to use the holds by pushing down on his foot or pressing his hand. His main skill is to try like mad though his approach to climbing is very all at once, continuous and super slow. It is as if while all his will pulls him up, an extra contrary amount he somehow summons up to pull the other way, to ensure the climb will indeed be a mission fit for him. Before long his body is sweating and vibrating.

A foot per minute we traverse the face together so by now sweat coats holds he lays across and over so he cannot see them or move. My face is right next to his, almost in his head, manic, maniacal to get through to him. He pants like a steam train the inhabitants of the big house behind might have travelled to London on.

"Go for it."
"Go for it!"
"Go on Alex, lift your leg…"
"Yes, that's your leg!"
"GO ON, lift it!"

Up it goes…not properly on but helping some… enough for a fat hand to wipe the top of the boulder. Tense muscles, still doing the 'push me pull you thing' he appears about to explode like a party balloon. He swims over the top, epitome of a 'gritstone udger'. The pressure he has built up comes rushing out in an enormous smile. He's bloody done it.

Not knowing if he'll wander off over the edge of the block, I hold his hand. This encourages him to grab me. Alex gives me a huge hug. My hands rest on his sweaty back, he smells a touch unusual. Looking down at his face I don't think I've seen anyone look so happy. He groans – a contented being. He continues to hold me. It may have looked to an onlooker that I was embarrassed but what was really going on was that I just didn't know how to hug at this level. It is only once I finally let go of my reserve that he finally gives me the big grin again and lets me go.

This is what mountaineering is all about…and what a view too.

Next day he comes back, but this time he's not alone. Alex has brought his girlfriend to meet me. He stands proudly before her (between us). I feel part of the tribe now and beam back, grateful for the big love.

The Angels' Share

When brandy is made, the liquor that escapes through the ceiling is known as 'The Angels' Share'. The greater their share, the finer the brandy is said to be.

To climb new climbs was always a special treat. There is nothing quite like solving how to climb a natural feature from scratch. My favourites have always been the ones that seem impossible on first acquaintance.

When I visited Black Rocks, I often stared down a beautiful, unclimbed steep bowed slab, wishing the natty crease in its super-rounded top was good enough to be used.

Traversing below the slab with that crease is a fabulous E6 climb I'd done the first repeat of on sight called *Velvet Silence*. It's shallower angled than the slab. Even with an arête to use to apply traction it's still tricky, involving a signature move where a kick of the foot simultaneously counterbalances your hand as it swoops out to the arête: horrifying unless you relax and really let go.

Both lines start over a bulge with an ancient gutter carved into it that threatens to flip you over if you slip off the unclimbed, pure friction ramp above. On first acquaintance on a top rope, primed 25ft above hard path, in a posture no more physical than sitting stroking a cat, I could almost have wept that the move was not quite there.

Using ruler and clock, moves can appear impossible, but momentum is interesting stuff – it can even make unusable features into holds. When you can weigh less, move using holds you are no longer on, fashion the grip you need purely from motion, odd things happen. A wall of death rider relies on the horizontal even while on the vertical since without it he would not be where he is. On the rope, this move to the crease and beyond was like that: "*Impossible but only just*".

I'd mused for days now on how to move from this position, where if I moved at all I simply fell off. At the café, in bed, on the bus, the momentum and my mind's grasp of it played around. Then looking at a bird fly by… with my mind no longer on it, I knew all of a sudden I'd just done it in my mind, if strangely not how, it was like an email with lost content.

Silence is not empty. A silence at Black Rocks is entirely different to that at Burbage South. Black Rocks calls for a velvet stroke, not a smack on

The last move of the Burbage South project Wizard Ridge. Though it is a double dyno it is the easiest move on it. The crux hold lower down you use in 7 ways. Nail holds, blind moves and extreme flexibility required. Photo: Stephan Denys.

leather or featherlight silk. Detail free velvet musing continued, finally the internal swoosh of the move emerged. The penny dropped, spun...strangely rolled uphill.

You fall off and move up at the same time...!

I'd never thought a fall could provide the impetus for a move.

Back at the crag, on a rope, below the move in hard copy, the crease does not look so far away now. The move is so turbulent all one can do is listen out: falling slowly away from the slab a very fast but gentle inward pressure on the subtlest of dimples lifts my body so smear can just be weighted, meaning a mere half second later the stone will be in a different place – quelling the urge to press too much or give up and fall outwards, a kind of rising flop done quickly allows tips to momentarily tease the start of the crease.

Sitting comfortably on the best of sofas, the real effort is invisible but, I might add, this single move has taken an hour to percolate out. Here and there are inscrutable brush marks: nature's calligraphy of choreography. I sit up and try again. Once ready my body falls away, jabs, fades and scampers like a wave landing on a beach. I sit on top of the gorgeous great boulder looking down a blank featureless bow of green sandstone. The feeling for the move already starts to fade in my body. My mind cannot, should not, document any detail. At the speed of brandy flavour leaving my mind, I sense the move slowly evaporating into the trees.

Blow grit dust chalk off, away with the rope, towel, toothbrush. The walk down loads the 25ft fall.

On a rope the move could breathe without fear.

As before on first ascents what is to come runs through. Trust is not, mistrust is not. Stood in the runnel there's still a vague but stable sense of my centre of gravity's bespoke whoosh at the crux.

...Moves low down remain in a useful subtle feinting vibration placing meticulously for the wave section. Suspended as my body, pressing as gently and as strong as I dare, the crease comes under my hand, but this time with more initial grip on the side of the crease the stronger rotation about the centre line of the body unleashes a full lizard scamper: *Tap..tap.....slap..slap...*

Abruptly the same stone turns from inscrutable barrier to comfy seat... and very satisfied eyes can look down at *The Angels' Share*.

E9

2005, London, somewhere I never thought to venture to live. Then, somehow finding myself here, it's amusing I'm still surviving on the boundary of E8 and E9. Hackney that is. For the moment, while writing this book, I live in *The Bunker*, a breezeblock-walled, virtually daylight-less artist's studio, with two warrior mice, Eric and Ernie. Through recycled frosted patio doors in my bedroom, blurred, works a photographer who supplements his income at the weekends by flogging gourmet mushrooms at farmers' markets on a stall called *Spore Boys*.

When I first received the results of my SPA application I was surprised to find that I did not have enough experience, and, like Simon Nadin, was declined an SPA. Once I realised there was another page to the log book, I filled it in with other climbs of mine. Eventually granted an SPA, I'm able to occasionally teach how to tie figure of eights and abseiling to the largely reluctant at Mile End Climbing Wall.

One day cycling back along the canal no-hands, sat well back, tracking cleanly, two women come towards me chatting. Looking my way, any moment now they'll surely move over, just, just a little... two big bollards and a tight gap or Umm...aahhH... The switch to hands on mode comes too late and short of ramming the cheerful pair I've no option but to bale directly into the canal. The two surprised women watch amazed as they see me ride without deviation into the water. I leap out instantaneously. With the speed of it all and still feeling warm, I assume I'd managed to avoid actually getting wet, am strangely surprised to find myself totally soaked.

It was auspicious I fell in where I did. It was right by the lock keeper's cottage. Opening the lockgates at the time, the keeper had the best view of the incident and a barge pole with which he hooked out my dripping Claude Butler. He lent me some big clothes and gave me a hot cuppa.

Communication with friends and family was the only casualty. The display on the mobile settled into a *pea soup fog*. It was as if I was being treated to a litmus display of a past London; the spirit of 1830s Victoria Park downloaded from where it had waited in the murk below.

Every morning when not at work, I cross London Fields, where bodies from the plague are buried, for a coffee at 'La Bouche' where you can learn to receive new haughty glances. But there are creatures from all walks hereabouts. The wrinkled are not merely crenulated but appear as if their facial zones have been in dispute for some time. Spirit, a local Afro-Caribbean man famously campaigns to retain tenure of his shop's lease. The Turkish supermarket with good deals on avocados releases the customer with a fast: "Thank-you-goodbye". Artists polish turds, a climber pretends to write, attempts to self-actualise.

Today, daily meditation in the park proves tricky.

I feel confused and sad. The idea of 'sitting' is not to shut out the internal dialogue but to watch it pass. Dispassionate, the mind can release its grasp and so encourage a capacity to rest without being distracted. However, where I've sat is directly in front of an intriguing sight. In this Tibetan tradition, eyes are kept open. Here, they are not just open 'to the energy that can fill the wisdom channel' but also to a vision of a man astride a kid's bike rocking to and fro.

"Stay on your cushion even if your house falls down around you", so in the molten chaos of death as senses leave you one by one, the innermost consciousness can remain.

The man has been sat on the bike for a good ten minutes.

My breath…in and out it goes. His feet are planted on the ground and roll the bike back and forth. His knees are up under his armpits. The tyres are almost flat. He is miniature but stocky. The effect is that he appears as if he is patiently attempting to shrink to fit the bike.

Standing up before I've time to resist the instinct to, I investigate and ask, "Are you mending it?"
"No", the man replies.

The bicycle is his son's and not for the first time he is attempting to ride it. But he shows no sign of actually going for it, so I offer to show him some useful tips. He tells me all about his family and his work and then his family again. He's avoiding my offer.

The patch he is on is quite rough.

"Let's get on that better pavement over there," I suggest.

His English is not very extensive, nor my Urdu. I've never taught anyone to ride a bike, though did teach my brother how to swim, parents out, by pushing him into the deep end. Likewise a physical approach is the main instruction method here.

He is clearly worried. He says he tried before but is quite old. So we set off. He walks the bike under him while I hold his shoulders. He's not sat squarely on the seat, steers too much, too often, and looks to the front wheel for moral support. He likes to set off slowly, which of course makes it particularly easy to wobble, especially for a man on a young kid's bike. My first intervention is to advise him to sit back a little to reduce wobbles.

"Look further ahead…"
"Imagine your centre of gravity goes through the middle line of the bike".

It is miraculous to see this stranger slowly learn how to ride. It tickles me to watch him gamely weave and rescue himself at the last moment. He was getting the hang of it.

The trick from my point of view was to wait till he was nicely vertical and had a little speed before slowly releasing my grip on his shoulders. Then off on his own for four soft pedals, he trundles away. We have a few more breaks. Each time he wipes the sweat off with his handkerchief. You normally see a grin like that on a young lad and this was no different. I congratulate him and we talk about the next big step.

A new launch protocol was devised. One foot (the left) would push off the floor, while his best foot (he is right footed) pedals off. Each go, before he starts, rather than whirling the pedal itself, he rolls back the whole bike till the pedal is at the desired position. With something of a combination between an order and a cheer from me he sets off on a slight downhill and with an obvious excitement he nearly makes a turn. He practises lifting his feet up for longer while rolling down the incline; first for two, then three, then four counts. His confidence and his balance improve. He looks further ahead now and pedals faster. Suddenly he is pedalling merrily, wildly in control.

His kids arrive.

Mouths open, amazed eyes watch their dad cruise around. Ali, the new bicyclist, shouts over to a substantial woman on a nearby bench I'd previously not noticed: his wife. She brings over a 2-litre bottle of lurid orange pop and offers me one of those very thin, wobbly plastic cups. Her husband puts his arm around me and pours me a cool drink.

247

It is not long before I have a distinctive headache that I had never experienced before. This and the warmth of Ali's words: "A student always remembers his teacher" come with me. Past where the alkies hang out, my legs make several steps past a large variety of peppers. A couple of steps more and I order a Latte – time to resume work on my book. In the shiny alloy of the coffee machine, I catch a reflection of a fresh smile that has replaced a sombre mood. I've been tangoed.

CLUB FOR ONE

Not alone on Nature's brow.

Time's dead on the bridge,
as you chomp the fruit of Now.

Party on the coffin lid,
surging off the grid.

Hot rubber smears
taut on apex toe.

Grasp and let go.

An eternal dancer
in the vertical ballroom.

Smart-stepping forward,
open and breathless;
steer for the Deathless.

Gritstone Senna

We all need heroes,
I've got mine.
He comes round to my house
and cries.
Stands
head and shoulders below the rest.

The real person,
the one squatting behind
those biggest numbers,
is child-like and fragile;
enormous presence
housed in a small frame.

He won't accept
arbitrarily imposed
metaphysical or
psychological
boundaries.
I've seen him draw
blood from gritsone.

I'm baffled by his logic,
and laugh to conceal
my ignorance
I am not alone.

Sometimes a sad clown
calls round
needing shelter from massive emotions...
he is cursed
with the knowledge
of un-met potential.

Martin Veale, January 1997.

Full of Myself

Climbing, like motor-racing, if unbolted, is risky. The rhythm of classic Japanese F1 track Suzuka allowed Senna to unsettle the car at just the right pace, just enough, grabbing all the grip, rotating the car, violently feathering the throttle – tweeked to be instant – perfectly. Before dips, or hanging on till after sections where the car loosens, he catches the car exquisitely on the grip he knows is coming up, leaving some residue in the set of the car for the next corner. Tricks off curbs, ways to steer left to go right – like Ondra style brachiation – fall into each lap's unique racing line.

Senna drove in an awarescape. The sound and feel of the lap known, the virtuoso way MP4/12c played grip, enabled him to coax the car into a blurred nether world of warp speed, reaping the moment's bonus. The car disappeared, his love for racing freeing the quickest lap possible. As Senna said himself, "Suddenly I realised that I was no longer driving the car consciously, I was driving it by a kind of instinct, only I was in a different dimension".

Inside the looking glass, a place where the mandrake sits in an armchair smoking, it would be no surprise to see Frank Zappa and Ayrton Senna playing paper scissors stones.

Senna and Zappa will always be 'Dark Peak' to me – technically bombproof, painstaking, super-determined but the epitome of spontaneous and spirited. 'White Peak' I consider geared most to outcome: neat, dogged, professional, doctored, moneyed, strategic. When Senna's subtle intuition was neutered by the new formula's 'White Peak' active suspension – where a car's computer balances the car instead – I could empathise having experienced the coming of the "White Peak" in climbing. Expansion bolts, 'beta' about climbs sequences being taken for granted and specific training divorced from the crag being applied as remedy to the 'disease' of weakness, an emphasis on delicate technique to conjure up grip in the heat of the moment, on a dangerous unknown line, was demoted.

Both Senna and Zappa faced money and corporate interest head on, but at a personal cost. Senna, when confronted with FIA supremo Balestre, (ally of championship rival fellow Frenchman Prost) moving pole position to the dirty side of the track, allowed his personal ethics to slide, deliberately taking off Prost at Suzuka's first corner to win the 1991 championship. Practising *End of the Affair* was a similar White Peak moment for me. Then came *Indian Face*. I'm sure I could have done that ground up, in time.

When asked: "Who was your greatest opponent?" Senna, recalling his early days in karting, replied it was a driver called Fullerton, who was, "The most complete driver I ever knew". Then he smiled, repeating the name, stretching it out to become "Full-*Ayrton*". It was Fullerton who had inspired him to become more whole, holy himself. (At least that is what I took Senna to mean). "Karting, that was *real* racing", Senna said with obvious relish. Climbing on brick and concrete were my karting. When Senna and Zappa died tragically early I felt like I was one of the last of the Mohicans.

British climbing *may* be a storm in a teacup but what a teacup and what a storm. Not the tornado of Czech or Elbsandstein climbing quite, but internationally notorious nonetheless. If we care at all about our climbing history surely somebody has to point out the elephant in the room: its possible inaccuracy?

To some who watch history unravel from a distance, it is the twists and turns of the drama that intrigues them not its authenticity. I get the feeling many dislike the frequently unflattering, cumbersome truth, hungering instead for the mythical sustenance they find in magazine copy, where falsehood shines with a glossy patina, history blurs.

We all want to do well, but some need to do extraordinarily well, better than they can accomplish right then and there. But when magazines rely on advertising revenue for their existence from the same companies that sponsor climbers, the temptation to claim early or overgrade arises, in an environment where a firm basis for unbiased journalism is crucially undermined. Carry more advertising revenue and sponsorship in, convulsing the media mix, and eventually the fragile little deer history teeters on the edge.

Moving images are just as open to manipulation. In '87, filming for *Stone Monkey* we only had the use of a Betacam for one day at Burbage South. Rain came too soon to film *The Braille Trail* then, but the unclimbed prow to the right (what was to be claimed as *Parthian Shot*) was dry enough to have a go on a rope. Not cut out for the super steep, the pocket on the crux a tad beyond my lock, I surprised us all, not least me, and did the moves on that first day. Well almost…in actual fact I didn't quite snag the first big dyno to the jug. The edit works well to give the impression that I did. It is easy to give off an impression that differs from the facts when professional needs demand. I said it would be two years before I would be anywhere near leading it.

Back in the 80's it would have been nice to feel myself at the top of the unbolted game of rock-climbing for a tiny bit longer, maybe travel sweet on the proceeds to free Caldwell bound Yosemite big walls, but there would soon be others who claimed lines beyond what I had done.

The big issue in establishing the truth of any damp controversy is a total recall of the facts. If a cherry falls from a tree and nobody is there to hear it, did it fall? Where do the boundaries of Porky-shire lie?

It is easy to see a fix sometimes, some fixes positively reek; famously Schumacher parking his car on St Devote to scupper qualifying. But some fixes may not be so obvious. The banned traction control, said to be hidden in the innards of the German's Benetton at the beginning of the 1994 season, could be said to have pushed Senna to set up an overly twitchy Williams, beyond even his limit – what may have cost him his life.

If you think all this digging around in the past is trivial then may I remind you when climbing on potentially lethal routes an incremental difference in difficulty borne of falsehood can unleash a hugely different outcome. It only matters to a few of us, I suppose, those of us who've made it our life for a while and those who love it.

It is difficult to know how much to trust one's own and other's doubts. Take a chance encounter Ben, Jerry, and I had with another climber at Cheedale tin shack Café. Over cake we talked about what we'd been up to. When Cressbrook Dale came up, Jerry's stance changed, ears pricked, he asked this chap what he'd done. Monotone matter of fact, a long list was reeled off, including one of the hardest problems around, Moffatt's *Superman* Font 8a+. This guy was either better than his other routes suggested or had an imagination we lacked. At this, Jerry, barely containing himself, seemed to grow a shirt size! Answers to enquiries as to just how he'd done it did not ring true to me. The usually instantly recognizable mimicry was sufficiently muted as to seem absent. It was interesting to see the same incredulous look dawn on Ben and Jerry's faces, as slap by slap detail omitted crucial thumbs, foot positions, and other checks and balances. I'd tried it, seen Moffatt and Moon do it – what was aped didn't seem the same to me.

Sometimes evidence of a fix is more forensic. One climb I tried on a dry day after a dry snap. By the brush marks it was obvious which the only holds to use were, however it was impossible to see how pulling on them would accomplish anything, since the solid lattice crust of fresh grit on the surface of the holds rolled under your hands, making them unusable.

Climbing was turning professional but money was as ever in short supply in the climbing world. Some played that game well, so perhaps I and others that quibbled, were simply jealous of others success. Commercialism did not suit me, or me it, with my metaphysical pomposities at the time. Mortgage due, whenever I whined on about these things, (including Ben and Jerry rather than me being sponsored by Stone Monkey clothes), the genial undoubted Sean Myles, (whose impressive CV includes *Captain Invincible, Rodney Mullen, Monumental Armblaster, Dwm Roof, Ogwen Crack, (RM +DR* he nabbed off me!)) teasing, would call me, "Saint Johnny…"

At one of Niall Grimes' famous Ape Index lectures in Sheffield, John Dunne was offered the right to reply to the sceptics. On chat show *Trisha* a lie detector is used to attempt to sift fact from fiction. Maybe that machine would've helped John to receive acclaim untainted and for Grimer (Trisha!) to call the doubters out from backstage to face the music and apologise…

John Dunne in an interview in *Summit* said, "I'd rather be called a complete wanker or a fat bastard than a liar. But I have been, and that's that. But in the long term, I'm the one that's laughing." You can understand his frustration given all his climbs *were* genuine. From my side, one useful outcome of dealing with disappointment and sadness is to have had the opportunity to practice some patience and acceptance (quite badly), but it would be great to put this all to bed now.

It was nice to leave it all behind and waste the last of my money from the sale of my house in S7 on racing motors…beep… beep. Cheating in motor-racing was already a traditional part of the sport to be expected. As a privateer novice it was a simple joy to aim to be my best, fed too by the spicier glee of aiming to be the outright quickest. Competition wasn't just about getting stronger having more power, but about learning, being brave, clearer by accepting what was there, finding novel ways to go strangely quick.

I love it. I haven't the resources now but at legal speeds I manage to enjoy preparatory games in my 306 *TDS*! Balancing a golf ball in a brandy glass glued to the dash I practise being smooth, flattening the road picking out the fine detail that repays you with grip on demand. Learning how to counter-steer, to delicately weight all four tyres to steer in or by using bumps. Sometimes I aim to clip far distant markings on the road steering only once. Lately I've learnt to brake, accelerator still applied making the car dive more, giving supernormal momentary grip but demanding a very delicate share on the brake before quickly finding the clutch.

I don't want to invest time/money developing a stronger more fragile engine/body to overcome the rock/crag. I want to explore the flaring grip by dancing off the cuff. Cranking up the decibels of indifferent music doesn't make it better however big the gong or cheque for the performance. If you want to listen to the silence you don't need a stereo with nothing on to turn up. It's not the wobble it's the wobble on the wobble.

Looking to stumble across the real thing again, in 2011, I find myself hiding away from it all in a narrow dark passageway at High Rocks. The line I'm cleaning meticulously, so the ascent and subsequent ones are enjoyable, is at a crossroads of passageways. It is raining on the main crag. It is nice and cosy indulging my cleaning habit in here, and quiet, apart from the sound of kids exploring the labyrinth slots of especially solid sandstone; perfect to enjoy the discovery of a ripple smear going with a warp side-pull, a press for the heel of my hand making a strange dish crucial to slap a pinch.

Please do not lie. Please, please do not chip. Clean your shoes. Do the dishes. Put the rubbish out. Be a good bear. Even deeper into the dark passage there is another slab line of pristine hard rock. Out of view, under dust, it has a chance. I peek under it for secret relief.

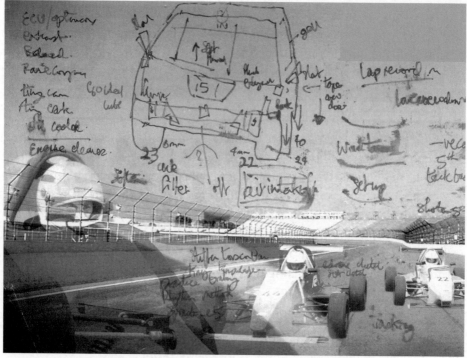

Above: Pug not rotated quite enough but will come round once over the crest. Two laps to go...
My nemesis, the Narconon XR2 is in my sights. Below: Some secret scrawl to decipher...

Cutting Corners

Racing a car is like being on a hard gritstone crux for a long time but in a musical instrument: if tyres are strings hanging on tarmac, rumble strips are the percussion. The feeling of connection you get with land when driving on the limit is unrivalled, while everything is rushing by, it's just like floating. As the true flow of track and car merge, your mind acquires the silent candour of the land…*BOOM, BOOM,* errr…. errrr.. bubabbababa……. Aarraaa...aaaara.

Finally I'll race not watch. My Dad first brought the family to the circuit in 1977 when we watched Jackie Icyx in a V12 333 Ferrari, hounded by two Chevrons, scream through Paddock Hill Bend. Brands Hatch is a venerable scratcher's track, home of the ultra competitive Formula Ford festival. The fiercely fought Stock Hatch Championship run by 750 Motor Club is the most popular UK championship and I'm in it. Sat down you can joust with Swifts, Golfs, 106s, 205s, XR2s, even an XR3 on classic old school circuits like Oulton, Cadwell, and Donington Parks. (I'd really like to race a Radical SR8 really if anyone is interested in making a few quid...)

On the way down the M1 from Sheffield, where I'd been at the wake for Meeta, not only sadness but a pastiness affects me. My lilac 106 XSI hair-dresser's hatchback, (my ride to crag and track for the season) insists on veering left on braking, as if it knows where it's headed and is frightened. To sort the veering out I ring Nick, the mechanic who prepared the car. His phone is off. Later, it goes straight to voicemail. Tax run out, passing traffic police in a garish Volvo, negotiating a traffic jam on the M25 at Heath-row, my mobile rings. Cameras interrupt our conversation. Phone battery is running out. "Your credit is running low. Please arrange a top up"…F..k – right – off.

When we finally get to speak properly, Nick's cheery, but not sufficiently serious perspective, relaxes but makes me irritated. He had just fitted new bloody brakes!

"I think it's the calliper… wait a sec Nick, another blinking camera".

I see a sign with a chequered flag, pull off the motorway. Signing on at the circuit, I'm right next to a filthy mood but hold it together: meditation working, medication unnecessary. Formula 4's belt around the glade, marshalls in orange uniforms, club motorsport heartland. Back out of the circuit tearing down country lanes braking to try and free the calliper, eventually it's clear there'll be no change. A garage is just shutting. I ask to charge my phone. It is not possible. I've given in, almost cheery to laugh at the gnarl. A calm pleasant bloke, self-possessed of similar atoms, gives me directions to Sidcup, SC Motorfactors. Listening bewildered, I follow mood and amazingly directions to the end of my tether. I decide to get a new calliper. More cash changes hands.

Inside the car I notice John Allen's car keys poking out of my rucksack… No. **NO**! I ring him with the last of the phone's charge – no answer. Upset preserved, I whine horribly, then listening to myself…breathe, become philosophical. Reversing I draw up next to another car and wind down the window.

"Do you know how I could send my friend's keys to Sheffield?" I ask a perfect stranger.
"The Post Office..?" they suggest.
Unjustifiably indignant I blurt: "But it's Saturday."
No time, it may be open, maybe not, more tension.

OK, back to Brands.

The only spot left in the paddock is by a mud track leading to the Rallyschool. Accumulated dirt has submerged the wire mesh fence's bottom. I park front on to the fence, then climbing out past the roll bar, realise doing the brakes will be messy facing that way, so have to turn the car around. I've had e- nuFF.

The registrar told me I must locate my transponder number to allow my lap time to be recorded. A burger. Sit on the outside of Paddock Hill Bend. Wow. Maybe it is all a vain mirage but that 7 was only just clinging on. That classic symphony of tyre, Tannoy and exhaust remind me why: I *can* get it together! On Toca 2, Playstation, set on 110%, I can win here, setting the SEAT Cupra, front engine, front wheel drive tail happy, low but fairly soft side to side. Thinking how to set up the little pug, I remember it doesn't even brake straight and doesn't have adjustable suspension anyhow.

Walking back across the paddock has me rattled a little. Everywhere, natty 'Radicals', 'Fury's', rasping Hot Hatches remind me I'm the new boy.

I text Julie to let her know the situation, she's on her way, wildly cheerful as usual.

Breaking the ice and needing a hand I ask northerner Stuart Pearson XR3i if he could help me later on. Waiting for him to arrive at his leisure, my effort with the A3 Fablon back panel reveals my butterflies in visible wrinkled bubbly form. 750 MC sticker, transponder sign, obligatory promotional stickers all on, purple/blue pug looks a parody.

My paddock neighbour's son Matt has taken six months to prepare a stock 205 1.6, pukka in its light yellow/blue Renault livery. They are upbeat Essex folk. Matt attempts to polish yet more speed into it. Kevin, XR2i, enquires what I'm up to. His young son offers to clean the whole car for £5, I fane dumb, he reduces it to £3. I insist *clean* means in *and* out. He grins. His Dad is sorting me out with a smile and is now covered in brake dust from the dirty wheels. I must learn more, earn my spots, compete with a smile. Finally car is ready-ish.

The last race of the day features throaty MG V8s racing a nimble Midget, lying 4th, getting amazing speed, using all the track. Fantastic.

Julie arrives from Hoxton. We put up the tent, arrange a vast array of cushions, karrimats, Thermarests and duvets, and go for supper. We watch a full moon by the Darent. Bushed, turn in early...

7.30am – Race Day.

Sound of A20 nearby, jets overhead, zip...outside it's a pea souper. We get the first teas from the café, yawning, a tractor tows the gravel comber, another scrubs the tarmac clean.

We walk the track. Paddock Hill is steep, scarred with marks where cars with downforce running super low ride heights have bottomed out on their gearboxes. The screech of them spinning is still there if you listen.

It's steep up to Druids Hairpin. The line in differs dramatically if you need to defend. Brands has a wide variety of curbs, some unrideable, some with faint lips you can hook tyres to maximise all important exit speed. Our lap takes 45 minutes but I can see how to make it much quicker!

I'm in Heat C, must fit in the new drivers' briefing and squeeze the car through scrutineering. Along with 90 other cars, belts, roll cage, extinguishers, master pull switches, suspension, brakes, and lights will all have to be tested. It turned out Nick had wired in the fog lamps to the brakes. Bonnet catch needed removing. Fire extinguisher had come loose. Finally I'm cleared. I'm given a practice only ticket. My safety clothing is ruled satisfactory though I lack a balaclava, but Firé rock shoes are stared at mistrustfully. "You at least need *Nomex* socks". Julie takes the wheel, steers it into the bay, while I run for my trainers.

For an elegant driving style to emerge a car needs to be tuned to a track. A cursory glance at my car shows this hasn't happened. In fact, not only have I never driven a track, save at an SPA style induction at Silverstone for a National B Licence, I've not driven the car before yesterday. Last to register for the race, Pug, *151,* with its three stickers even costs more. I'm officially at the very bottom of the food chain of British Motorsport.

A long breezeblock tunnel feeds under the circuit into the pits proper. A red-faced marshal waves me in hurriedly. Intense young men with archipelago beards twitch around their Formula 3's. On request I slow for a steward who says, "Three quarter throttle". I think he's insinuating: "You're a novice so take it easy out on track". It begins to rile me but in fact he just wants to take emission and noise levels and I can go mental in under five minutes.

Up behind Kevin's XR2i, the other qualifying group in Bike-engined Sports Cars pass back to the paddock. A round woman ushers us out on to the pit lane to line up. I find myself fumbling with electric windows, pulling straps down on the red four-point harness. Oil temperature is low, make a mental note to start engine earlier. Efforts to keep calm have left me not nervous, but also not excited. Finally we're waved out onto the track, pedal beneath my right foot makes a noise…drop in, down right into *Paddock*, car yaws away to the rumble strip. Into *Druids* even with cold new brakes the car surprisingly brakes perfectly straight. As expected from *Toca 2*, car loses front-end grip in the middle, pinches on exit. Tyres will balance up as they warm.

Into *Graham Hill* I let the frontrunners past to leave space to put a quick one together. Mid-corner wash out, I use grass on entry, feint (first steer the wrong way like on a motorbike) to aid turn in, but I'm unbalancing the car too much. Adverse camber, apex blind, into *Clearways* undulations come quicker. Rhythmic steering, modulation of throttle unlock the use of the curb to tighten the car for an earlier exit out of the bend on to the pit straight. Smoothness releases extra revs… be patient, let car roll out to nibble the grass …3rd….4th. I catch the limiter (car sounds different helmet on).

Tearing into *Paddock* over a blind brow, hard on the brakes from 110 mph plus, car floats, balancing eventually, it drops and bites as the corner banks. Car chops sideways, straightening out on the curb. Feedback instantly logged: speed, placement, angle of approach quietly mull over in the war room of my mind. To do Paddock perfectly, as the father of a fellow competitor will observe, "is to experience one of the greatest thrills of this life".

Just 20 minutes to learn a new track in a new car, in traffic, yet it feels cosy, frustration gone. A 'yellow' flag is out – I notice it, even know what it means: slow – incident. Time to reflect: a softer way steering over bumps will start to wake up the engine. Less curb here, deeper there, later here, so on to the main straight a sense of the whole track ahead is there.

Now for a super quick one… sense of the possible can introduce itself to the improbable, beware the unpredictable..! Past the pits, typical, the chequered waves, end of session.

A woman in a motorhome asks me how I'd done in qualifying. She looked me up. John Dawes. Not in the 80's or 70's, there I am: 65th, which puts me in race 2 out of three, 10th row out of 16, on a 1:03.61, 3.5 seconds off fastest. Seemed crap to me, but it seems I've out-qualified her husband who has camber and is in his fifth season.

An unscheduled driver's briefing is called. I trot over there, not feeling in the least out of place any more. My fellow drivers are less hooligan than I'd thought. All the competitors listen to a heavily made up woman in her fifties, the Clerk of the Course, who says she has a whip for the naughtiest drivers. She reads out who must report to race control. 151 is not on her list.

Before the race at 2.10pm, we've time to watch races in the other classes. Watching stripped-down 500bhp MGB V8s race nose to tail, excitedly I suddenly realise, in under an hour I'll be on the grid.

Now then, how to start best? The pit straight is anything but straight and not flat either. I'm placed on the inside, 18 cars ahead, 10 cars behind. On the flat, 4,700rpm usually gets 106 away best – keeping a touch of wheelspin, briefly slipping the clutch to keep the revs up. As momentum builds, the sound of tyre on road stays at the same pitch till clutch fully releases. So what revs here? How much wheelspin if any? Do I short shift early? If slow do I block? How aggressive should I be?

…A marshal ushers us into our grid boxes. The Pug left high at the back to turn in more readily, must have looked like it wanted a good spank sat on the grid. A slight illegal creep before the lights will help. 4000 revs, steering down slope will help to get it off the line.

The two-minute board goes out. Window up, straps tight, calm wandering mind. Breathing quietly, looking ahead, a sea of cars, each filled with a maniac eager to win. Three cars crashed out in practice.

One minute. Some gun their engines…those with open doors close them.

Thirty seconds. Cacophony. I'm thinking of the crowd, the hassles to get here: all the wrong things.

Novice black cross on my boot. Red lights… suddenly no lights…I'm still waiting for green. Bugger, taken aback car sits spinning wheels, great start doesn't materialise but its a little better than the XR2 ahead. I short-shift taking 2nd gear early. Jostle, weave, there's no space to exploit, sat in a long caravan up to *Druids,* the car in front brakes early concertinaring me back. …locked tyres… smoke in the mirrors… waiting for the crunch…but it doesn't come. Riding the curb tight, giving space, down the hill there're no gaps for separate lines: three abreast, then two, single file cars peel into the left hander, trainee *Red Arrows*.

Now, I can go for it. Into *Clearways* quick in order to defend, compromises the exit. Leaders are gone. They're so much quicker in a straight line. In the mirrors faster cars place themselves to advantage.

Through *Paddock* itself I'm quicker than the others around me but lose a place, have no idea how I could've avoided it. Ahead Le Tissier XR2 screws up his braking, I go inside. Although he's gone wide, he gathers speed down into *Graham Hill*. First giving him a little room then pinching him I take the shortest distance to head him off. Le Tissier is left behind… but down the straight he closes up once again. Power on earlier, exit neater, by the end of the straight at *Paddock*, he's still behind. Braking super late, unsure quite what will happen, Pug goes in at the right speed but on a foreign line its dynamics are strikingly different, sending me in all *Dukes of Hazard,* but still ahead. Nick, (who'd sold me the car as one to learn in) said you can take it in 4th. (A fanciful 3.8th gear is what's needed). Steering lock to lock it likely appears to the uninitiated as if it's not sliding at all but if it had full grip and went where the tyres were pointed Pug would have all four wheels on the infield grass.

Some slides wash up my arms before they have time to grow, a few before they even germinate. Car more stable, slides that would've happened accounted for become invisible, transform into pace.

Six laps of 13 gone, in front a pair battle, patient here, aggressive hands over eyes nutcase there, speed comes to reel them in, another racer chases my behind. Use all the road – concentrate. This new pace urges me too fast into *Paddock*…I wait and wait before turning in for the grip, anticipating the sound of gravel scraping the bottom of the car. It doesn't come. Next lap there, a shade earlier/gentler/longer on the brakes, the better balance yields higher apex speed. By *Druids* crisp accurate entry speed and a little use of left foot braking brings the rear around like a delicate use of handbrake (some power left on stops driven wheels locking). The challenge from behind has faded, I'm almost on them.

By Lap 11 up ahead the Nova and XR2 are having a grand scrap. I pull them in by full four car lengths up to *Druids*. At the bottom of the hill, 3mph on them, by *Clearways* we're snapping at their heels. All the way around the last lap of the race their cars get steadily louder. Not greedy in *Paddock*, smudge not sludge, smooth/aggressive through *Druids*, 3rd early down to *Graham Hill* making use of the lull in grip on exit by *Clearways*, giving it all, in faster from far left while giving them space, I müller the curb blending my speed using the brake till right on their bumpers. They kiss, Nova goes onto the grass. Past the Nova, I chase the XR2 in. By the line there's a wheel in it.

In the pits I wonder why definite skills I've developed have not born fruit. The other cars just seem quicker. Car and I'll grow together, set up well with the right kit. (Forgot to set the tyre pressures as advised that first race, 28 front 32 rear. End of season I'll end up on 24/39 so wayward is the Pug by end of race).

Scrutineers weigh all cars, check their ride heights. I'm pulled off to one side to be reweighed. Half an hour passes while the rest pass. Whoops, it's

20kg under. A steward hustles me to the Timekeeper's office where they keep the gnarly female Clerk of the Course.

Race control looks down on to the start/finish. One wall is plastered in CCTVs trained on each bend. Four jolly officials sit facing the track. I'm invisible. Baked airhostess with clipboard awaits… I ask to fix myself a coffee. While I look attentive she explains the rules…at length. She points out the penalty, asks if I'd like to lodge an appeal… I'm missing the F4 race.

Once back at the car I twig I've accidentally parked it where the winners are garlanded. The winner of the Formula 4 race is strutting down the pitlane towards us. A smirking marshal avoids eye contact but stretches out his arm dryly, presenting me with the exit.

(No points *and* the race must be counted in the rounds that go towards my title bid).

Julie arrives greeting me as if I've won. A friend of the winner of the race, Matt Rozier, congratulates me on a good race. Down-spirited I say: "Rather go for a blast in mid Wales, The car's … blah, blah".

A large damp cardboard box serving as my garage reminds me I'm just starting off. I would always have regretted it had I never done it. As long as I can remember I've wanted to do this. Now I appreciate the benefits of adjustable camber[50] more power from an ECU, weighting the car's corners the same, testing at a track to qualify better, the need for a trailer so I could risk contact if I had to (I drove the Pug to every round). When we watch the final its clear how much quicker the top cars are.

There were sixty-seven competitors in 750 motor club's Stockhatch Championship in 2004. Pug and I manage to win a place in the final of 24 cars on three out of eight occasions during the season. The best I ever ran was at the end of the season at Lydden Hill, on a drying track. I posted 9th quickest in qualifying. Afterwards, asking the team-mate of the leader of the championship (whose 106's suspension cost more than my whole car!) "What tyre pressures do you run?" echoing from the back of the decal plastered artic comes the season's crowning glory, "Don't tell *him* too much".

I had them worried..!

[50] The inclination of front wheels that ensures a tyre gives its greatest grip by presenting a flat contact patch at the crucial moment. However, the higher degree of camber, the poorer the braking in a straight line.

The season for all its considerable hassle had been grrreat. Highlights included:

…For eight laps keeping a caravan of five faster cars behind me at Donington by using all the curb to go sideways into the Old Hairpin and by left-foot braking after the pit straight. A broken water hose was all that stopped me.

…At Pembrey going from 24th to 8th in three laps had Poolie jumping up and down screaming, then the disappointment of a red flag. That weekend I found out three abreast round Honda Corner doesn't go. The future Clio winter champion goes down one verge, me the other at over a ton. Turf on sand threatens to roll a car if it goes sideways…

… At Brands Hatch's final race I overtake into Druids and the blind Paddock Hill Bend. Later I go off at *Paddock* trying it almost flat-out in top.

…In a *Semsec* meet at Lydden I lead a slick shod race Mini till my treaded tyres go off. We had the crowd on their feet every lap according to my new pal, race mechanic Steve, who used to prepare Colin McRae's engines.

…Testing at Mallory. In the damp the massive slicks of the JCB Ferrari Daytona let the driver down, he spins trying to follow me into the amazing, wheel to wheel correction entry to the flat-out Gerrards. Tyres down to the canvas when I come in, Pete Felix, the lap record holder in the class, to my delight, having watched each corner on the circuits CCTV, said "There's not much left to come from your car". (The little Pug was eventually stolen from outside The Fricsan and is now probably a small cube. It wasn't a great car but I *loved* to race it.).

Car £750, £1,850 to prepare, race equipment, entries, licence, another £1,800, means that for less than £4,500 you can race on the UK's premier circuits too, if nothing breaks and no one hits you... One issue I should've borne in mind at the beginning of the season was that Stockhatch is for cars with 1600cc 8v or 1400 16v engines. I had bought a **1360**cc 8 valve.

Where will this going round in circles lead?

Tour de France

We often have a good time working at Mile End Climbing Wall, hugging a hoodie, keeping hands off attractive clients. I've good friends around the world now but what is the point in all that? What is accomplished apart from a brief assuaging of loneliness or bathing in momentary glee? Increasingly, the only thing that makes me feel really happy is doing things for others. There is the problem of what is going on too. What can you do for others that really counts long term? Life *is* short and its end brutal, the afterward either a flat note of white noise with no ears or a transmigration of the soul, or something else.

Maturing, shrinking, the compelling gnaw of Buddhadharma sets me on a journey to a retreat near Montpellier, southern France. It had been a case of a book winking at me from the shelf…

It is too late to fly, TGV is too expensive, the only thing for it is to ride down there. I pedal out through Hackney, down Mare Street towards the City… out to Elephant and Castle and Deptford. In Decathlon searching for a waterproof, without a bike lock, the manager lets me bring in my Claude Butler Ortlieb-panniered sprinter into the store and asks me what I'm looking for. I spot a nasty home-brand extra large red jacket, perfect. On its second price reduction, it is almost in my price range, but after the manager enquires about the escapade, he sells it via his personal account, at trade, £8.

Finally, with everything required, I break out through the skin of the megacity. Through Kent, *a* garden of England not *the* garden, provision hasn't been made for the harmless traveller on a cycle and for several stretches of the road to Dover, trucks hurtle past far too close, nearly answering the question of what happens after death.

I sidle off the main road as soon as practical. Down one meandering cool lane I stop to pick cobnuts, almost ripe, from a hedge. An hour later there is something entirely groovy about riding up into the huge metal cave of the ferry on my own. No longer feeling the need to dismiss, impress, extort or ignore, up on deck I look back at the iconic sheerness of England and pull out a bulgar salad from a plastic bag I've prepared for this very moment.

En France mon petit choufleur…paperwork away, where to head to decided, winging along at a good pace, never straining nor slacking, making sure to balance the bike crisply, avoiding rough patches of road I reach into Picardie for somewhere to sleep safely, a £6 fishing tent home.

Hands are feeling a little numb. The flat city handlebar riding position is wonky for a trip like this and the cycling shorts I've bought seem to have been designed to carve the wearer a new arse. Riding mostly without hands, the bike starts to travel upright automatically.

Sun overhead, it's no picnic, soaked T-shirt wrapped around my head is bone dry by the next village. Bread and cheese, an occasional tomato, water filled up from the village fountain, dozing in the dappled shade of trees at noon, I make grand progress, 80 miles some days. Then I see the graves. Line after line of stones. The Somme. I pitch up at a caravan site and treat myself to *Omelette et frites*.

What was won there in those fields but quickening technology and the thrill of power?

Morning again.

"Il fait *chaud*…uhh?" They could only tell I was not French by my clothing…It's good to be alive, unknowably so, here, lucky to have choices. Traffic absent, down one long straight, the incline is so perfect, tarmac so silky, that freewheeling down the centre of the road between two painted lane markers, I can safely close my eyes for minutes at a time without fear of running off the road. Wrists laid on handlebars, tummy on seat, legs over panniers, feet rudders, the distinctive sound of corn clattering softly in one ear contrasts with the wheat whooshing in the other.

It all seems a wonderful dream but I cannot keep eyes shut forever. Soon I'm swimming in the Loire in deceptively beautiful cadmium water. By a bridge over the river, rebuilt many times as wars ripped by, I listen to a stone by stone account of its history, in French, winning me a surprise supper. Afterward, the kindly couple invite me to visit a chateau the next day. It was the one that appears in Hergé's Tintin, more remarkably for me built by Catherine de Medici, an ancestor who brought *French* cooking to France!

Lerab Ling, where I'm headed, is a Tibetan Buddhist monastery. I already knew some of the people attending the retreat from Rigpa on Caledonian

Road in North London. I'd searched it out after reading Sogyal Rinpoche's *The Tibetan Book of Living and Dying*.

To me, young kids always looked like they've been aware before. Some dogs are like poets. This makes the view that our awareness doesn't entirely disappear when we die likely to me. If we do indeed reincarnate and don't understand how the illusion works, suffering from thinking that this is all there is, fighting to have it continue whatever way your mind has become used to already, suffering seems inevitable. Ignorance of that process if it could be known seemed a foolish luxury.

If everything is connected up like in *The Matrix*, *The Force* a reality, then Depeche Mode's *"Everything counts in large amounts..."* must be true. To truly help others – even hoofed and winged types – agreeing with Buddhist thinking I could only conclude that the problem was ignorance of the reality of life and death.

The **Big D** isn't peanuts.

Primal therapy had woken me up to why I felt emotionally awry. Mum came from a lineage of perfectionists, but we're well over that. Dad and I, close and open finally, have talked about being emotionally distant. Aged seven, during the war, Dad was sent away to Worcestershire where emotionally he had to fend for himself. So self-reliance, good as it is, would naturally form part of the Spartan, if moneyed way, it would be for me. Public school sent me off into space. Climbing had drawn me back some, friends' patience more still. Now all these strands had led to the possibility super-highway, my life was surely now much more my own to give. Was I on my way finally?

...Running a little off schedule for the retreat's start I'd bought a train ticket. My train not for an hour, the porter upgraded me on to the TGV persuading the conductor into putting my bike in a special locked compartment for valuables and registered documents. (The TGV doesn't take bikes!) Speeding/leaning train was cool, quiet and luxurious. Six days cycling to Bourges, two thirds of the way down France, now just six hours to complete the journey to Montpellier, on time for the retreat.

I was amazed one day to be sitting next to a chap who once famously whipped a car with a branch for failing to start. Neither of us, though certainly drawn to Buddhist ideas, warmed strongly to the décor of the temple and when I poked an instructor with: "What is the point of enlightenment if you can't race cars?"[51], my new neighbour confessed he thought it a valid question. I was asking, can you have your cake and eat it? Could you enjoy life and not cause suffering? Skirmishing for a physical solution to allow me to follow my passion for racing, to square with my beliefs and conclusions about the world returned me again to the project of the vegetable car.

Physicists and mystics say physical reality has no intrinsic existence. Things make an appearance then disappear, a field of modulating frequencies. When I think of this it makes me want to know the whole story, to find out what really could stop the sufferings and satisfy all we/me's, the it/all not. That'd take a long time…unless it *has* already been done, can be taught and one practises it, religiously...

[51] Apparently when Trogyam Trungpa first arrived in the States the first thing he did was to see how fast his friend's muscle car would go.

Strange Cargo

After selling my terrace in Sheffield, I had some cash left over and decided to race a car, as you know. It had eaten quite a bit. I didn't intend to buy another house to mollycoddle so bought a van instead with the notion of touring and getting fit. It had not worked out at all well. Almost immediately it was broken into in Sheffield, new bike and climbing rack stolen. Then in Wales, driving along Cleigiau, a bumpy hyper-twisty road over the hills, disaster strikes again. A video of me one hand solo on *Downhill Racer* E4 and of crags parkour set to William Orbit's *Strange Cargo* falls from the parcel shelf, jamming miraculously between gear stick and steering wheel, consigning the van to a dry stone wall death.

The nearest place for the van to be laid to rest is a lay-by at Bryn Bras Castle, where Lloyd George wrote his speeches. I ring the bell of a large pink house that must've been the gatehouse in days gone by. By chance I knew a russian princess who lived there! Her partner Llewellyn came to the door, holding back three rescue dogs and casually said I could wait. I stayed there for eight months in the end! It is my fate for a dark Lurcher called Morgan to befriend me and my cheese. He can undo the extra security devices fitted to the fridge and also pick the ad hoc locks barring access to his favourite but forbidden sofa. Once *Cathedral* wrapper discovered on the floor is put into the bin, I'd find him lounging, like Terry Thomas on the sofa, body unapologetically immobile while one eye tilts up showing you he knows you know, but also that he doesn't care.

During the solstice, blue-blooded, Fiona enjoyed hot naked baths in the garden with a glass of absinthe. Her daughter was not so laissez faire. On our first meeting, she took exception to something sassy I said, grabbed me and bit my leg. Another occasion I was giving Fiona a massage. She walked in on us. "You slut…" she exclaimed to her mother. Llewellyn once said I was smarmy but I think secretly he loves me very much. It was great living there, off and on, writing this book.

I eventually found myself living in a public house. Yet again. The construction of the pub used the first brick in the valley hence the name: *Fric*-san. A brass plate across the Caernarfon road recalls what happened years ago. Explosives were stored there when it was the old slate railway depot. An explosion threw a railway sleeper a mile, 500ft up on to Cleigiau lane where an X on a slate marks where it landed.

Even stone cold sober, the wonky steps that led down from the pub to the caravans made you feel drunk, particularly in the twilight encountering one of the peacocks perching on the handrail. Lasting out the winter in the caravan, the clatter of the wind encouraged a modest lack of direction in my life to assume tremendous proportions in my head. The pub had a second name on a sign on the pub wall: *The Snowdon Inn*. Under it in Fawlty Towers' tradition the only letters remaining advertised:

"A commo tion available".

Strangely it's the second time I'd lived in a public house that had a big disaster – the first was at *The Snowdrop* in Lewes, where the most serious avalanche in England happened. That was an enjoyable time; chilling with a mellow local posse, exploring the fantastic sandstone. It included putting up a 7a climb of the same name.

There was a surprising amount of privacy at The Fricsan. Crispin kept his canadian canoe there. Sometimes I hauled it onto the Seiont. Behind the pub is a sacred lake with an island in the middle inhabited by a family of ancient heron. For awhile I toyed with the idea of rowing courting couples there at sundown for a little extra cash.

Outside on the patio, there was a great spot for coaching climbing skill and when it was icy you could run and grind the tables. If it rained, cockney neighbour Clive, Mark, diligent head barman and big John, hard rock enthusiast, pulled tarpaulin over a permanent scaffold frame, providing the basis for hazard and merriment as it filled up with gallons of Welsh rain. Inside, hell or high water were the locals: avant-garde jazz, bongo-bongo, Drum 'n' Base or happy hardcore, you'd find ex-quarryman Hugh caught tapping his feet, quietly spoken Kevin or wry Duncan's angle border the bar. If the pub had one thing that set it apart more than the friendly welcome, it was the superb quality of the live music, whether far flung like foremost Cajun band Sarah and the Francadians or local luminaries like Gwilym Morris, Kev Fox, Rob Jones or Red Stripe.

Open mike nights were far more than Karaoke. Arwel, inspired just two weeks before by a local, learnt to drum brilliantly and had us all roaring in approval. I suspect there was not a more relaxed excitement to be had in a pub anywhere. Even if the pool cloth was tidy as the pool played on it, The Fricsan 2010 was a dive; intermittent leak above a corner of the room, bands' signatures on the ceiling, carpet an ongoing epidemiological experiment, the flickering candle electrics unconvincing. Come Christmas Ted didn't want twinkling decoration. It all kept the middle class away.

…The pub, my surrogate living room, was now busy returning after cooking pasta in the caravan. *Playstation* with *Toca 3*, still perched under the widescreen needs to go back behind the bar.

Ann Bierd's (a friend who no-one will let change, a little like me, or anyone in fact) and my role is often to break in the dance floor, but tonight rebellious breasts already jounce to Tom's mechanical mix. The place regularly changes utterly, keeping one on your social toes. Tomorrow the rest of the paragliders are arriving for their convention, the day after bikers, then fun Cardiff Climbing Club, then hippies for a merry birthday festival. Regular visitors are reggae crew *Natty Dread* from Oxford, gigging for a charity project in Ghana. The developing rapport between the locals and them is a heart-warmer. Huge hip hop caps askew sit on the head of a man swaying like a boat on a rough sea, Tony, the elder, pumping it up from the mike… and, oh yes, the wiry owner is sometimes about. If he is in, the music you hear will be from behind the bar most likely, horrendous *"diddly-dee…"* See him hunch forward, mischievously rolling a bottle vertically in his hand: "Right, lock the doors, it's time to get the ashtrays out".

My First Job

My first job: "Cor..!"

I didn't need a reference as I'd once danced New Year in with the boss, and not tried to molest her, and she knew I could move, which is what you need in a shop.

While I finish my book I enjoy donning a pinny working at Saffrwn, a good food shop in Llanberis high street. It is a workers' co-op. We sell baguettes, homemade soup, local organic vegetables, groceries and herbal remedies.

I work on busy Fridays when all the vegetables are in and people are getting ready for the weekend. Juggling the till, with ghosts ringing up the phone, cooking, cleaning and stocking puts me into overdrive. Working with the public is 'interesting'. Shoppers vary from helpful and friendly to incomprehensible or downright hostile. Activity comes in waves, trouble in threes.

A harmless enough woman who regularly comes in loves to bark at male me. One memorable day, she was having a bad one…someone hadn't understood her earlier…had continued without doing so – I'm not sure quite what, but my word she was on it! Half way through our experience, a man comes in. He rushes hot around the Tatws and Kale, grabs eggs and cheese, slams them down on the till. As I punch in the digits, the till computers back angrily. I press the **Err/Cor** as trained, continue, ask for: "8 pounds 44 pence please…" Aghast, he says accusingly: "That's not right." He was absolutely furious. I check. Sure enough he *was* right. I apologise, eating humble pie, including the crumbs. I turn the spluttering soup down and punch my fingers at the numbers again. Gently ask: "6 pounds 65 please…" He pays with the right money and leaves.

Sam, the manager tells me, "You dealt with that well Johnny". Seeing me still a little upset, she distracts me with another task: to bank. I put the few cheques and notes in the pocket of my pinny and head off diagonally across the street. Who should be coming towards me but the sharp-featured, highly-strung arty man I'd just diddled on the till. We happen to be walking on collision trajectory. He spots me but suddenly I realize the paying-in book is still in the drawer, turn tail and trot back to the shop. By the time I retrieve it and turn around, angry man is right in my face. His kettle is no longer pretending to boil and is whistling.

"Are you taking the piss? This is ridiculous. You've overcharged me again. Do you do this deliberately? I'm pissed off", he informs me.

What had happened is that he had bought a box of cheaper local eggs, understandable as the box was below a sign for them but the box itself was a regular one. I apologise, self-flagellating appropriately. Fair enough, the guy was right again.

"Wow", I say to Sam, shocked as the wake settles around the Kohl Rabi. She apologises for the egg labelling fiasco but is pleased I kept my cool.

Soon after, a woman who is an expert on bats and enjoys a josh at my expense comes in circling around the shop in order to decide what she wants. She looks hopefully at a female customer at the till: "Is he messing you around?"

"No *actually* he's really good at his job…thank you", she says giving me a smacker on the cheek.

I enjoy the emasculation and the soothing equally! On some of the customers who have come to enjoy it I practise my rude French waiter technique, others get a massage if we're not too busy, some I quietly leave to it. All can buy great food and milk cheaper than our Spar-ring partner up the high street.

Thank God it's Friday I think. Climbing partners should be a little easier to find.

Usually two weeks or more between going climbing, such is the vile weather, which seems to reserve its best efforts for when I'm in the shop, I get no fitter to try the unclimbed seven pitch traverse of Scimitar Ridge.

I climb sometimes with the Wraith. He is low key and really enjoys climbing in itself. To go to crags we are familiar with, try climbs I never did at my height feels like a special treat. Tremadog's *Sultans of Swing* required a full bloodied storming; cunning rests, reading moves right first time, using swings to and fro and raw pace to blast past sequences, hanging fingers crimped over thumb, knee barring or shaking out on jams, not putting in extra gear in mid sequence, E4 feels hard carrying extra. With no reserve, an ad-hoc hand-me-down rack mixed with Wraith's, I can't avoid a rich pump. Sat on the top, the ravens play in pairs, diving in and out of the gullies. The sun strokes my skin. Wraith is puffing away gratifyingly.

It might be too rainy to climb this weekend but at least tonight in the pub should be fun. It is nice to sit here in the shop in the dark for a moment, the day's work done. I have pulled the shutters down, brought in the sandwich board, swept, torn off the Z reading, counted the coins and notes and cheques to enter into the computer, covered the bread (as reminded), put the soup in a clean pan in a sink of cold water to keep and turned off the weighing machine and fridge light. I never used to understand why Zippy drank hot water, but it has a totally different flavour than cold.

Riding back along the old railway line to the end of the lake, I like to keep my hands warm in my pockets. Llewellyn gave me gloves but they've gone astray somewhere. I haven't done the whole ride no-hands yet. At the end there is a long tunnel. It has some nasty divots and at its edge lurk big blocks. There is virtually no moon, so no heroics tonight.

Lover

A fearless moral inventory, as the Twelve Step Programme puts it, would include, for me, the observation that wanting but failing to get what I want makes me angry. True success, rather than climbing infinitely hard, would be to be free of all anguish like that. As I climbed better did I come to feel more alive, care more about others and learn to let go of mental luggage? I think so, climbing hard does knock some of the rough edges off you. At your limit, you learn how to hear when your mind is chattering as it happens, but just as truly, climbing as hard as possible can bring a ceaseless chatter of its own.

To be the best is like being a water boatman raised up on the summit of a bubble on a pond created by gas brewed in the depths below. Once the bubble bursts, the water boatman finds itself back at the same level as the other boatmen, skating mysteriously on the surface tension but in a farty atmosphere.

Striving for perfection was a constant growing up. I would endeavour to gain mastery of each skill asked of me by circumstance, one after the other. Thereby, and this is the point, as skills linked up like pieces of the developmental jigsaw, I presumed I'd become whole, gain control over life, that I would become happy. Once all the brilliances joined up surely I'd be fine. But becoming brilliant distinguishes one, invites competition, even jealousy. It is a pungent distraction.

Comparing oneself to others is no good. A taller climber able to reach the first holds has already completed the first jumping move I'll have to do. The same climber unable to jam his longer lower leg between flake and smear will not be able to rest where I can. I know unction about either situation holds no truth or benefit at all, though it still comes now and then. Ambience, surprise, the spirit of the move, the blessings of camaraderie, are there as gifts. It is true, taking on more challenging climbs can ripen these qualities; tearing off or slowly grinding away the muddying effect of comparison. Ultimately a clearer presence of mind free of 'better than' will outperform striving anyway. What I think now is that acceptance allows you to be part of the wider world. Only when one continually accepts how one is can peace finally pervade.

Sixteen-year old Czech sensation Adam Ondra is not only superlight, flexible and strong but has an easy fluency on rock. He has a speedy precision which I've never seen before. Seemingly chaotic, flick-flacking legs resolve to help him hit holds knowingly, his weight often exquisitely off to one side, already set to latch the next by brachiation. I love watching him move, it almost means there's no need to climb yourself. But I would love to do a climb in my dotage that put the wind up him – steam up his Harry Potter specs.

Is the universe learning? In the 3D movie *Avatar,* the new level of visual trickery reminds me of how reality's resolution of itself can develop. Catching sight of the avatar floating in amniotic fluid through the transparent vessel, it tickles me when I realize it looks just like Adam Ondra!

In 1988 where progress would take the sport was still life's secret. I watched entranced each day as Jean Baptiste Tribout, Jibé, came closer to completing his long term project *Le Spectre du Sur-Mutant*, which will be an early 8b+. In 2010 I unexpectedly encounter a content Jibé behind the counter of his shop in Lourmarin near Buoux. So to have him then animate how he saw a youngster climb an 8c on sight, emphasising in that way only the deeply French can, his eyes popping, hands twinkling, was a special treat. What he had to say about the youngsters was interesting too.

"They are brave, missing out bolts" and "They flash 8b boooldair, so 7c is stamina, 7b a rest". He also points out that now the best are bound to be better than before with a larger pool of participants from which talent can emerge, as for all sports. Youths cradled under blank roofs, tender tendons growing till repellent to injury, an Ondra (a tall person that *could* actually climb) was in the stars. *Les Mutants sont arrivés!*

…I look at a young lady through the pane of the Mirabeau café; as smooth as her skin is to mine, so the gulf between Adam's youthful body and my own. Jibé also pointed out, "As you get closer to your old limit it gets harder and harder…" I agree and say "One after the other all the old injuries turn up and say, 'Remember me..?' "

For some reason, after being dormant for many years Buoux has reawoken. Jibé told me that only last week all the moves on the old 80s project above *La Plage* had been done. He told me by whom, but I did not know him and since have forgotten his name. "His friend is even stronger!" Jibé said. The day before when I'd succumbed to a hot 6c+ I'd watched a young climber from Grenoble on the wild unclimbed bombé[52] give it a good go. It starts with the same move as *Action Directe*, Wolfgang Güllich's ground breaking

[52] A bowed feature of rock starting very steep, growing slabbier.

9a; a footless leap across a roof for a mono, sure to be 9b+ or something. Buoux deserves a fierce, cutting edge testpiece.

Finally sunny and warm today, my American friends six foot six T-Quay (who I'd first met at TCF ledge in 1988, when I'd apparently barracked him up his first 7a, and on sight) and his wife Andrea and I walk along the lane below La Plage. A big buff, scruffy Peugeot, courses towards us, en route to the auberge below *Bout du Monde*.

"That was Antoine Le Menestrel, I think", I say as the dust clears.

"What's he doing later?" Andrea asks… T-Quay and I look at each other, raising our eyebrows. I pretend to peer into my sack for a crystal ball!

Later, primed for more "Spankâge" from the rock, still power-pumped from not warming up enough, again, with trepidation I gear up at the foot of *No Man's Land* 7b and we get our answer to Andrea's unusual question.

Marco (Jean Marc Troussier), who put up *Taboo Zizi*, my first 8b in 1988, turns up saying kindly: "Today the cliff is alive with legends…" Amongst the trees I spot the same life-lined papery face I'd seen pass by in the car earlier. Happy eyes sparkle out from under a ragged cap. Some part of me recognizes *La Chapeau Multicoloure* as one I'd seen decades before. The man I'm still not certain is Antoine, looks like a plumber who enjoys his work; modest, gently cheeky, he looked to have left his *Rage de Vivre* behind.

Still I'm not quite sure if it is him.
He talks first.
"Where do you come from?" he says.
"North Wales" I reply. (Strictly speaking I'm a sofa surfer).
"Have you ever been there?" I ask.
"Right Wall" he says.
"How long ago?" I ask.
"Very long time ago" he says.
"Was *Lord of the Flies* there then?", I ask to clarify when.
"No, no, no".

We decide it was probably 1981. It was him.

They are doing the moves on his *Harlem Desir* 7c, "…juste pour le plaisir" he says. Antoine is sweet, slowly charismatic. When we have each finished our climbs, me having fallen, to what I imagine is his mild amusement, the time to pull down our ropes naturally coincides. Pulling my rope across the traverse, back up the trail of quickdraws, I'm already timing it, without noticing, so both our ropes near the belay at the same moment. Antoine's voice raps a little higher, more bubbly to show he has noticed too. Coming down together, orange and purple ropes sail down, lacing the blue sky with colour and whip into the trees together.

"That was like making love with you Antoine", I joke, poking fun at the professional dancer and choreographer.

A long moment passes as Antoine freezes. Then holding up the rope pensively he says, "Do you know how we call this in French?" as he starts to coil it. "*Lover*... like in English!"

I laugh. Our ropes had *Antoined* pour un moment speciale.

They sling their sacks on to go.

"How long you stay?"
"Maybe we see you again?"
"Bye, bye…"

Later, below the Menestrel brothers' handiwork; *Chouca, Le Minimum* and *La Rose et Le Vampire*, it's almost pleasurable nostalgia to still feel the mild familiar twisting of my guts the presence of the full clan of French mutants gathered at Bout du Monde sets off in me. It makes me shy, but I don't feel bad. Now it feels simply physiological rather than psychological. I relax and watch an unfeasibly plush young woman finesse *Chouca*. She climbs beautifully, but doesn't stop at the belay, continuing on to *Bout De Chou*. As she slows a chorus of "Allez… Allez…" builds. It would upset anyone's balance, she falls, but without shouting.

Ben Moon has moved beyond the S7 treachery with a successful clothing company. Jerry owns a B&B and surfs. Sean is working in IT in Salt Lake City. I'm back here in Buoux to reel in my middle age spread but the climbing is powerful, difficult to read, can be awkward, painful. Can it make people like that? Jangling, I don't know whether to laugh or cry as I pick my way down the path through the crazy tangle of tree roots to join T-Quay and Andrea. 'Not worthy feelings' my ego has physically translated to my body pulsate as if they *were* my own. Then I remember again they have nothing to do with me. Soon there is only a quiet feeling, smiling, walking through the dream.

The Transients

I feel like I have totally failed to explain who I am in this book. At my friend Leo's fancy dress 30th I went without changing my clothes. It was a *Chavs and Toffs* party, not quite the *Haves or Have a Yacht* party my life might have thrown up, but I can't imagine that those kinds of parties would have been as interesting anyway. Although people at the party said I made a good Toff, my reception was even friendlier when Adam Long (2nd ascentionist of *The Angels' Share*) and I swapped clothes. Humble garb was much more fun; to be distinguished was somewhat of a pain.

Seeing everyone again, older, you realize how we are here for a blink. What we do with what we see in that time is ever so important. I feel like I can really feel how so. Acts of good willing rooted in true understanding just totally out-gun all else. If I could just remember that... and do them.

Some moments are not especially remarkable but remind you of what a particular situation it is to be alive.

I sit below The Crook's new find in the Gwynant Valley. Today Crispin, Noel and Big G are with us. For all of us to get together these days takes the securing of family passes, finding times when no one's away surfing or

Big G amusing Crispin and Noel on the long walk into Strone. Photo: George Smith.

working, but today we're together. Pritch's even been around, did *Flying Buttress* with The Hodge in eight hours, an amazing alpine effort.

Sat watching the mock glorious shenanigans of us old timers milling below this natty wave of dolerite that my new *Honorary Limestone* E4 6a takes, the way two decades has passed is palpable. A naturally big target, George somehow avoids pokes and jibes but as Noel, earnest, polite looks up preparing to climb, Big G announces, "…and now for the main attraction!"

All the trips away, retold stories, pictures in my mind surround my gaze like a merry cool cloud. I can feel this won't be here forever and savour it deeply, as if it were a special reprieve given by The Reaper to experience something that happened before death…just one more time. Hearing Crookie emit that familiar, forgotten "Hooff…" as he feels a disappointing jam, seeing Crispin take off his torn, resin-splattered trousers, treating us all to an inventive, determined performance in loose grey Y-fronts makes me feel clearly how we're all just a passing miracle, unlikely as a Gingham rainbow. These are our days, those next I hope will be great?

It's not that I'm no longer ambitious. I've got Leo's amazing arête *Rare Lichen* E9 6c in my sights and two other newies harder than anything I've done. Boots through, midges about still, I have to go away, but I'll be back soon, since this year seems to be the year of crag **X**, Y and Z.

Text from G: proceed to craig llugwy 682 629 uphill from carreg minianog crimpy vertical wall of perfect rock G.

G's renowned for turning up new climbs in interesting locations. Aha…but virgin crag **Y** is right behind G's house in Fachwen so my route up its fine central groove had to become: *George The Big Explorer* E3 6a. The harder line to the right I led shortly after my friend, the *great ginger hope* Calum impatiently tried it first on a rope: giving me the benefit of seeing how it was for him. It was a *Schoolboy Error* E5 6c.

Z is on …….. where a friend's back garden, amazingly, still harbours in 2010, a 30ft cliff sporting unclimbed steep arêtes and cracks…Both Noel and George have showed me fantastic cliffs in Scotland on their phones; Noel's one is near Simon Nadin's home, George's a big, brilliant largely untouched granite tor near Aberdeen, the Mither Tap.

If those were X, Y, Z: what about **M**? Here's mine. **M** is in the Malverns; hills made from a pre-Cambrian metamorphic rock that outcrops here and there along the three mile length of the whaleback escarpment. It is a place like no other; full-on Elgar country but beautiful to see, and smell. By a post box on the uphill side of the road in West Malvern, a path curves up past a mass of wild garlic to a unique traverse in Broomhall Quarry. It starts below an unclimbed, overhanging crack, Egyptians to a tricky crimp, slaps out to an arête of heels and poor holds, to a long crux slap for a poor sloper. Come into an undercut, sloping edges to finish twisted tenuously at a seam, *Celebrity Juice* V7.

I've still got it.

Herpes that is…

So that's enough about me. Let's talk about you.

What do you think about me?

Notes

A. Here is what he wrote in reply: Dear Johnny,
I read you piece with interest. I do not usually bother with tittle-tattle, but, the only comment I have is with regards to Scritto's. The only object I have memory of taking the hammer to was the hanger of an ancient bolt made from what I can only describe as of 'sardine tin' lid genre. It was then possible to get a wire over the stud. The flake on *Scritto's* just came off in 'me 'and guv', not by persuasion of Stanley. Please get the facts correct! Yours, Ron Fawcett.

Photo Notes

a. *Silk* E6 6c on sight. It was like many routes on Stanage I'd tried to solo again and again. Like on John Allen's elegant friction scoop *Grace and Danger* E6 6c, you must look at a smear, fathoming immediately if it was good enough to use, if the position above was reachable and held, all the while continuing to bear in mind the realities of the fall. The crux stand up needed a subtle inward push on a very high smear. Trying *Silk*, though new, was no different than trying established routes without practice or foam mats. They were both rock you had to read right. Doing this sort of risky soloing regularly, matured that day, and with the weather dry, put me in the frame of mind to do *Silk* easily, afterwards allowing me to take off up *Ulysses*, fearlessly, for its second ascent.

b. Martin 'Basher' Atkinson holding the ropes on the oft-looked at arête left of *The Rack* at Millstone. It had three tiny golo studs from an aid ascent I threaded with three millimetre cord and a blade in the edge of the hand-like feature on the left side of the arête that seems to be reaching for the edge. I was aware of the scree at the base as a 'Get Out of Jail Free Card' if they stripped.

c. There was nonsense spoken about pebbles having broken but in Stone Monkey you'll see I used none. Underneath is a shot of the first ascent. Standing on the hands off was a moment the Peak became open to me. Hands off rests, strangely, are a feature that refrain on many of my climbs.

d. *Sad Amongst Friends* E7 6c. Even though I'd made some friends in Manchester, with whom I seemed to get on OK, I felt inexplicably sad a lot of the time, like I had an alien in my chest. To hang out and try this brutal line, camping out at the base, for three days, slowly getting higher and higher, was a good way of coming back to someone I could be. Happy to be sad amongst those friends. The finishing move mantels a ridiculous nob of rock that should not be there. Like on many of the best routes there is a hold right where God if he was a route setter would put it after a reflective cup of tea. Photo: Neil Foster

e. Kaluza and Klein were two scientists intent on theory of everything. I thought I was too. It landed me in hot water on a snowy day. Three iterative moves requiring a relaxed style in a frightening situation astride the arête.

f. A doctor on the ropes and the world's best hitcher. I go back up having fallen off. I climbed down from the top to inspect and prepare the finishing holds, but never quite managed to summon up the guts to slap right for the pinch. Just as well. How I was trying the move wouldn't have worked.

g. This huge, by Peak standards, wall was a shock to see for the first time. On proper holds forcing you into great shapes with good pegs that don't interrupt the climbing it epitomises what I like about grit quarry walls. 7c+.

h. Climbed mid-summer, we (please remind me who I was with!) woke early. I topped out at 5.30am. Be careful to not kick the Rock 1 out in the changing grooves section like Andy Cave did. Welsh E7.

i. Bounce your foot into a slight dish, lightning quick, share, to set up for the dyno. The first 7a on slate. The way the right foot lands on a slight dish determines the fate of the next two moves entirely.

j. I would like to try this in EBs sometime to see if it is possible. Every type of bridging right after one another with some interesting holds thrown in. For a while I was determined to do the pitch on a Rock 3 at the half height underclings foregoing bolts.

k. Paul had placed the 3rd bolt above *The Rainbow*...so as not to ruin the boltless climb. Beyond my reach, attempting to dynoclip it like I had on *Raped by Affection*, this time I missed, falling god it's a long way. Ninety foot. I ended up 5ft above the path. Paul 10 ft above me. The concussion I sustained took a week to subside but at the time did not stop me going up to complete the lead, this time wearing a red pompom hat for protection.

l. One line snakes through the back wall of the zawn. Only attemptable on sight since it is so steep. It was a 'wild card' choice of somewhere likely to be dry sat in Pete's on a rainy day

m. A glaringly obvious line with features visible from Wen Slab you could mould yourself onto in your mind's eye. The right hand start, finished by reversing the first pitch pulling under into the Cryptic Rift, would be a sturdy deep water solo.

n. When Ben Moon took up Paul's and my offer of a visit to Harris we pointed him to this line. At the base was a wet mica slab which we cautioned him against. He went straight across it like a well-seasoned ledge shuffler.

o. Gambler John Rosholt, on Jardine's *Owl Roof* 5.12c, a notorious off-width roof crack, was a professional poker player. He quickly became a good friend. I was shocked to hear of his unexplained disappearance, his van found empty in the desert. Owl Roof was my first off-width, I managed to do it with one fall, its best ascent at the time. Pulling up from a footless arm bar on the lip to foot jam serially up the crack then invert had me prostrate in Camp 4 on a bench for a day.

p. Hopping speeds up the brain, teaches you how to make grip on the hoof and looks ridiculous. Note the plastic bags in the heels of the Tennies to help me use the boot's toe. The hop across from the boulder, bottom right, is the most crucial move to get right on this one foot special at Stanage. Photo: Simon Nadin

q. I broke my right hand and was reduced to one-handed climbing. It was fascinating seeing what would go and how hard; *Asp* normally E3, interestingly, was easier (at 7c) than *Kirkus Corner* E1 (8a with left hand only). Once recovered I experimented using my right. A good one was *Master's Edge*. It wouldn't go on the right side but did up the unclimbed left side by fantastic fluxing presses and pulls, though I haven't linked the three sections.

r. *The Sron*, one of my favourite crags in Britain. Stays dry and steep. *Knuckle Sandwich*, E7+ *The Scoop* E7 6b, 6a, 6a, 6b, 6b, 6a,6b,5b *Occasional Table* E6 6b, the first pitch of *The Nose* free all featured on sight climbing on glorious warped gneiss. Photo: Gordon Stainforth.

E9

⊛ INDIAN FACE
6c

THE VERY BIG
AND THE VERY SMALL [8c]

* The Angel's Share
7a

[8a+]
Coeur de Lion 7a, 6c, 6b

* THE Quarryman 6c, 6B, 6c, 7a

E8

* Gaia 7a
Slab n' Crack 6c
End of the Affair 6c

⊠ Hardback Thesaurus 🔓
6B

⊛ Llanberries
7a

⊛ THE 39 SLAPS
6B

DAWES OF PERCEPTION
6c

* Living in Oxford
7a

△ Knuckle Sandwich [8A]

Bobby's Groove [8A]

THE Untouchable [8A]

THE MEDIUM

⊙ Snakes & ladders [7c+]

Fire Escape

⊠ COME TO MOTHER 🔓
6a, 6a

E7

WINDOWS 7a *

🔓 * Sad Amongst 7a
Braille Trail 6c
Bright Lives 6c *

Kaluza-klein 6c

Dharma 6c

* Janus
6c

Phil's Harmonica
6c

△ The Scoop
6B, 6a, 6B, 6B, 6a, 6B, 5b

* WHITE LINES 6c

* Juggled Hare 6B

* silk 6c 🔓

UEA

Charlotte Rampling 6B

* Heath Robinson 6B

WEATHER REPORT 6B

THE Cool curl 6B

Adam Smith's 6B

Committed 6c

🔓 White Water ⊛ Honorary Grit 6c

Fingertip # Phenomenon

* Saltation 6c * moira

Twin Cam 6c

Wall Street Crash 6B

Offspring 6B

* perplexity 6c

⊠ Conan, the librarian
6B, 6B, 5c

⊛ Rupert Road 🔓
6B, 6B, 6B, 6B, 5B

Satsumo Wrestler 6B

⊛ Mini Hatta 6B

⊠ THE RED SOFA 🔓
6B

* NON STICK VICAR

* Untoward 🔓
6B

* inertia real 6c

E6

* Downhill Direck
6c

⊙! Pagan Man 6B

⊛ Rimsky Korsakof 🔓
6a

E5

1980   1984   1985   1986   1990

☆

Wizard Ridge +
Numerous
Projects
...

RotatorCuff

Map of Injuries!

'90
concussion
(cure 4a
sick mind!)

1978

'82 Pelvis
+ nose

'93

punched
a wall

'86

'85

'84

* gRit
# slate
⊕ Rhyolite / D
⊠ Quartzite
△ Gneiss
◔ Limestone
⬡ Sandstone

On Sight

* Drummond Base
6c

(Lived in
◔ The Snowdrop   * Smoked Salmon
[8a] with the new!) 7a/b
SOUTHERN SOFTIE
[7B+]

* Zen Boy
7a

◔ BLETCHLEY PARK [8a+]

※ Professor Whittaker 6d
6b, 5c

* Avoiding the traitors
* WarmLove
7a/b

Quarryman's Wife
6B/C

KING OF THE Mezz
6c

* Sentinel Groove
6c

* Jumpin on a Beetle
6c

⬡ The Colonial

⊛ Poky little Puppy 6B

⊕ Bolton WANDERER
5a,5 C, 6a, 6b, 6a, 6b, 6a

⊛ Kung Fu Panda
6c
⊛ Schoolboy Error
6c!

◔ INDIAN RAILWAYS

* The Boulder 6c

2000

21/12
2012
(End of the
World!)

Black
hole
⊛ ← ⊛ ← Sun

Acknowledgements

I was going to say to people that all that stuff about writing being difficult was clap-trap but in reality it is a brutal challenge. Without friends, professionals and healers of various kinds this book was never going to happen. Heartfelt thanks to you all.

Thank you George Smith for a great preface. It set the bar unnervingly high.

Noel Crane, Johnny Allen, Trevor Hodgson and Uppingham climbing buddy Ed Douglas, thanks for reading early transcripts and giving me dry friendly feedback to guide me off in a professional direction. Nick Dixon for praise and encouragement. Al Alvarez for his wise silences and favourable noises. Andy Newton for later support, indeed all the many people who encouraged me to "get it finished…"

I'm proud to include Paul Mitchell's poem Club For One and Martin Veale's Gritstone Senna. Others have offered me literary ingredients that were too long or didn't quite fit but which will appear on my website. Thanks to them, Chris Plant in particular.

There have been plenty of challenges along the way. An early version on a data-stick fell off my keyring. Resigned to it being lost, to having to rewrite large potions of the book, I was elated to have Harry from Bangor University hand it to me in Pete's. He'd found it lodged in a wall after I had given up looking under every rock at the Cromlech boulders. Don't forget to claim your half...

Two computers bit the dust during the writing of my book. To David and Llewellyn at Bangor University Psychology department and to Chris Wright at Snowdonia Active, a loud bellow of thanks to you all for your considerable skills and support. To Simon Panton. Mark Lynden and friends at Caban be sure I appreciate all you have done for me.

It is hard to write a book sat out in the rain so a great grunt of gratitude goes out to my good friend Ted Sylvester for my time at the caravan at The Fricsan. Before he had the joy of me Fiona and Llewellyn did wonders putting me up with them, (or something like that). There is no way that without their generous hospitality I'd have had the financial circumstances to get my bearings squarely on what I wanted to say. Without Steve the mechanic, both a home and reliable car would have been much more difficult, much appreciated. And to all whose sofa's I've come to love.

To Tristan Johnson up in West Yorkshire I wish all the best and thank you very much for your scanning work. A big thanks go to Cordelia Molloy for her hard work and skill in getting the photos in the book up to scratch within a very tight deadline.

Editor Julia Gorton generously ran her professional eye across the draft with warmth and clarity, offering us an understanding ear, editorial wisdom and gratefully received hospitality. Thank you.

A special man hug goes out to Neil Foster. Without his dedicated recording of what I was up to back then the major portion of action shots wouldn't exist. You can't go back and truly catch the drama again. But there are many photographers to credit who have kindly offered me their work for free. To Zippy, Tim Glasby, Glen Robbins, Alun Hughes, Skinny Dave, Jan Davies, Jim Perrin, John Kirk, James Avery, Simon Nadin, Martin Crook, George Smith, Craig Smith and my brother Mike, thank you all very much. Chris Williams for access to his dad Paul's collection. Thanks too to Jon Retty, Heinz Zak, Sean Smith, Paul Pritchard and Phil Kelly long may you all sail in her, whatever she may be. To Alan James thanks for being so well observed in your cruelty and for lending us the cartoon. To anyone whom I've lunched out on and failed to remember I'm sorry, concussion is a little devil.

Jon Barton and Jane at Verterbrate Graphics, thank you for barcoding the ISBN, twice! Simon Panton at Ground Up, thank you for the Twll Mawr topo shot and well seasoned advice. Ben Pritch, cheers for the mexican food and video grabs. To Iwonna and Tadeusz Hudowski at the Alpine Club library, thanks for the hand holding and magazine sifting. The two Richards at Cordee, I'd like to thank for educating me about the real workings of the book business. John Graham at Go Outdoors for his openness to my situation. Without Richard Robinson and John this book would not have come out till xmas 2012 and that's too late because the world will have ended!

Thanks too to Pete's Eats, Caban, Saffron and all their customers. My appreciation to all those who have listened to me try passages out.

The term 'vanity publishing' surely suits an autobiography entitled *Full of Myself*. Writing any autobiography will always be a somewhat precious endeavour and it is Al Williams I have to thank for steering me into a more realistic frame and showing patience where it was well needed. His work at the mixing desk always speaks for itself.

To the climbing pioneers before me, those who did sponsor me, the technologists that conjured and made my gear, and to the mystery that made my body I salute and bow deeply.

And so to the editor in chief, my dear Julie Hiam. I've learnt so much working with her: to keep calm, when to sing, when to have a nice cup of tea. Painstaking, patient, talented and knowledgeable, I recommend her as an editor to anyone seeking to sharpen their book's thrust.

Thank you everyone.

I dedicate this book to my dear Mum and Dad.
After a rocky patch I feel we have a sweet time now.
Wish you both all the best for many years to come.